Cellaring Wine

Cellaring Wine

Managing Your Wine Collection ... to Perfection

Whimsical illustrations by William Bramhall

JEFF COX

Storey Publishing

Edited by Dianne M. Cutillo and Marie A. Salter

Art direction and cover design by Cynthia McFarland

Cover illustration © Riley Illustration: William Bramhall

Whimsical interior illustrations © Riley Illustration: William Bramhall, pages ii, vi, 3, 7, 10, 13, 14, 17, 22, 27, 30, 32, 35, 44, 49, 50, 54, 56, 59, 67, 71, 78, 80, 102, 107, 125, 166, 170, 172, 179, 190, 197, 211, 219, 224, 230; all other illustrations by Brigita Fuhrmann

Text design and production by Karin Stack

Production assistance by Jennifer Jepson Smith

Indexed by Susan Olason/Indexes & Knowledge Maps

Printed in the United States by Von Hoffmann

10 9 8 7 6 5 4 3 2 1

Library of Congress Cataloging-in-Publication Data

Cox, Jeff, 1940–
   Cellaring wine : managing your wine collection to perfection / by Jeff Cox.
      p. cm.
   Includes index.
   ISBN 1-58017-474-4 (alk. paper)
   1. Wine and wine making — Amateurs' manuals. 2. Wine cellars — Amateurs' manuals. I. Title.

TP548.2.C69 2003
641.2'2—dc21   2003045641

To the vineyard workers, who toil so that we may drink wine.

Contents

Preface

In *From Vines to Wines,* the companion book to this volume, I detailed the process of choosing the site of a vineyard, selecting grape varieties for the site, growing the grapes, and making wine from them. In this book, I describe the journey of the finished bottle of young wine — whether made from your grapes or a bottle you have purchased — to its ultimate destination on your table as a perfectly aged wine, faceted not only with layers of fruit but with the accoutrements of age: silken smoothness, generosity of flavor, and the fragrances of bouquet that only arise with sufficient time in the bottle.

If, as I said in *From Vines to Wines,* wine is the child of the marriage of a human being and grapevine, then to know that wine in the fullness of its maturity is to know the child grown to the full power of its adulthood. Well-aged wine is as different from the product that first went into the bottle as an adult is from a child. Its youthful appeal may be diminished, but its complexity and depth can be infinitely greater.

Wine can achieve these heights only if it is handled properly during its years of maturation. That takes a wine cellar. Although I loved fine wine as a young man, I never thought about having a wine cellar of my own until one November nearly 30 years ago when I visited friends in France.

• • •

A more volatile couple can hardly be imagined — he a reserved, upper-class Englishman, she a fiery, libidinous Frenchwoman. After a few days of listening to them bicker in the confines of their Paris apartment, I was thankful that they offered to drive us all down to her mother's château near the city of Angoulême so we could spend some time in the countryside. Her mother, who must have had considerable wealth, was in Paris at her own apartment for a few weeks, and so the château was available for us.

Angoulême is in the department of Charante, where Cognac is made, about 300 miles southwest of Paris. To the south of Charante are the departments of Dordogne and Gironde, which hold the culinary and vinous treasures of Périgord and Bordeaux and offer plenty of opportunity for day excursions. We left Paris early and made a noontime stop in Saumur, where we visited a winemaker. After we sampled his very good white (but astringent red) wine, he led us to one of his *chais,* where a staircase descended into caves carved three levels down into the underlying chalk. The air in the caves was close, and the bottles of wine stored in the lowest level covered with the dust of decades. "During the war," he said, referring to World War II, "we hid all our wine and valuables down here, to keep them from the Nazis." The Nazis never did discover the entrance to the caves, he said, because it was then hidden under the manure-encrusted floorboards of a horse stable.

We arrived in Angoulême at night, exhausted. The next morning, I rose early to look around. The château was a grand house dating from the early eighteenth century. Behind the house was a copse of trees that turned out to be, on close inspection, overgrown filberts, and a clos with a vegetable garden and a gate in its wall. Through the gate, a path led through a pasture of ripe-smelling grasses and dried weeds to a nearby dairy farm. Later that morning, and every morning for the two weeks we stayed there, one of us would take a silver pail and walk the quarter mile path to the farm, where rich whole milk still warm from the cow would be poured foaming into the pail.

I reveled in the niceties of rural France. The estate's caretakers collected our dirty clothes and laundered them outside, scrubbing them on a washboard in a tub of soapy water kept hot with boiling water from a cauldron hung over a wood fire. We purchased meat and eggs from a truck that pulled up every day about noon. The butcher let down a long flap on the side of the truck and climbed into the enclosure, the flap becoming a counter on which he set a basket of fresh eggs, ham, steaks, and chops for us to choose from.

The house itself was intriguing — two stories with long hallways that ran the length of the building, opening onto rooms filled with antique French furniture. Although the kitchen was updated with a refrigerator, gas stove, and oven, it was easy to see its original appearance in the ancient tiled walls and flagstone flooring.

On my second afternoon there, I wandered into the clos to see what was growing and discovered a set of steps leading down to a cellar-level room under the château. An ironwork gate barred the entranceway to the cellar. A large padlock secured the gate to an iron rod cemented into the masonry. Inside I could dimly see a table, some shelving, lots of cobwebs, and a number of dusty wine bottles lying on their sides.

Excited by my find, I ran back up into the house to see if Corrine had a key. "Somewhere here," she said in her thick French accent. "When we were kids, my cousins and I would always try to break into the cellar to steal the wine, so my father put up that gate to keep us out. I'm sure the key is here somewhere." And though she looked high and low as I waited impatiently, she couldn't find it.

Several times before I left the château for good, I went back to the iron gate to see if I could dislodge it from its hinges or pick the lock. The dusty bottles inside seemed like treasures beyond measure, lying undisturbed for years in the cool, dark cellar. I imagined the wine inside softened and smoothed by time, ripened into what surely must be the finest sip of ambrosia on the planet. I saw them there in the dark, inscrutable vessels of promise, tantalizing and taunting me, but locked beyond my reach. Corrine's father had done his work well. Although he was many years deceased, his gate stood proof against looters like me. That's when I became determined to someday have my own wine cellar.

• • •

Now I do have my own wine cellar, although one with perhaps less ambience than Corrine's father's. It's darn near a social necessity here in Sonoma County, where wine is the local industry and subject of much talk, discussion, debate, argument, inquiry, and even gossip. Almost immediately after moving here 15 years ago from eastern Pennsylvania, I joined a group of three amateur winemakers and found myself elbow deep in fermenting must before the moving truck even arrived with my furniture. I became acquainted with, and then friends with, many professional winemakers. On the not-so-infrequent occasions when they invited friends over for a meal and to share some wine, those friends brought treasures from their wine cellars: One night Penny opened a bottle of 1935 Simi Zinfandel, which she inherited from somewhere when she was still in her thirties. Another night John brought a 1964 Beaulieu Vineyard's Georges de Latour Private Reserve Cabernet Sauvignon, one of André Tchelistcheff's masterpieces. Tom opened a bottle of 1985 Dehlinger Merlot, with a rich bouquet of age. Rod brought a 1970 Swan Vineyards Gamay, with a distinct blueberry flavor; we later discovered it wasn't Gamay at all, but a variety called Valdiguié. And then more truly spectacular bottles, all French: Mike's 1918 Haut-Brion that opened beautifully but lasted no more than 15 minutes before fading away in the glass. Peter's 1929 Bouchard Père et Fils Chablis (69 years old at the drinking and still fresh as a March breeze). And David's 1919 Musigny, 79 years old and like a bouquet of lovely pressed flowers, delicately scented, sweet, and beautiful. And then the ultimate bottles: the 1928 Château Latour, finally reaching maturity after 70 years, its depth and richness intact but silkened by time. And the 1947 Château d'Yquem Sauternes, whose sweet golden liquid smelled like the faintly perfumed gown of a sleeping Venus — and if you think that elaborate description overstates the case, I suggest you try a 50-year-old Yquem and come up with a more accurate one.

None of these exquisitely sensual experiences would be possible without a wine cellar. The cellar is not just a repository for wine. It is a school — no, a university — where young wine learns how great it can become. Properly operated, the wine cellar becomes a mechanism whereby today's modestly priced bottles become tomorrow's valuable, historic treasures. Each well-aged bottle is a window into the past, a visit to a time gone by, a reminder of a specific summer, an evoker of memories, a delicious peak experience for the palate, a glass of cheer in a world too often sad and somber, and a comfort to us as we, too, age into fruitful full maturity.

Acknowledgments

I've been seriously interested in wine for over 30 years now, and the list of people who've helped me understand the subject would be long indeed. Special thanks, however, go to Bob Thompson, the writer who has believed in me and helped me along. Dan Berger has been a friend and unwitting teacher, as I've listened closely to his opinions. Richard Arrowood has never failed to be generous with his insights and time when I've asked for his help. Peter Hardell allowed me space in his wine cellar before I had one of my own. Rod and Lynn Berglund have been friends who've generously invited me to many dinners where old and well-cellared wines were opened. Leo McCloskey has given me deep insights into the biochemistry of wine. Mike Rubin shared his ideas about how wines age. I could not have written the chapter on building the wine cellar without the expert help of Anthony Micheli of Micheli Construction in St. Helena, who has built many wine cellars in the Napa Valley, and John Cottrell of Petaluma, Sonoma County, whose expertise in building is incorporated in that chapter. I'm delighted with Bill Bramhall's witty drawings and give him my heartfelt thanks.

Very special thanks go to Dianne Cutillo, Marie Salter, and the folks at Storey Publishing, who believed in this book and encouraged me. My visit to North Adams was heartwarming as I saw their camaraderie and enthusiasm, and it reminded me of a fondly remembered time when I also worked for a book publisher that helped authors realize their dreams in print.

PART ONE

Why Collect and Cellar Wine?

A properly aged glass of fine

wine is one of the few peak

experiences we can enjoy on a

daily basis. We provide the cellar

with the wine, and the cellar

returns it to us glorified.

CHAPTER 1

Why Collect Wine?

People usually delve deeper into wine because they like it. It tastes good, and it makes a fine accompaniment to food. A glass or two is relaxing after a hard day's work and may even be good for the health. Once you begin to enjoy wine on a regular basis, it's also more convenient to select a bottle from a stash of your favorites than to run down to the store before dinner and take potluck from the store shelves. And so the first reason — and still one of the best reasons — for collecting a few bottles of wine is so you don't run out.

Wine is one of those subjects, like cooking or gardening, that continues to open up before you as you explore it. The more you learn, the more there is to learn, until, a long time into it, you realize that you'll never exhaust the subject. No one can taste all the wine there is. No one has yet mapped out exactly how a grapevine transforms rainwater and sunshine into the complexities of sweet grape juice, or how yeast, the simplest of God's creatures, changes this juice into even more complex wine. No one can possibly fathom all the variations of climate and soil from vineyard to vineyard that create wines with the unique taste of the place where their grapes were grown.

Because of this complexity and the many levels of quality found in wine, a fascination with wine can quickly grow from a few bottles in the kitchen cabinet into a number of cases in the bedroom closet. From there, it's a short step to many cases on shelving in the basement, and then to a well-stocked, fully operational wine cellar. I know; I've made this journey. As one's interest

in wine intensifies and one's knowledge grows, so does the collection of wine in the cellar.

TO INDULGE THE COLLECTOR'S IMPULSE

Part of cellaring wine is the collector's mania. I've felt the mania most of my life. It started when I was about eight or nine years old and got interested in baseball. Living in Manhasset, Long Island, we were natural Yankee fans (the Mets weren't born yet). The more I knew about the Yanks and the other major league teams, the more baseball cards I collected. I just had to have Mickey Mantle's card when he came up in 1951. Yogi Berra was a favorite of mine, so I bought packs and packs of bubble gum (the ostensible reason for buying these packs was the bubble gum, the baseball cards were a bonus; in fact, of course, it was the other way around) until I got Yogi's card. This mania ended about six or seven years later, when I was finishing up high school. The tragic ending of this story is not atypical. Returning home from college, I looked for my cards — a collection of perhaps 200 dating from 1948 to 1957 — but couldn't find them. I asked my mom if she had seen them. "Yes, Dear," she said sweetly. "The little neighbor boy was over visiting and found your cards, so I gave them to him. Did you want to keep them?" The little neighbor boy has probably built his dream house in Hawaii with the proceeds of those cards. And yes, my mom burned all my comics, too. When I get to heaven, I'm going to have a stern talk with her.

The collecting mania can strike the wine lover, too. As my interest in wine grew, I saw there was a great hullabaloo about certain wines — the Merlots of Château Pétrus, 'La Tache' from Domaine de la Romanée-Conti, *Trockenbeerenauslesen* from Schloss Vollrads in the Rheingau, and so on. I wanted to taste them, to discover for myself what all the shouting was about. At one time, I was also in love with certain automobiles: the 1958 BMW 507 Touring Sport, for instance, and the 1955 Mercedes Benz 300SL convertible. Whereas these cars were well out of my financial reach, the wines weren't. It occurred to me then that there weren't many luxury experiences within the reach of folks with modest means but that good wine was one of them.

Toward the end of the 1960s and the beginning of the 1970s, you could find a bottle of Château Margaux for under $20 — and that was considered very expensive. I picked up the 1970 Château Lafite for $25. I remember buying a bottle of 1926 Château Pichon-Lalande for something like $28 from Sherry-Lehmann wine purveyors in New York City in the early 1970s. As my collection of little vinous treasures grew, so did my need for a wine cellar to keep the choice bottles safe. If my own mother could give away my baseball cards and burn my comic books, no telling what friends could do to my wine.

TO LEARN AND TO SHARE KNOWLEDGE

Friends I know from other parts of the country who aren't very sophisticated about wine often drop by. Sometimes they want recommendations for wineries to visit, wines to try, and bottles to look for, and I'm happy to give them suggestions and even call a winery for them to arrange a visit. I figure this is their opportunity to learn about good wine, and by seeking my advice, they show me they want to learn. Other folks come with preconceived ideas: "I like Sutter Home White Zinfandel. How do I get to Sutter Home?" I personally don't mind if they like white Zinfandel, which is a characterless, sweet, fruity wine one step up from Sprite. That's their business. But I'm not going to try to convince them that there are treasures far beyond white Zinfandel. It would be presumptuous of me. Besides, I have a soft spot in my heart for white Zinfandel. Here's why.

* * *

The soft spot developed when I moved to California's Wine Country in 1985. The most beautiful vineyards were the old, head-trained field blends planted by Italian settlers in the late nineteenth and early twentieth centuries. These were mostly Zinfandel, usually with some other varieties like Carignane, Alicante Bouschet, Mataro (the old-timers' name for Mourvèdre), and even a few vines of white grapes like Golden Chasselas mixed into the vineyard, hence the term *field blend*. Many winemakers in the early 1980s made rich, red, intense, luscious, fruity, concentrated, massive, inky, explosively flavored wines from Zinfandel and Zin field blends. Some Zinfandel made by winemakers with a more restrained approach reached heights of quality that belied their low price. These were not widely known or popular around the United States, although within the Wine Country, wine lovers enjoyed them.

During the mid-1980s, the French varieties of Chardonnay and Cabernet Sauvignon were queen and king, respectively. Top-quality Cabernet was bringing up to $1,000 a ton (it's many times that now), and Chardonnay was not far behind. Field blends of Zinfandel and vineyards that were 100 percent Zinfandel, on the other hand, brought half that amount of money. Vineyard owners were tearing out the ancient vines and replanting with the higher priced varieties. Also, new outbreaks of phylloxera, a vine root louse that was devastating vineyards first in Sonoma County and then in Napa County, necessitated wholesale replantings of sick and threatened vineyards. However, those century-old field blends and old Zin vineyards had never succumbed to phylloxera, most likely because the Italian settlers had planted them on phylloxera-resistant rootstocks.

Just as these treasured, gnarled, ancient Zinfandel vineyards were being torn out, along came the Trinchero family, which owned Sutter Home and introduced white Zinfandel, a wine made by lightly pressing the juice from Zinfandel fruit without rupturing many of the cells in the skins that hold color compounds. The juice is then fermented off the skins, this red grape being treated like a white wine. The end result was the pinkish, sweet quaff that immediately found a huge market. Sutter Home turned from a small family winery into a wine giant, buying up all the Zinfandel it could find. Suddenly vineyard owners had a new opinion of their old Zin vineyards — these things could make money! And so, although some old field-blend vineyards were lost, many were saved by the marketing magic of white Zinfandel.

It got to be that around the country, people knew Zinfandel as a white wine. I remember going to a rather upscale watering hole in eastern Pennsylvania around 1990 and hearing a woman at our table ordering "Zinfandel, please." The waitress looked up from her order book and said, "You want that up or on the rocks?" And of course, when the wine came (up, thank goodness) it was white Zinfandel. The praenomen "white" had gotten lost out there in America, and the nation had come to think of Zinfandel as a white or blush wine. Fetzer Vineyards even felt impelled to label a wine "Red Zinfandel," which caused an immediate reaction among wine buffs here in California — they would have laughed if they weren't so horrified.

Real red Zinfandel slowly came to be appreciated through the 1990s, and by 2000, top-quality Zins were selling in the $20 to $30 range, both a mark of how little top-quality Zin there is and an indication of its inherent value.

TO PURSUE QUALITY

Another reason for collecting wine is to nab some of the good stuff before it gets away. There's a saying here in Sonoma County that the really, really good wines never leave the county. This phenomenon reflects the quality pyramid: The higher the quality of the wine, the less of it there's going to be. That's because winemakers tend to select out the really excellent wines and keep

them as separate lots. They may blend them into one of their premium blends, such as a Meritage of Bordeaux varieties (Cabernet Sauvignon, Cabernet Franc, Merlot, Malbec, or Petit Verdot). Or they may bottle them separately and release them as reserve wines. If a particular vineyard produces exceptional quality year after year, its wine may be released as a vineyard-designated wine. But in all these cases, wines of top quality are selected out and kept separate from the run-of-the-press wines.

The more astoundingly good the wine, the more chance it's going to be selected out, and thus increase in rarity. One example is the 1999 Archery Summit Estate Bottled Pinot Noir, which was selling for a rich $82.99 a bottle at one market I found. Such a wine may well be worth the money if you can afford it. Its aroma of spice, roses, and black cherry leads to a hugely concentrated flavor that reveals layers of chocolate, cherry, plum, and licorice. If you like it, you'd better jump on it, because only 215 cases were made. That's a miniscule amount of wine in a world where the big boys and girls produce wine by the megaton; those 215 cases can be snapped up in a week or two. So, it's not that the really good stuff never leaves the county, but rather that locals hear about the good stuff first and take their cut before the rest of the world learns that it exists. You can get in on the fun no matter where you live, however, if you know the inner workings of acquiring wine; you'll find that information in chapter 2.

THE "FUTURES" MARKET

In recent years, more and more wineries sell wine on "futures." The deal is that you pay now for a wine that may not be delivered for one or even two years. In return for having your money to play with before they have to deliver any wine, wineries usually set an attractive price on their futures wines. My first venture into this game occurred in summer 1982 when I plunked down $125 for a case of 1982 Calon Ségur, a fine Bordeaux that wouldn't arrive on these shores for two years, owing to the two years it would spend in barrel. No one knew it at the time, but 1982 turned out to be a fabulous year in Bordeaux, so fabulous that when 1983 rolled around, the wine merchant sent me a letter saying that the 1983s were going to be even better than the 1982s, and that I should swap my 1982 Calon Ségur for a case of the 1983, straight up, no money changes hands. I did a little checking, and while 1983 seemed like it was going to be a good year in Bordeaux, no one thought it would approach the quality of 1982. The wine merchant was trying to get that 1982 back so he could resell it at high prices now that people knew how good it was. Naturally I refused, and it wasn't too many years before I began seeing 1982 Calon Ségur being sold for $125 a bottle, which was what I had originally paid for twelve bottles on futures.

TO PRESERVE OR ENHANCE QUALITY

Once nabbed, good wine needs proper storage or it will lose quality through exposure to light and heat. The answer, of course, is to have a wine cellar for your big scores.

When wine is first released, it's usually at its least expensive. As wine ages and acquires the character of bottle age, it may become more expensive because it may become better wine. But not all wines become better with age. We will discuss how wine ages in chapter 3, but right now suffice it to say that wine is usually — *usually* — least expensive when it's first released. Having a wine cellar of your own allows you to buy wine at good prices and age it yourself.

Since there are few absolutes about wine, it may not always be cheapest when it's released. If the wine doesn't sell well and there's a glut, you may find it discounted a year or more after its release, the same way that last year's automobile prices drop when the new models arrive. And be aware that buying direct from the winery doesn't necessarily mean getting the lowest price. Wineries sell at the equivalent of the "manufacturer's suggested retail price." Big wine shops and supermarkets are usually the ones doing the deep discounting.

IT'S AN INVESTMENT

Which is another reason for collecting wine. It can act as an investment: Wine can increase in value, and you may be able to sell it down the road for a great deal more than you paid for it. But this will happen only with certain bottles of very sought-after wine. Most *vin ordinaire* will decrease in value with age, even if the wine has improved by its time in the cellar, simply because people want the big names. But not every wine you lay down in the cellar will become a treasured bottle, dusty with age, its contents transformed from youthful pungency to smooth, luscious wine at its peak of quality. You have to know what you're doing if you plan to age wine for resale later on. Chapter 3 will give you good insights into what you have to know if you're going to cash in, rather than take a financial (and gustatory) bath.

EXTRAVAGANCE!

There's a related reason for collecting wine that has less to do with the price of the bottle than the amount of cash in one's bank account: the snob appeal of owning wines that are difficult to get. Distasteful as the thought may be, that snob appeal plays a big part in who gets the high-priced bottles of wine, and why. I recently attended a wine auction here in California where high rollers paid outrageous sums for fine wine. It's all for a good cause, of course — the proceeds go to help the farmworkers, mostly Mexican, who do the heavy lifting in the production of these fine wines. I was watching the bids go up for California's cult wines. These trophy bottles are made in small amounts by celebrity winemakers. If you can even get a bottle, most run between $400 and $500 or so for one 750 mL bottle. If you look for them on the Internet wine-shopping sites, you'll find prices reaching $1,000. Who can afford such extravagance?

Plenty of people. I talked to one well-heeled man from Colorado at the wine auction who said, "What would you do if you had $240 million in your bank account? Okay, you buy the big house, the big car, you invest, you contribute to charities and to political parties, but you still have hundreds of millions in the bank and more coming in all the time. Do you think I think twice about buying a case of wine for $10,000, flying in a planeload of my friends, and pouring the wine for them?"

Well, that's a nice altruistic thought, but I suspect the thrill is less about giving your friends a wonderful wine experience and more about, "Look at me. I can pour you a glass of wine that's worth more than your car. Ha!" Still, if that's what thrills you, who am I to naysay it? I will say that with cult wines at those elevated prices, you probably don't get what you pay for. The same holds true for the famous garage wines of Bordeaux. These are small production wineries that tend to make big, intensely expressed wines. Like their California cult counterparts, the wines made by the *garagistes,* as they're called, may be good, but not necessarily a heck of a lot better than many other wines sold at far lower prices.

This all came home to me at a recent tasting of a dozen and a half California cult wines, set up by a Napa Valley winery. The tasting was given for wine writers and winemakers. We tasted the wines blind: That is, they were wrapped up in paper bags so we didn't know which was which and wouldn't be influenced by the wine's reputation. One wine in particular was thoroughly execrable — almost undrinkable — we all agreed, and scored it last. Another was exceptionally delicious, balanced, full of concentrated fruit from the entrance on the palate to the long lingering finish, and the group scored it first. When the paper bags came off, the execrable wine retailed at $450 a bottle, while the winner was $40 a bottle. As I said, you don't always get what you pay for when the wine is sought after more for its limited availability than for its intrinsic quality as a wine.

TO CULTIVATE YOUR TASTE

Another reason for collecting wine is to learn about wine. As you select certain bottles for your cellar, you begin to define your taste. After a number of years, your cellar will accurately reflect your own preferences and will become in a sense your personal description of what constitutes good wine.

But this matter of taste is a dicey business. I've learned through many, many hours of tasting with people who are well educated in wine that from time to time, someone will like a wine that I find undrinkable, and that conversely, someone will hate a wine that I find to be a grand expression of its fruit. As the Romans said, *"De gustibus non disputandum est"* — loosely translated, "There's no arguing with taste."

A problem may arise when you really love a particular wine and serve it forth with great enthusiasm and predictions of pleasure to your guests, only to have them smile thinly and nod in half-hearted agreement, probably to be polite. When you give your opinion first, guests are put in the position of having to decide whether to agree or disagree with you — and that can be uncomfortable. D. H. Lawrence hit the nail on the head when he said, "I cannot cure myself of that most woeful of youth's follies — thinking that those who care about us will care for the things that mean much to us." Best to serve a wine without much comment and let the guests discover its qualities for themselves. Then their praise for it will be unconstrained by your opinion and may even include praise for the host who has such good taste. And that can be a not inconsiderable pleasure.

As Samuel Butler said, "People care more about being thought to have taste than about being thought either good, clever, or amiable." Having taste means that you are educated to the relative merits of things and appreciate what's good. Ralph Waldo Emerson wrote in his journals that "[a] man is known by the books he reads, by the company he keeps, by the praise he gives, by his dress, by his tastes, by his distastes, by the stories he tells, by his gait, by the notion of his eye, by the look of his house, of his chamber; for nothing on earth is solitary but every thing hath affinities infinite." The wine cellar stocked with wines you've come to love is a reflection of your personality, another way to tell friends, coworkers, and all those you care about who you are.

At this point, I offer a strong warning about simply collecting wine regardless of its merit or simply because it's expensive. That's just acquisitiveness. Always avoid wines you don't appreciate.

That doesn't mean that your taste must follow fashion or the list of "100 Best Wines" from *The Wine Spectator* or anyone else's list of favorites, for that

matter. Cultivating taste means discovering what you like, regardless of what the rest of the world thinks. If you like Mogen David, then drink it. Just don't expect me to like it. I'll respect someone who likes a solid $8 bottle of wine far more than the fool who buys a $500 bottle of wine because it shows what a big spender he is and how he can have the wine that you can't.

The more wine you taste, the more you learn about wine, and that learning process is facilitated by having a well-stocked wine cellar. Not only will you become familiar with wines from different regions, countries, and parts of the world, but you'll be able to define the differences in flavor of the various grape varieties. As you age wine, you'll be able to know the flavors of these varieties when they're youthful, and how these flavors and aromas change over time. It's no more astonishing for a well-educated wine lover to taste a wine and say, "I believe this is a good Burgundy, perhaps a Nuits-St-Georges, with a good bit of age on it, maybe a 1989," and be correct, than for a well-educated antique dealer to say, "That is an English candlestick with the English lion rampant theme, produced in Bristol between 1850 and 1858," and be correct. When you know what something is, it's easy. But it takes time and the ability to taste a lot of wine without swallowing it all.

TO HAVE GIFTS AT THE READY

Having favored bottles laid down means you always have gifts at the ready, although when giving wine from your cellar to family, friends, and acquaintances, you will find yourself on the horns of a dilemma: Some bottles are just too prized to be given away (translation: you want to drink them yourself), but others aren't quite good enough for a gift. It comes down to how much pain you're willing to endure. The more it hurts to give a bottle away, the more that bottle means to you, and the more it might be appreciated by the recipient. However, the Bible admonishes us not to cast our pearls before swine, and so it makes little sense to give a $120 bottle of Caymus 'Special

SELECTING A BIRTH-YEAR WINE

Fortunately for future generations, California rarely has a bad vintage of the longest-lasting wines like Cabernet Sauvignon, Merlot, Cabernet Franc, or Meritage blends of Bordeaux varieties. Okay, 1982 wasn't very good, but you'd be hard-pressed to find a really bad year since then. Received wisdom had it that 1989 wasn't a good year in California. Well, it did rain just before the harvest period for white wine, and a lot of Sauvignon Blanc and Chardonnay rotted on the vine, but the tough-skinned red varieties were fine. In fact, 1989 Cabernet Sauvignons are drinking really well right now when they're 12 years old, and I expect them to improve some more.

Similarly, many people thought 1998 was a difficult year — and it was, with rain late in the spring and early in the fall. But winemaking has come a long way from the era when all a winemaker could do about bad weather was wring his hands and pray to the weather gods. The 1998 vintage may not be one for long cellaring, but you need to drink something while you're waiting for the good vintages to age into sumptuous maturity.

French wine has more definite good and bad years. Even with first growth wines, good years can be absolutely superb, and bad years can be not worth drinking. Be aware of this if you're going to lay down a birth-year wine for an infant who won't drink it for 21 years. If it's a great year for French wine, like 2000, go ahead and cellar French for the kid. If it's not such a good year in France, you're usually safe going with the California wine. Italian and Australian wines tend to be more even in their quality, much like California, although Italy has its odd cold and rainy summer, and 2002 was a disaster because of hail in Tuscany. Remember that reds will usually be more age-worthy than whites, although that isn't always the case (see chapter 3). Check vintage charts before making your final decision.

Selection' Cabernet Sauvignon to the neophyte or casual wine drinker. They would probably be just as happy with a fruit-driven, easy-drinking, modest member of the fighting varietal clan — that is, bottles in the $8 to $12 range.

Because good wines will age for years, even decades, a wine cellar is a place to store wines to be given as presents on special birthdays. I have a friend whose daughter was born in 1985, which happened to be a very good year for Cabernet Sauvignon in Sonoma County. I purchased a magnum of 1985 B. R. Cohn 'Olive Hill' Cabernet when it was released in 1987, created a "happy 21st birthday" label and pasted it on the back of the bottle, and sent the wine to my friend. When his daughter reaches 21, in 2006 — just three years from this writing — he's going to present her with the wine, 21 years old, one hopes as beautifully blossomed into maturity as the young woman herself.

In fact, it's traditional here in the Wine Country to lay down a bottle, magnum, jeroboam, or even a case of a birth-year wine for a newborn. That's great if your birth year happens to be a very good vintage, less great if the year is less than stellar. Who wants to wait 21 years for a wine that went over the hill after year eight?

AESTHETICS

Aesthetics is a driving force for many wine collectors. A great wine can be a work of art. But its evanescent nature makes it more like music or dance — here for the moment and then gone with the wind (or the roast beef) — than like a painting or sculpture. Still, there's a strong connection between wine and art. Hess Collection winery on Mount Veeder in Napa County, California, is a bona fide fine art gallery as well as a winery. Château Mouton-Rothschild in Bordeaux has been putting reproductions of paintings by famous artists on its labels for years. Kenwood Vineyards in California has been doing the same thing, and now Imagery, a small but highly regarded winery in Glen Ellen, California, not only puts reproductions of paintings on its labels but also hangs the original paintings in its tasting room. Imagery wines are available only at the tasting room (and a few lucky restaurants that the winery owners favor).

The Labels

Even without artwork, labels themselves can be classy-looking works of art. The typographer's art is on display on many French wine labels, and the calligrapher's art can be seen on many in France and the United States. Some have a modern look; others have the look of an old engraving. Labels, in fact, provide one of the aesthetic pleasures of collecting wine, and those who cellar their wines should give attention to storage systems that don't scuff or tear the labels, or worse, subject them to conditions where labels become moldy.

COPIA

The connection between wine and the arts became stronger with the opening of COPIA — The American Center for Wine, Food & the Arts in Napa, California (see Resources, page 237). This multimillion-dollar facility includes artwork, display gardens of organic produce, and events centered around wine's place at the table and in the well-lived life. Visitors to the Napa Valley should be sure to stop at COPIA to see what events are happening there.

The Mystery

COPIA offers more proof, if more were needed, that there's something exquisite about a bottle of really fine wine. First of all, there's the pleasure that the wine inside the bottle promises — and it is only promise, because one never knows just how pleasurable it will be until the cork is drawn and the wine poured and tasted. That enticement and excitement is part of the wine's cachet. Inside its dark green or dead-leaf green bottle, the wine is black, mysterious, hidden, waiting — perhaps for years and years — for its moment to arrive. In fact, a bottle dusty with accumulated years in a wine cellar is especially treasured.

I remember buying a bottle of fairly well-aged (maybe 15 years) Port in a New York City liquor store and noticing that the bottle was dusty, as though it had lain in a cobwebbed cellar for ages. But a little rub with my thumb didn't wipe the glass clean. I mentioned this to the store owner, who said, "Oh, they spray that stuff on the bottles. It's a mixture of dust and glue. Makes the bottles look ancient, doesn't it?" So not every dusty bottle has acquired its dust honestly.

The Bottle

The glass bottle itself can be a beautiful thing. High-priced red wines are usually put into high-priced bottles. The marks of quality include a shape that tapers slightly from the shoulders of the bottle to its base, becoming smaller at the base. Feel the bottom of the bottle for the indentation called a *punt*. Less expensive wine bottles have a flat bottom with no indentation. If the glass is thick and the punt deep, and especially if the slight bulge in the center of the bottom of the punt has a fractured edge, you are looking at quality.

The heavier the bottle, the thicker the glass and the more expensive it is. Some wineries go for extra tall bottles, which makes their product stand out on the market shelf, but makes life difficult for folks like us who cellar our own wine and have to deal with these odd-sized bottles that stick out too far, making their perch on the wine rack precarious, or, if they're stored in cardboard cases, project out so it's impossible to close the case.

Sometimes wineries will have bottles, especially the larger sizes, etched and hand painted with their labels or designs that make the bottle really special. There are businesses devoted to doing that here in the Wine Country, including California Etching and Bergin Glass Impressions, both in Napa. I spoke with Jill Spragio, art director at Bergin, and she said that the big etched bottles are used to solicit high bids at charity wine auctions, for wine distributor incentives, and as marketing tools for wineries — hence, the big, etched bottles you see sitting on counters and back bars throughout California. They can also be used for wedding presents or any special occasion. The designs are etched into the glass using a small sandblasting tool, leaving raised and sunken areas. These are then painted with enamel paints and dried.

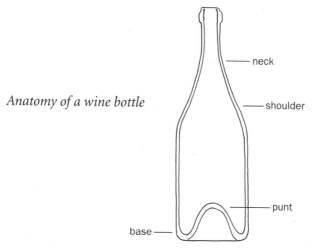

Anatomy of a wine bottle

neck

shoulder

punt

base

THE ORIGIN OF THE PUNT

I've heard many explanations for the punt, including these:

- It's there to collect sediment that falls to the bottom when an old wine is stood upright.

- The punt enables the waiter to hold the bottle with one hand, thumb inserted into the punt, while he pours wine into the glass he's holding with the other hand.

- The bottom of the bottle is indented so that when bottles are laid end to end, the neck of the following bottle can rest in the punt of the forward bottle.

- Even the usually accurate *Oxford Companion to Wine* says, "Most champagne and sparkling wine bottles have a particularly deep indentation because of the need to stack inverted bottles one on top of the other during the traditional method of sparkling wine-making. Punts are obviously less useful for still wines — although they can make 75 cL capacity bottles look bigger and more impressive — and deep punts can provide useful purchase for the thumb when serving wine from a bottle."

I think all of this is nonsense. It's silly to think that punts are there to make the bottles look more impressive.

The punt is an artifact of the glassmaker's art. It's there because when thick glass is formed into wine bottles, the punt is where the molten glass is perched during its formation. When wine bottles were handblown by artisans, they would be cracked off the molten chunk of glass from which they were formed, leaving a slightly fractured edge in the center of the punt. If you have such a bottle, it was undoubtedly made many, many years ago, because today, even fine wine bottles are made in factories.

About four years ago, Bergin began silk-screening labels onto bottles using enamel paints that are then fired. "The paints are actually annealed onto the glass," Spragio says. "These labels don't mildew in the wine cellar, they don't tear, and they don't slough off." All wineries have to do is get the silk-screened bottles back, fill them, cork them, foil them, and sell them. Because of cost factors, most of the silk-screened bottles are ordered by small boutique wineries with 250- to 500-case runs of wines priced $20 per bottle and up.

Silk-screened, enameled, oven-fired labels have a lot of advantages over paper labels that can so easily be destroyed by the ravages of time. Also, etched and painted or silk-screened labels make the bottles as collectible as the wine.

FOR PLEASURE!

Among all the reasons to collect wine, one reason stands out: Wine is an exquisite substance. The ancient Greeks and Romans, along with many other cultures, sang its praises. In ancient Judaea, Jesus changed water into wine at the wedding feast of Cana and left us his legacy in a bit of bread and a draught of wine. And if you have not read *The Rubaiyat* of Omar Khayyám lately, give it a peek. Among its gorgeous verses we find these lines:

> *Drink! For you know not whence you came, nor why:*
> *Drink! For you know not why you go, nor where.*

And then the poet poses a question that is intriguing even today:

> *I wonder often what the vintners buy*
> *One half so precious as the stuff they sell.*

Exquisite. Precious. Delightful. These adjectives can apply to wine, but they also apply to anything that pleases our senses. A Beethoven symphony is pleasure for the ears. Loving caresses please the sense of touch. A Rembrandt painting is pleasure for the eyes. A rose gives pleasure to the nose. Chocolate pleases the palate. Wine pleases more than one sense, however — it gives pleasure to three senses, at least. Its lovely color pleases the eyes. Its fragrance pleases the sense of smell. Its flavors, for fine wines have layers of flavors, please the sense of taste.

Stoppered up in a classy package and laid down in a wine cellar, resting but improving as it rests, wine is truly a gift of the gods.

Look what it does for us. Wine enhances our meals, increasing our enjoyment of them. Dining is a prime social activity — a person eating alone in a restaurant is rarely a joyful sight. Wine relaxes us at the table and at our social gatherings, bringing forth stories, mirth, and sometimes, truth, for *in vino veritas*. It enhances our appreciation of life, and in its own way makes life that much more worth living.

I can speak from personal experience when I say that a wine cellar is a trove of pleasures yet to come. I know that within its dark vault lie the accompaniments to delicious meals and future festivities, toasts to successes yet to happen, gifts for friends I haven't met, and cheer for those occasions when cheer will be needed. It is the glint and polish upon my future. It is my validation of today and a declaration of my faith in a benign tomorrow. It is something to look forward to.

CHAPTER 2

Selecting and Acquiring Wine

What's the big deal about acquiring wine? You just hop in the car, go down to the store, and acquire some, right?

Well, no. There's a lot more to it than that. Going to the supermarket or liquor store may be fine for folks who don't have a wine cellar. They just pick up a bottle of wine they think will go with their dinner that night. In fact, something like 95 percent of the wine that's purchased in the United States is consumed within a few days of purchase. Most ordinary wines are probably at or near their best when they're purchased. Oh, the wine might benefit from being laid quietly in the closet for a few weeks, just to get over its travel sickness (wines that are shaken up by travel need a few weeks to calm down and regain their grip), but the travel sickness effect is a modest one at best. Most wines on the supermarket shelves, especially those in the $8 to $12 price range, are made and meant to be consumed fairly soon after bottling.

An interesting side note: Because most supermarket shopping is done by women, many modestly priced wine labels are designed to catch the female eye. If you think that statement shows gender bias, don't blame me. Wine is just one of thousands of products that marketers pitch to women, just as they pitch others to men. Wine, like any other product of commerce, is subject to marketeering.

Some of the *vin ordinaire* on the supermarket shelves may improve with a few years of bottle aging, but most is made for the short haul. In fact, it's a conscious decision on the part of most supermarkets to sell wines that are ready to drink right off the shelf. These markets aren't going to stock their shelves with wines that will age well and are suitable for laying down in a wine cellar because such wines are still tight right off the shelves. Shoppers who want a bottle of wine for that night's dinner will be disappointed in a hard, tight, tannic, unyielding wine, no matter how glorious it will be in 12 years. Even folks with wine cellars won't be drinking perfectly aged fine wines every day. We need some everyday wines to fill the gaps between memorable bottles and to drink while we're waiting for our cellared wines to mature. So, it's a good thing that there's a wide choice of wines that are ready to drink and easily available.

However, what we're talking about in this book is acquiring wine for our wine cellars — that is, wine that we believe will improve with time. That will take more time and effort than simply nabbing a bottle at the supermarket for dinner the same night, but like most activities in our modern world, whole industries are set up just to take care of the needs of folks who want to lay down a few bottles. The most important asset you can have for finding wine to cellar is your own taste — your palate preferences. Realize, though, that these preferences are a moving target. My first taste of wine, for instance, happened when I was about seven or eight years old and my parents let me taste a glass of their wine. I remember the winery and even what the label looked like because that taste engraved itself on my memory so indelibly. The winery was Virginia Dare and the label carried a picture of a young woman. I had no idea who she was, although I later learned that she was the first child of English parents born in the New World (in 1587). I also later learned that Virginia Dare wine was made from the Scuppernong grape (*Vitis rotundifolia*), a native of North Carolina (and other Southern states), just as Miss Dare herself was. The only problem was that the wine tasted so horrible (gasoline is a good descriptor) that I distinctly remember thinking to myself, "Why would anyone drink this stuff?" At that age, I preferred Coke. Entry-level wines are usually simple at best.

I must have been a college freshman before I tasted another wine that I thought was at least palatable. It was a bulk wine made by the Taylor wine company in upstate New York called "Lake Country White." It must have been made from the grape varieties called Diamond or Niagara — white versions of native American *Vitis labrusca,* whose most well-known member is Concord. The defining taste of these grapes is that aromatic, sweet, grapey, Welch's Grape Juice flavor called foxy. It was juicy-fruity and syrupy but still a small step up from Coke and Virginia Dare.

My next discovery was a huge leap forward: At age 23, I tried a bottle of French Beaujolais, a fresh, fruity, modest wine but made from *Vitis vinifera,* the classic wine grape species of the Old World that includes all the finest wine grape varieties, including Cabernet Sauvignon, Chardonnay, Riesling, Merlot, Pinot Noir, Cabernet Franc, and Sauvignon Blanc, among dozens of others. This, I thought, was a delicious wine. It became my standard of quality for a number of years. I tried California wine in the late 1960s, but the best I found was jug wine called NSM, explained further as wine from Napa, Sonoma, and Mendocino counties. It was awful plonk, hard, devoid of fruit, and bitter. Other jug wines were worse. I didn't have access to the good California wines that were being made at the time.

By 1970, at age 30, I finally broke through into German Rieslings, Alsatian Gewürztraminers, and the other wines of France: Bordeaux and Burgundy reds and whites. Through the 1970s and the first half of the 1980s, I educated my palate about wine and myself about how grapes are grown and wine is made. Alden and Aurora were the first grapes I planted at home, but Aurora bore only scantily, and Alden's generous crops were annually infected with brown rot that spoiled the fruit before it ripened. I soon planted a wine grape, the French-American hybrid Chancellor, that is hardy in the USDA Zone 6 area of Pennsylvania where I was living and didn't have the disease problems of Alden. I would have planted *Vitis vinifera* but knew that the vines wouldn't survive winters that occasionally got down to 20 below zero. Finally I was growing grapes, getting them ripe, making wine, and enjoying it. The wine wasn't Château Lafite, but it had a rich fruitiness that my friends seemed to enjoy even more than I did.

The learning curve that had been almost straight up until age 30 began to level off. As my knowledge of fine wine grew, so did my passion for wine. My taste became more refined, and I was able to tell at a sip much about the provenance and qualities, including cellar age, of the wine in the glass. Finally, in 1985, I just gave up trying to indulge my passion for wine on the East Coast and moved to the Wine Country of California, bringing several cases of Bordeaux with me, which became the foundation of my wine cellar. I recently drank up the last bottle of 1982 Calon Ségur that I'd purchased before my move west. It was 19 years old and perfect.

Once settled in California, I discovered just how much I didn't know about wine. Again I began learning in great gulps and swallows of information. I'm still learning something about soil, climate, grapevines, fruit, and wine almost every day.

I recount this time line to illustrate what I said before: The most important asset you can have for finding wine to cellar is your own taste — your palate preferences. Educating your palate is primary. How can you know what to cellar if you don't know what you want to cellar and why you want to cellar it? So, where do you get this education?

CONSULT THE EXPERTS

Many people rely on the educated palates of others. Take your pick among the wine journals. The most influential are *The Wine Spectator* and *The Wine Advocate,* especially the latter. *The Wine Advocate* was begun around 1980 by Robert M. Parker Jr., a Maryland attorney. He has an uncanny ability to remember the taste of wines — thousands upon thousands of them. He devised a 100-point scoring system to rate wines (it's really a 50-point score because 50 is the bottom mark and 100 is the top). He publishes his opinions about the wines he tastes in *The Wine Advocate,* and his opinions are honest, trenchant, and carefully described. Similarly, a handful of people rate wines for *The Wine Spectator,* using a 100-point scale. You'll find wine ratings in a number of publications, including *The Wine News, The Underground Wine Journal, The Connoisseur's Guide,* and *The Wine Enthusiast,* among others. These ratings are important as a general indication of quality. Few of us can

taste all the wines tasted by the panels of these publications, and so we may rely on their assessments to get a line on wines we haven't tasted ourselves.

The problem with using these ratings as your guide is that you are taking your opinions from someone else. It's well-known that Parker enjoys bold, robust, concentrated wines, and he gives high marks to those kinds of wines. It's his opinion and he's entitled to it. James Laube of *The Wine Spectator* gives high ratings to California wines that show a certain profile of quality, especially richness and concentration of flavor. But those ratings only reflect the opinions of two men. There's a whole world of different opinions out there. Here's what one Napa Valley winemaker wrote to me about the necessity for diverse opinions regarding wine:

> *Our industry is much more diverse and complex than the opinions of two strong, very effective writers expressing their individual points of view. Because they've been so effective in their writing and their dedication, they have captured the consuming public's admiration, overlooking*

the fact that there are other styles of wines that are gentler, friendlier, with finesse and elegance that will harmonize better with food — each style being outstanding. We all want to let the world know of the different ramifications that wine has to offer.

Using the palates of Parker and Laube as your own may be fine for the occasional wine buyer, but not for the master or mistress of a working wine cellar. That cellar should reflect your personal tastes and preferences.

Along with his opinions on the quality of a wine, Parker usually gives an indication of when he thinks the wine will reach its peak of quality. Again, however, some people like wines when they are young and fruity, others like

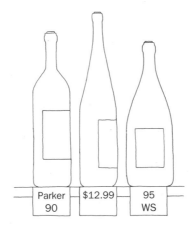

Shelf talkers, *the little tags near the bottles of wine on market shelves, may give clues to a wine's value or quality.*

them better when they are very well aged — and there's someone with a preference for every stop in between. Here's an example of what Parker has to say about a certain Châteauneuf-du-Pape: "This serious, concentrated, muscular Châteauneuf-du-Pape requires 2 to 3 years of cellaring, and should keep for 15 to 18 years." In other words, the wine will increase in quality for about 3 years, then its quality will hold fairly steady for the next 15 to 18 years, after which it will decline. But Parker's opinions aren't graven in stone. You may think such a wine will keep increasing in quality for more than 3 years, and that at 15 years, the wine might thin out too much. You might come to these conclusions because of your experience with previous Châteauneufs. Your opinions need to be based on experience, which is the foundation of an educated palate. Parker's and Laube's opinions certainly are, and they are always there as a backup. But there's no substituting another's taste for your own when you are creating a wine cellar.

The ratings of Parker and *The Wine Spectator* influence the wine marketplace tremendously. Their ratings have a big impact on price. Most of the wine-buying public have probably never read a single issue of *The Wine Advocate* or *The Wine Spectator*. But they use the publications' 100-point rating systems for a guide when they're buying wine because the marketing and public relations departments of wineries, chain stores, mail-order clubs, and retailers from coast to coast use them to promote wines to the public.

Novice wine buyers innocently go by the numbers. They deem anything that scores less than 90 points not worth drinking. Parker knows this and it doesn't make him happy. "Scores are abused by retailers," he says. "I would have trademarked my scoring system years ago had I known how popular it would become. But I believe in the 100-point system. The British way of scoring wine — fine, very fine — is a cop-out. If I give a wine 90 points, I need to back it up with good, well-written tasting notes that communicate a wine's weight and accessibility."

Most novice wine buyers who go by the scores of Parker and *The Wine Spectator* don't understand that those scores represent a bias toward wines of "ultra-ripeness, majestic richness, and provocative intensity," in Parker's words. Not everyone thinks that such ultra-ripeness is a good thing. "Everybody wants these terribly extracted and over-oaked wines," one wine retailer told me, "but have you ever had one with dinner?" Parker insists that while his 100-point (perfect) scores are given to rich wines, they have to show balance and symmetry. "It's all about intensity and balance," he says. I'm sure Parker and the panel at *The Wine Spectator*, among others, know what they like and rate it high when they taste it. But the net result is that personal opinions of wines, as represented by scores, have been magnified far beyond their inherent value. When wines are given a high score, prices soar.

That's because the better the wine, usually the less of it there is. Demand creates price increases. So when people go for wines that have high ratings, they're paying a premium price for the label. However, labels can fall in and out of fashion. If people have great difficulty getting a wine, they're more willing to pay exorbitant prices for it (witness the $1,000 a bottle prices asked for some of Napa Valley's so-called cult wines on Internet wine sites). In many cases, demand drives the winery to make more wine. Once it becomes widely available, though, the trophy hunters usually start looking elsewhere.

My take on cult or trophy wines is that while many can be excellent, they're not worth the money.

Truth be told, a wine retailer told me, trophy hunters have to pay huge sums for their wine when they can get them at all, and they aren't really concerned with their cellars as a source of wine for their table. "They're happy because they have the wine in their cellars, not on their dinner tables. The wines are trophies," he said.

So, as the consumer, try to ignore the ratings and find out what you like — what gives you the most pleasure in the glass — and find out who's making those wines. Wineries tend to be consistent from year to year. When you find a label you like, try a bottle every year; chances are you'll like it. Stick with wineries you know are good. They may not be the most expensive, or highly rated, wines around. But they'll be wines that suit your taste.

DISCOVERING YOUR TASTE

It's important for you to discover what you like in a wine, but how do you do that in a way that makes sense? If you drank a bottle a day, you'd taste only 365 wines a year and that would hardly put a nick in what's available — and you'd damage your health as well as your bank balance. A glass or two of wine daily is a healthy amount; more is not. So, you must try to maximize the number of wines you taste and minimize the amount you actually swallow. The number of wines is maximized by attending wine tastings. The amount swallowed is minimized by the sniff-swirl-taste-spit formula (see page 81). Not every drop that enters the mouth needs to go down the gullet.

Wine Tastings

Go to wine tastings. Join a private group or find a wine shop, restaurant, or other establishment that holds tastings on a regular basis.

Private groups can be fun. They usually comprise a group of wine-loving friends. If you don't know of one, start one. Six or seven people is a good number. If everyone brings a bottle, you'll have six or seven wines to taste. Fewer people may hardly make the effort worthwhile. More than seven and the tasting group (and wines to taste) may exhaust the host and hostess as well as the palates of the participants.

If the purpose of your tasting is to become acquainted with certain wines, there's no need to have a blind tasting (where the participants don't know anything about the wines in their glasses). But it's smart to have a theme. Let everyone know well in advance about the theme and make it broad enough to avoid duplication of bottles. If your theme is "Condrieu" and your liquor store only stocks one Condrieu, it's a good bet everyone will show up with the same bottle of wine. A better theme might be "Zinfandel." Here you have a choice of bottles from the Sierra foothills east of Sacramento, Sonoma's Dry Creek and Russian River valleys, Mendocino County, Sonoma Valley, Napa Valley, Contra Costa County, Paso Robles, the Central Valley, and lots of other California sites in between.

If the purpose is to evaluate the quality of wines of a certain type, say Zinfandel, then a blind tasting is in order. The bottles are placed into paper bags and numbered. The participants know they're all Zinfandel, but that's all they know. That way participants aren't influenced by the labels. The wines are tasted and notes taken, scores are assigned to the wines (you can use the 100-point score or, more typically, scoring can be done on a 20-point

scale, with 20 being the highest score), and then the scores are toted up. Everyone discusses which wines they liked, didn't like, or were indifferent to. Then the bags are removed and the wine labels revealed. You'd be surprised at the number of times modestly priced wines will score right up there with the pricey ones.

One of the most interesting tasting groups I've sat in with was the gang that showed up for tastings at Michael's Wine Cellar, a wine shop in Corte Madera, California. The proprietor, Michael Boyd, would collect six or seven wines of rare quality — Bordeaux from the 1950s, Burgundies from the 1960s, and other old and promising treasures, including older California vintages. He'd total the cost of these bottles (the cost was kept down because he bought them wholesale) and divide by the number of people in the group, usually eight or so. Thus for the reasonable cost of a seat at the tasting bar, you could taste wines worth many hundreds of dollars. I never missed a chance to attend one of these because they were so educational, not only about how the wines aged, but also about the wineries that produced them, the vintage years, and how the same grape variety can produce very different flavors in different parts of the world. Because I probably would never get to taste these wines again, I kept a little notebook with my impressions of each wine. I encourage you, when you do a tasting, to keep a notebook and take personal notes for yourself. Even if you don't refer to these notes very often, the mere process of writing down the name of the winery, the year, the variety, the appellation, and your impressions of the aroma and flavors of the wine will help engrave these facts on your memory.

Your Local Wine Merchant

Another way to educate your palate is to get to know the proprietor of a good wine shop — someone you can work with and someone you like personally. Ask him or her for recommendations, try the recommended wines at home, and let the proprietor know what you think of them. After a while, the proprietor will begin to get a feel for what you like and will be able to tailor recommendations to your taste. The wine shop proprietor will also be able to give you some idea of how long to age the wines you like.

Because I lived in Pennsylvania for many years, I used to travel to New York City to buy wine. Pennsylvania's medieval system of state-controlled liquor and wine shops meant that wine could only be purchased in one of the state's retail outlets. There was no incentive for the state to supply wine lovers with choice selections, and so the liquor stores carried whatever brands the Liquor Control Board decided to do business with. Not only that, but if you were caught at the state border bringing liquor or wine into Pennsylvania that was purchased outside the state, you could have your car permanently confiscated. It happened to a friend of mine. And so, feeling a bit like a smuggler, I'd make my runs to New York's Sherry-Lehmann wine shop for European wines and to Park Avenue Liquors (located, oddly, on Madison Avenue) for its selection of California wines.

Over the years, I got to know one of the employees at Sherry-Lehmann fairly well — Hy Gelfand. He was a short, portly man in late middle age who knew much more about European wines, especially French ones, than I, and I relied on him to give me suggestions. I remember showing up at the store one day and asking for him. He came out to greet me. We shook hands and then stood there for a moment of awkward silence, broken when he looked out over the racks of wine on the shop floor and said, "Yes, wine is of interest." Besides discovering much about French wine, I also learned from Mr. Gelfand that the perfect way to break an awkward pause is to say something profoundly obvious.

QUALITY, NOT QUANTITY

Now I live in California, where you can buy liquor, wine, and beer along with a fill-up at many gas stations. The supermarkets and convenience stores sell wine. But I still buy most of my treasures at wine shops — Sonoma Wine Exchange in Sonoma, Bottle Barn in Santa Rosa, St. Helena Wine Merchants in the Napa Valley, Root & Eastwood in Healdsburg, Kermit Lynch in Berkeley, and various stores all over San Francisco.

One of my favorite wine shops is Enoteca Wine Shop ("One Location Worldwide!") in Calistoga, California, operated by Margaux Singleton and Frederick Schrader. Stephen Tanzer of *Food & Wine* calls it "one of America's

top wine shops." *Town & Country* says, "rarities from small producers the world over, taste-tested before stocking." And *Travel & Leisure* proclaims the shop to be "for oenophiles," which I'd say characterizes anyone contemplating creating a wine cellar. Enoteca has wines from $9 and up, but most of its wines are up, up, and away. A recent newsletter offered "our annual oo-la-la box" of four bottles of wine for $912. Included are one bottle of Shafer 'Hillside Select' Cabernet from the Stags Leap part of the Napa Valley, an Hourglass Cabernet (only 45 cases made), a Jones Family Cab from Heidi Barrett, a currently "hot" winemaker in the Napa Valley, and a Château de Valandraud from St-Emilion, a so-called garage wine from France (because it's made in such small quantities, it's as if it were made in someone's garage). I like looking around this shop, even though most of the wines are out of my financial reach.

Although my resources, like most people's, are limited, I still spend a certain amount of money on wine each year, and I always keep this slogan in mind: Great wine in, great wine out. Cellaring cheap or inferior wine will not improve it. Rather than spend $120 for a case of bulk Cabernet Sauvignon, I'd rather spend $120 on a single bottle of an excellent Cab, such as Stag's Leap Wine Cellars 'Fay Vineyard' from the Napa Valley, a Chateau St. Jean 'Cinq Cépages' from Sonoma County, or Bolgheri Superiore Ornellaia from Tuscany. A wine cellar is not about quantity but, rather, about quality. A cellar with 50 bottles of really great wine is much more attractive than a cellar with 500 bottles of undistinguished wines. Besides, one of the most common mistakes made by owners of new wine cellars is to want to fill them up right away, to see all those bottles looking so nice in their neat stacks, even if that means stocking them with mediocre wines. Build the cellar and the wines will come. Just don't rush it. Save your pennies for wines worth cellaring. Besides, if you fill it up right away, where will you put the wines worth cellaring that will keep coming season after season? Avoid guides that say a good wine cellar should contain 20 percent Bordeaux, 15 percent California Cabernet, 10 percent Burgundy, 8 percent Côte Rôtie or other Rhône reds, 5 percent sparkling wine (either French or American), and so on. Nonsense. That's formulaic and has nothing to do with your personal taste. One of the finest wine cellars I ever encountered was owned by a friend in New Jersey who cellared only Bordeaux from great years.

AGE MATTERS

Anyone contemplating building a wine cellar needs to know how much age will bring his or her favorite wines to the place where they're most appealing. In very old wines, the fruit can fade away, leaving impressions of oak, acidity, and dried leaves as the dominant organoleptic factors. (You may find the term *organoleptic* cropping up in wine discussions. It's a 10-dollar word that means "pertaining to sensory impressions.")

Some people have a tendency to over-age wine — to let it go until it's past its peak of pleasure. That's based on the reputation of the great French Bordeaux and Burgundies, which, in great years, really do seem to last forever. But it may not be true for wines of lesser greatness. Your job as a wine cellar owner is to find out which wines will age, which won't; which wines you think are great, which you don't; and at what stage they most appeal to your palate, at what stage they don't. This means acquiring a great deal of information not only about wine, but also about what you personally like in wine. That may sound like a simple assignment ("I can't say what I like, but I'll know it when I taste it"), but it can become very detailed and complex.

A lifetime spent exploring wine will continually reveal treasures of information about subjects you didn't even know existed when you began your inquiry. When I started my love affair with wine, I knew that yeast ferments grape juice to make wine, and that was it. Now I know that there are many kinds of yeast, each of which imparts a different flavor profile and yields a different result if used to ferment the grape juice. Some of these yeasts will make great wine, and some will spoil it. Bacteria are involved, too, which tame the stark bite of malic acid and smooth it into soft, refreshingly tart lactic acid. If you inquire further, you'll find that scientists are working to modify the genetic structure of yeasts and bacteria to turn them into life-forms that will do what the scientists want them to do rather than what nature intends for them to do. And this leads into deep levels of microbiology and ethics that are now full-time occupations for many people around the world.

The more you study wine, the more information you gain. The more information you gain, the more you understand wine. The more you understand wine, the more refined your taste becomes. The more refined your taste, the more passionate about wine you become. And isn't it wonderful — doesn't it make life worth living — to have passions?

You can get more information about a particular wine by buying two or three bottles of your selection. With a single bottle, you pretty much have to make a proper guess as to when to drink it. You'll find out whether you were right or not when you open it, but you'll have no basis for comparison. If you have two or three bottles, or a case, you can open one every three or four years. When you feel the wine is delivering all the pleasure it can give, then you know it's time to finish off any bottles you have left. Having multiple bottles allows you to follow the development of a wine, which educates you so you can make better choices of which wines to buy for cellaring in the future, and how long to age them.

Having a good wine shop nearby helps in acquiring wines for cellaring, but even the most lavish wine shop can hold only a small percentage of the wines that are available on the market. That's why it helps to belong to a mail-order wine club. The folks who run these clubs scour the world for wines they think their customers will like, and so there's a selection process to weed out the real dogs. Sometimes these clubs offer exceptional wines at impossible prices. How can that be? Won't cheap wines turn out to be thin, unappealing, characterless wines?

Not necessarily. Wineries are like auto dealerships. When the new vintage is due to arrive, they want to sell that unsold inventory, even if they have to reduce prices. Therefore, savvy wine club operators can get some very good wines for very attractive prices.

Another reason why you might be offered good wine for cheap is that it may be a varietal that hasn't caught the public's fancy yet — and probably will before long. Have you ever heard of Charbono? Valdiguié? Roussanne? Most people haven't, and yet these varietals, and many like them, can produce superior wines. They just won't sell at superior prices.

Sometimes a year will come along in which ordinary producers will find themselves with some extraordinary wines. The climate was just right. It rained or didn't rain at the right times. There was enough sun at the right times. The weather was perfect for ripening. Suddenly, *vin ordinaire* becomes *vin extraordinaire.* In 1991 in California, the harvest season was very cool and slow, and harvest was long delayed. I personally harvested my Cabernet Sauvignon from Sonoma Mountain around Thanksgiving, when it's usually in the fermenters by the beginning of October. The long, slow maturation gave the grapes enormously long hang time, which allowed them not only to become ripe but also to become fully mature. All over Sonoma, Napa, and Mendocino Counties, ordinary vineyards produced extraordinary wines. Their prices reflected their ordinariness, but the wine in the bottle was worth much more. Mail-order wine clubs apprise their members of such occurrences and offer the wines at reasonable prices. Even cheap Bordeaux from 2000 is usually good.

Mail-order wine clubs sometimes also hype wines that may not be all the marketing copy represents them to be. That's why the savvy buyer needs to find a mail-order source he or she trusts. A few experiences of being burned — spending good money for lackluster wines — should turn you away from the dealer. A few experiences getting more value than you paid for should cement your relationship with a dealer.

I recently received some offerings from a mail-order wine club in California. The club is reputable. Not every wine they gush over will be worth all the gushing, but most are quite good. You have to read between the lines with the sort of material they send. I give you my take on some such copy on page 40.

Wine club newsletters can be very helpful in identifying wines with aging potential. Most of them do this by quoting *The Wine Spectator* or Robert Parker. In a recent issue of *The Rare Wine Company's* newsletter, the following wines were offered for sale, with notes on their aging potentials by Parker as follows:

1999 MONTEPELOSO 'ROSSO' (TUSCAN SANGIOVESE)
"This pure, symmetrical effort should drink well for 8–10 years."
1999 NARDO (SUPERTUSCAN)
"This tour de force in winemaking should age for 12–15 years."
1998 CHÂTEAU DE BEAUCASTEL (CHÂTEAUNEUF-DU-PAPE)
"Ideally, it needs another 3–4 years of cellaring and should keep for 25–30 years."
1998 CHAPOUTIER 'BARBE RAC' (CHÂTEAUNEUF-DU-PAPE)
"Drink it over the following 20–25 years."
1998 ROGER SABON 'CUVÉE PRESTIGE' (CHÂTEAUNEUF-DU-PAPE)
"Should age effortlessly for 25 years."

The long aging mentioned here by Parker doesn't mean that you should necessarily wait 20 or 25 years to drink the wine but, rather, that the wine will be good to drink anytime up until those limits. The only wine that Parker here suggests keeping for a while before drinking is the 1998 Beaucastel. But again, remember that these aging recommendations are Parker's and not the word of God (although some wine lovers do invoke that name when discussing Parker). You may find that wines aged to your taste are quite different from those aged to Parker's. Or you may agree entirely with him about how wines age, in which case you can simply take his recommendations as your own. That would be convenient.

My Take on Some Mail-Order Offerings

Here are some offerings I received from a reputable mail-order wine club in California. My comments on the newsletter copy appear within brackets and in italics.

1999 DROUHIN-LAROZE RED BURGUNDIES

"Serious Red Burgundies that should be in your cellar!"

The 99s from this producer have turned out to be excellent. They are the best wines this producer has made since their very successful 96s. [Well, that's not saying a lot. If the 96s and the 99s are better than the 97s and 98s, that's a 50-50 split.] The Domaine has excellent holdings in some of Côte de Nuits most coveted vineyards. [The Côte de Nuits is a prime part of Burgundy, but we have to take it on trust that Drouhin-Laroze holds excellent parts.] The wines are neither fined nor filtered and come from relatively old vines. [Those are good signs.] They have wonderful balance, purity and are true to their terroirs. [This means they have the flavors associated with the Côte de Nuits in northern Burgundy. To assess the truth of this statement, one needs to be able to identify those flavors and apply them to this wine. That's asking a lot before the wine is purchased.] They should age effortlessly for one to two decades. [Hmmm. By 20 years out, many Burgundies will be laboring to keep their quality. But maybe . . .]

LATRICIÈRES-CHAMBERTIN

From extremely old vines. Explosive nose of cherries, kirsch, and intense minerality followed by wave after wave of intensely sappy pinot flavors. [Since kirsch is cherry liqueur, how does it differ from cherries? I can understand a mineral component in the taste of a wine, but in the nose? The wave after wave of intensely sappy pinot flavors sounds like hype to me.] Not particularly complex at this moment but the components are here to permit that to develop over time. [Translate "not particularly complex" as "simple." Beware. Simple wines put into the cellar usually come out as simple wines.]

CLOS DE VOUGEOT

This and the Latricières are from the oldest vines of the domaine and this wine comes from a superbly situated parcel of Clos de Vougeot high on the hill, next to Alfred Haegelen's parcel adjoining the wall. [Well, I haven't been there, so the landscape descriptions mean nothing, but the fact that they are described at all augurs for an above-average wine.] I'm not a huge Clos de Vougeot fan; a lot of the time the wines can be very disappointing. [Good admission from the wine club writer; makes me think the copy isn't simply hype.] A key to success in this vineyard is the location of the parcel. Higher up on the hill and close to the Château des Clos Vougeot are the preferred locations. Deep ruby in color, with aeration, aromas of black cherries and black berries. ["With aeration" means that the wine's aromas didn't develop until it was allowed to open up for a while in the glass.] Wonderful core of minerality, earth, and spice. [Both "minerality" and "earth" refer to the guts of the wine — an earthiness that's appealing.] Very pure, very dense, yet suave. The finish lingers long after you taste it. A textbook example of what Clos de Vougeot can achieve in the right hands.

BONNES MARES

Not as thick as the Clos des Vougeot yet more poised and complex. [How, pray tell, is one wine more "poised" than another?] Reduced aromas [As in the chemical reductions — changes in molecular composition — that take away character?] of briary red and black fruits, minerals, forest floor, herbs and orange zest. Very intense but remains light on its feet. [Intense but poised and light on its feet — like prima ballerina Suzanne Farrell?]

Another great example of this vineyard that really marries power and elegance. I've had recently a bottle of 1978 and it was a knockout, and that wine was fined and filtered! A great value for Bonnes Mares. *[Truthfully, I've never had a Bonnes Mares I didn't swoon over.]*

CHAMBERTIN-CLOS DE BÈZE

Exotic aromas of berry, cherry, minerals, truffle, mocha, and iron. *[That's quite a nose! The smell of iron — sounds like a little hype going on here.]* Great intensity of flavors, yet at once elegant and refined. Wonderful persistence on the finish with the lingering flavors of berry and minerals going on and on. A classic Bèze that one should make room for in the cellar.

WINE AND COMPANY

Depending on the company you keep, having some very-well-aged wines to bring to a tasting or party does carry a certain prestige. Among casual wine drinkers who are not particularly educated about fine wine, a bottle of non-vintage Turning Leaf might be just as sought after as a bottle of 1991 Joseph Phelps 'Insignia.' In fact, uneducated palates may find a big old wine like the Phelps a bit strong and difficult for their taste; they may prefer something light, fresh, and fruity. Similarly, folks who don't read for pleasure may toss James Joyce aside as inscrutable. In a company of wine aficionados or winemakers, that Phelps will bring nods of approval and admiration. In fact, I have often seen such a group play serious games of one-upmanship with the wines they bring. The person who brings the oldest, rarest bottle wins. But of course, when the cork is pulled and the wine is poured for all, everybody wins.

Some may consider all this insufferable snobbery. I'd suggest that they are not candidates for having a wine cellar. All the time, expense, and effort spent on creating and operating your own wine cellar at home has to be enjoyable for you, or why do it? It also requires that you have some friends who are as passionate about good wine as you are. Nothing's sadder than the person who drinks alone. It's a hobby, it's interesting, it's erudite, and it's fun. It's exciting to have some old and rare bottles hidden away for special occasions — although occasions are hardly ever special enough for the really treasured bottles. Great bottles don't need special occasions; they *are* special occasions.

I have in my cellar a jeroboam (also known as a *double magnum,* consisting of four bottles' worth of wine) of 1987 Joseph Swan 'Ziegler Vineyard' Zinfandel — 15 years old at this writing. I originally acquired this oversize bottle because the Ziegler Vineyard Zinfandel of that vintage was such extraordinarily wonderful wine. I keep waiting for the right occasion to open it, but none has arrived so far. Since wine ages more slowly in larger bottles (I don't know why), this wine should be now just about right for drinking. Zinfandel is usually appreciated for its briary, blackberry fruit flavors. As it ages, it becomes more and more like any old red wine: That is, it loses its distinctive character and starts smelling and tasting like aged Cabernet. Most

---

TOP WINES OF 2001 *from* The Wine Spectator *and their prices at The Wine Club of Santa Ana, California*

- *TENUTA DELL'ORNELLAIA*
  BOLGHERI SUPERIORE ORNELLAIA, 1998 $144.99

- *CHÂTEAU CHEVAL BLANC*
  ST-EMILION, 1998 $289.99

- *CHÂTEAU CANON LA GAFFELIÈRE*
  ST-EMILION, 1998 $74.99

- *ANTINORI, GUADO AL TASSO*
  BOLGHERI SUPERIORE, 1998 $74.99

- *PIO CESARE*
  BAROLO, 1997 $45.99

- *CHÂTEAU SMITH-HAUT-LAFITTE*
  PESSAC-LÉOGNAN, 1998 $44.99

- *E. GUIGAL*
  BRUNE ET BLONDE, CÔTE RÔTIE, 1998 $28.99

Zinfandel is at its best — softened but with plenty of its youthful zest intact — when it's from 3 to 8 years old. Because my jeroboam is such a large bottle, the preceding 15 years have probably brought it to perfection. Probably. I must find a reason to open it soon — like money in my pocket, great wines burn a hole in my wine cellar.

WINE ALERTS

Some wine clubs will send you e-mail messages about small shipments they receive of very good wines, giving you a chance to nab a few before they all get away. The Wine Club of Santa Ana, for instance, in southern California, recently followed up *The Wine Spectator's* "Top 10 Wines of 2001" with an e-mail saying that they had seven of the ten wines in stock and they could be

purchased by pressing the "reply" button. They are a fine group of wines, but because they have the reputation and the publicity, they are very sought after, and their price reflects that, as you'll see.

Actually, The Côte Rôtie 'Brune et Blonde' from Guigal (which *The Wine Spectator* ranked as number 10) is rather a bargain at the price listed. Thus, there's a benefit from ordering from *The Wine Club* — a monthly newsletter that's actually a small newspaper, 36 pages crammed with wines for sale, with a circulation of 97,000. It's been published every month since 1976, and it's sent free to customers. Despite its friendly, familial attitude, *The Wine Club* is big business. Many of the newsletter's pages are headed with an interesting wine quote. Here are some samples from a recent edition:

In Europe we thought of wine as something as healthy and normal as food and also a great giver of happiness and well-being and delight.
—ERNEST HEMINGWAY

No thing more excellent nor more valuable than wine was ever granted mankind by God.
—PLATO

Some take their gold in minted mold,
And some in harps hereafter,
But give me mine in red, red wine
And keep the change in laughter.
—OLIVE HERFORD

Not only wine clubs and online wine retailers have newsletters — wineries do too. If you find a winery you think makes superior wine year after year, you may want to get on their mailing list for news of new releases, programs for customers, upcoming events, and other information. Many back labels on wine bottles have an e-mail or Internet address, but if you can't find that information, you can tap into the Web sites of the associations of wineries in both Napa and Sonoma Counties.

The Internet has proved to be a boon for wine retailers (see Resources for contact information). Prime Wine allows you to search their stacks online, then order directly from them. Winehouse.com is a Los Angeles–based bricks-and-mortar store with an online presence. The site has a searchable catalog, message boards, tasting groups, and reviews of many of the wines by both professionals and amateurs in the world of wine. Probably the best and most comprehensive online wine store is located at Wine.com. This store has a selection of more than 5,000 imported and domestic premium wines. It offers several very worthwhile features, including information on whether they'll ship wine to your state, online wine education, promotions and loyalty programs, sweepstakes events, and wine clubs and bulletin boards, as well as a long list of wine merchandise and accessories.

Many mail-order and Internet wine companies have specialties. The Wine Messenger features wines from small producers around the world. If you want wines that are already well aged or new, hard-to-get wines, The Chicago Wine Company has a good selection of both. Because of death, divorce, or just a desire to capitalize on years of collecting wine, really fine old cellars often come up for auction, and you can find some rare wines and good bargains at WineBid.com.

There's plenty more for wine lovers and those interested in learning more about wine on the Internet. If you enter wine-related topics in your browser's search engine, you'll find more sites than you'll ever need.

MAKE THE ROUNDS

Probably the most fun you can have acquiring wine is to do some traveling and visit the wineries. Excellent destinations include the Finger Lakes region of upstate New York, the eastern end of Long Island, southeastern Pennsylvania, Virginia, Missouri, Ohio, Washington, Oregon, and of course California. An added benefit is that places where really fine wine is grown tend to have a beautiful climate, especially California. Because wine is such a well-known feature of these places, they usually boast fine restaurants as well.

California is by far the most interesting place in the United States to go on a wine-buying vacation. In Sonoma, Napa, and Mendocino Counties — "Wine Country" — the scenery is spectacular, there's a winery with a tasting room around every corner of just about every country road, and the restaurants are world-class. Most people don't know it, but Sonoma County produces far more than wine. Oysters are farmed on the coast. Extensive fisheries ply the Pacific for fish and crab and, when the state allows it, abalone. Some of the best lambs and ducks in the world are raised on the hills near the ocean. There are large apple and orange groves. The region was once covered with redwoods, and many of the giant trees still stand. It's chock-full of small organic farms growing fresh vegetables for the residents and the restaurants. It's "where the palm tree meets the pine," according to a local song.

California's North Coast is not the only area of the state where fine wine is produced. The Central Coast from Santa Barbara to San Simeon and inland to Paso Robles is studded with wineries. The regions around Monterey County and the Santa Cruz Mountains are also home to many worthwhile wineries. To the east, the foothills of the Sierra Nevada Mountains grow some excellent Zinfandels, Barberas, and other varieties.

When visiting wineries in person, you not only usually get to taste what you're buying, but you'll also often find small production and library wines (older wines from the winery's own cellar) for sale that aren't available anywhere else. Tastes of wine in winery tasting rooms used to be free, but more and more wineries now charge a nominal amount for a few tastes. Sometimes this is $1 a taste; sometimes $5 buys you the right to taste whatever is open.

The most expensive, reserve, and single-vineyard wines that wineries produce aren't always available for tasting, yet these are probably the very wines you'll want to put in your cellar. If you explain to the person behind the tasting room counter that you're looking for wines to age, he or she just may suddenly find a bottle of the good stuff for you to taste. If you see a bottle that looks like it might be a real candidate for your cellar, go ahead and buy it and have it with dinner that night. If it turns out that your hunch was right, you can always buy more the next day, even over the phone. But don't hesitate. He who hesitates is often lost, as the better the wine, the less of it there usually is. I have been wrenchingly disappointed many times by failing to act on a good first impression, only to find that the wine is all gone when I try to buy some later on. I've learned that the really good stuff is rare enough that if you run into it, nab it then and there.

VISIT VINEYARDS

You can learn a lot about what makes good wine by visiting vineyards and wineries. Winemakers say that the quality of the wine is made in the vineyard, and that the job of the winemaker is simply not to screw it up getting it into the bottle. And it's true — you can't make good wine from bad grapes, although you can make bad wine from good grapes if you're not careful. Knowing that grapes like poor, well-drained soil with a sunny exposure gives you a clue as to why Shafer Vineyards 'Hillside Select' Cabernet Sauvignon is such a great wine (and well worth cellaring). The vines grow on rocky, parched soil with a southwest exposure. Doug Shafer says he has to meter a little water to the vines during the growing season just to keep the vines alive and working (it rarely rains in California's Wine Country from May to October, and then usually hardly more than enough to settle the dust). On the other hand, vines growing on rich bottomland along a river may produce a lot of tonnage, but they're not likely to produce high-quality wine.

Inside the winery, you may be shown the barrel room during a tour. Look at the barrel heads. In addition to the barrel-maker's name, you'll also see a letter branded into the oak: L, M, or H. These stand for "light," "medium," and "heavy" and refer to the degree of toast the cooper has given the barrel.

When barrels are made, they are charred on the inside. The heavier the char, the more toasty flavors the barrel will impart to the wine. The oak itself imparts woody flavors to the wine, and when it's overdone, oak can interfere with the flavor of the grape. As I write this, I have a bottle of Alexander Valley Cabernet open in the kitchen. I had a glass with dinner last night, and I think I'll pour the rest of the wine down the drain. It's so oaky that its predominant taste is oak wood. That's a defect. As the wine ages, that oakiness will only become more prominent and objectionable. Oak should be for a wine as perfume is for a woman: A hint is enticing but a heavy dose is sickening.

Be aware that when you buy from the winery, you pay full retail. That may be okay if it's the only way you can acquire the wine you're after, but if the brand is sold widely, you can often find the same wines discounted at large retailers. Make a note to buy the wine when you get home.

SHIPPING WINE

You can usually arrange to have wineries send wine to you, so you don't have to lug heavy cartons through the airports, unless your home state prohibits shipments of wine. If the authorities catch you getting wine through the mail in those states, it's a felony and you face serious consequences, up to and including jail time. That's right — when it comes to alcoholic beverages, state and federal authorities get their panties in a bunch. One supposes that they are strict in order to wrest every possible tax dollar from consumers, but there may also be a smidgen of the puritanical attitudes that brought us Prohibition about 85 years ago. The federal agency charged with regulating wine used to be the Bureau of Alcohol, Tobacco, and Firearms — so you can

see that wine was in some pretty seedy company. Since the reorganization of the government after the events of September 11, 2001, wine has been detached from cigarettes and guns and is now regulated by the U.S. Department of Agriculture.

To find out about your state's wine shipping rules, visit the Wine Institute's Web site (see Resources).

Keep in mind that just because it's legal to ship wine to a certain state, that doesn't mean all the common carriers will ship wine there. The Wine Institute's Web site has a "Who Ships Where" section, where you'll find an up-to-date list of common carriers that will and won't ship wine.

If you can't visit the wineries, you can acquire wine directly from them by placing telephone or online orders. Some wineries and wine merchants are national in scope and have warehouses in states where it's illegal to ship wine. If you order wine from them and live in one of the prohibited states, they may be able to fulfill your order from their in-state warehouse.

Also keep in mind that things change state by state, often every year. Bills are put forth to change the laws to allow reciprocity, to prevent reciprocity, to allow limited shipments with permits, and to institute reporting requirements for shipping. The Wine Institute's Web site is kept perfectly up-to-date, however, so you can rely on it for current information.

When wine is shipped to you legally, carriers often require an adult signature for the wine to be delivered. It's a good idea to know which carrier will be delivering your shipment, see whether they require a signature, and arrange for them to deliver the wine at a time when an adult is home.

When your wine arrives, resist the temptation to open a bottle right away. Wine has a way of entering "dumb" phases, especially after being shipped. It needs to rest in the wine cellar without being disturbed for a couple of weeks at least. Otherwise it can be prone to "bottle sickness," which occurs when the wine is agitated during shipping. Wine is a living substance and needs a few weeks to recuperate after shipment.

Sometimes the "dumb" phase can happen to wines after a year or two in the cellar. After a few more years, they may suddenly become brilliant again. How and why it happens is a mystery.

READ THE LABELS

One final word on acquiring wine: Learn what the words on wine labels mean, even the European wine labels. If a German wine label says the wine inside is *Erzeugerabfüllung,* you should know whether that's a good or a bad thing. (It means "estate bottled," so that's a good thing.)

Bordeaux labels reveal enormous amounts of information about the wine. The more closely defined the area where the wine comes from, usually the better it is. If, for instance, a wine says it comes from Bordeaux, it probably won't be as good as one that says it's from the Médoc, which is part of Bordeaux. Médoc wines, in turn, may not be as good as wines labeled Haut-Médoc (upper Médoc), because that's a more closely defined area. An Haut-Médoc wine may not be as good as one labeled with its commune, such as Paulliac, which is a defined part of the Haut-Médoc.

Finally, a wine from a château will probably be better than a wine designated only by its commune. And if the bottle says "mis en bouteille au château," that means it's estate bottled and comes from a very defined vineyard area, with attendant quality points.

Knowing the meaning of the names and designations on the labels means you can play some hunches. I've often bought a bottle of wine simply because something about the label looks classy, all the designations are good ones, the bottle is made of heavy glass with a deep punt, and something about the whole package says "Buy me!" It's nice to know that when the occasional bottle whispers like that in your ear, you can bring it home and give it a proper place to rest in your wine cellar before you open it. (See chapter 7 for more on labels.)

CHAPTER 3

How Wine Ages

The late Warren Dutton had a large ranch near Sebastopol, California, where he grew Pinot Noir and Chardonnay, among other varieties. Someone once asked Warren how long he needed to lay down one of his wines. "Lay it down?" Warren said. "Don't you know I make more of it every year?"

Actually, several winemakers have told me the same thing: The question they're most frequently asked is, "How long should I cellar this wine?" And of course, they have no answer for it, because the answer depends more on the person cellaring the wine than on the wine itself. Personal preferences rule.

The more you know about wine, the better your wine cellar will perform, delivering properly aged fine wine for your table anytime you want it. But it's not enough to know only about the bottle you have just acquired. If you knew human beings only as babies, you'd think human beings were relatively helpless little things. To really know human beings, you must know them through all the stages of their lives. Similarly, to know wine you need to know it when it's young and immature, as it ages, when it reaches as great a perfection as it's capable of, and when it's in decline. A bottle of Château Mouton-Rothschild is very different when it's first released than after it's several decades old.

Since a chief purpose of having a wine cellar is to age wine to perfection, it's important to know how and why a wine ages. Is an aged wine really better than one just a few years old? There is no categorical answer to that question. Early in the 1990s, I purchased six bottles of 1990 Lambert Bridge 'Crane

Creek' Cabernet Sauvignon — a single vineyard wine that had lots of forward fruit. Since Cabs take well to long aging, I left it alone until it was 12 years old. When I poured a glass from the first bottle, I was mightily disappointed. The gorgeous fruit had faded. The wine tasted thin and austere. I've now tried four of the bottles and they are all the same: disappointing. I should have drunk that wine when it was just four or five years old at most.

On the other hand, my winemaking pals and I made a Zinfandel in 1987 from the Long Vineyard on the east side of Dry Creek Valley in northern Sonoma County. It was a drought year, and the berries were small. They tasted intense. The wine was undrinkable, so I put it aside and tasted a bottle every few years. It remained tight, tannic, closed in, very concentrated; almost bitter. I am proud to report that now, 15 years later, the wine has finally relaxed, dropped its tannic structure, the fruit is revealed, and the wine is gloriously delicious and deeply flavored.

So, go figure. Is predicting when a wine will reach its peak just a wild guess, a crapshoot, a stab in the dark? The short answer is no. You can predict when a wine will be in full bloom. Will your predictions always be

100 percent correct? Again, the short answer is no. Most of the time you will probably be right, but because you're dealing with biology here, and biology is known to be capricious, sometimes you'll miss the mark. The wine will be either too young — too late to put it back in the bottle for more aging — or past its peak, in which case you drink a toast to what might have been and get on with life. So realize that and don't be too disappointed if your prediction wasn't correct. Most of the time it will be, and those times will give you great satisfaction in several ways.

First, you'll have the satisfaction of knowing that you were knowledgeable and clever enough to bring this wine to its full potential. Second, you'll have the great pleasure of consuming the wine in the fullness of its quality. And third, you'll most likely be able to share the experience with a friend, because older, well-aged wines, once opened, tend to be good for that evening only. By tomorrow, most will have faded away. And really old wines may not last more than a few fleeting minutes.

I remember stopping by my friend Mike's house to meet him and his wife for dinner. Before dinner, he produced a bottle of 1918 Haut-Brion. With care he drew the cork and poured the wine. It had a bouquet of fine old leather, rose petals, tea, a bit of old tobacco, and many other lovely, if ineffable, aromas. The taste was an echo of the fruit of long ago, pure silk; and the wine had lightened up considerably over the years, leaving much of its color as a residue on the inside of the bottle. Within 10 minutes, it became simple. By 20 minutes, it was flat dead. I thought of the scene in the movie *Lost Horizon* when the beautiful, young-looking woman leaves Shangri-la and once outside the valley, quickly grows old, weary, and dies.

CHANGES WITH AGING

What happens to wine that it changes so over time? Probably the most noticeable change is in the smell of the wine. A young wine has an *aroma;* that is, it smells of the fruit it's made from. Sometimes this aroma has a definite character, such as the herbaceous, green olive note of Sauvignon Blanc, or the meaty, sausage-like aroma of a concentrated St-Joseph from the Rhône Valley.

Sometimes the aroma is an indefinite smell of grapes termed *vinous*. Grapes that have a very individual, definable, and recognizable aroma include the heady, perfumy Muscat (of several types), herbaceous Sauvignon Blanc (called *grassy* by some), Cabernet Sauvignon (if the grapes are fully ripe, giving a spicy aroma with hints of green olive), Zinfandel (with bramble berry and raspberry notes), among others. Chardonnay is a chameleon — sometimes with aromas of fig, apple, citrus, or tropical fruits, depending on where it's grown and how ripe the grapes are. Then there are certain smells that arise from the fermentation process; the smell of yeast, for instance. These are all aromas and refer to the smell of the young wine. (See the Wine Aroma Wheel on page 233 to learn more about describing wine aromas.) *Aroma* is the smell of wine before it acquires bouquet.

Most often, *bouquet* refers to the smells that arise in the wine over time, although one component of the bouquet is an artifact of the fermentation process. One of the best aspects of having well-aged wine in your cellar is that you can enjoy the bouquet, especially of old red wine, and especially of old Cabernet Sauvignon. As other red wines like Cabernet Franc, Merlot, Zinfandel, and Syrah age, they tend to smell more and more like old Cabs, losing some of their fresh fruit aromas and acquiring the bouquet of age. The smells of the bouquet of age are manifold but can include a whiff of an old cigar box, well-worn leather, and dried flowers. The great California enologist Maynard Amerine says of this bouquet of age, "The nature of this bottle bouquet has not been established. It is not due to any specific ester, although esterification is probably a part of the process. Certainly it is subtler than most aromas. Occasionally it blends with, or even develops from, the aroma" (Amerine and Roessler, 1976). Although it is hard to define, once you partake of that inimitable bouquet of well-aged, fine Cabernet Sauvignon, you will want to partake of it again, and again. It is a pleasure so great that actually drinking the wine can become an afterthought. It is what encourages many people to build a wine cellar in the first place.

WHAT WINES AGE WELL?

Cabernet Sauvignon and other big, robust red wines, including Nebbiolo and Sangiovese of Italy and Temperanillo of Spain, are more likely to last for a long time in the cellar than are the more delicate varieties, such as white wines. A general rule of thumb is that the bigger the wine, the longer it can age. (Be aware, though, that there are many exceptions to this rule.)

The chief exception is Pinot Noir. The aroma of Pinot Noir is a more delicate affair, and with age, it can develop the loveliest bouquet. I remember a 1959 Chambertin that I drank when it was 40 years old. It smelled like a field of wildflowers on a sunny summer day — really, it was the most extraordinary smell. Only the greatest Pinot Noirs will last and last in the cellar, however.

White wines are a different story. Most of those lush, fat California and Australian Chardonnays won't last more than five years without beginning to lose fruit and gain the objectionable characteristics of oxidation and eventually *sherrification* (tending to taste like a sherry). Yet great white Burgundies, also from the Chardonnay grape, can last for a decade or more, and fine Chablis, an expression of Chardonnay in a cold climate on chalky soil, can last maybe forever.

One of my peak experiences in wine tasting was a glass of 1929 Bouchard Père et Fils Chablis that smelled as delicate and lovely as a fine bath powder and tasted as smooth as velvet. That Chablis probably began life as a hard, flinty, steely wine with a strong mineral character that you'd use to cut through the unctuous, buttery dishes of Dijon in eastern France. Why such a difference with California and Australia? The latter have growing seasons considerably warmer than those of Burgundy and far warmer than those of cold Chablis. The colder the climate, the more crisp and acidic the wines usually are. This fact has lots to do with understanding which wines will age well and which won't; I'll get to this a little later in the chapter.

Among other long-lived white wines that benefit from long cellaring are dry or off-dry Gewürztraminer and Sauvignon Blanc, less so Semillon. The highest quality, rich, sweet, botrytized dessert wines like Château d'Yquem and other great Sauternes and Barsacs, as well as some made in Germany, Alsace, New York State, California, and Australia, will stay well preserved because of their intense sugar content and high acidity. When noble rot *(Botrytis cinerea)* infects grapes, it extends its *hyphae* (long appendages with enzymes at their tips that dissolve cell walls) into the center of the berry, drawing out its water to use to build its fungal structures. As the water is drawn out, the sugar and acid remaining in the berry are concentrated. The rot imparts a delicious honeyed flavor to the juice, which carries over into the wine; it doesn't spoil the berry's sensory qualities, although it doesn't do much for its appearance.

Botrytized dessert wines are at their best when they approach the rule of 10-10-10; that is, they have 10 percent residual sugar, 1.0 TA (titratable acidity), and 10 percent alcohol. When such great balance is achieved or approximated, a remarkable thing happens when you take a drink of them. They seem to open up cloudlike in the mouth. Although they're 10 percent sugar, they hardly taste sweet. Although the acid is a highly concentrated 1.0, they

NOTES FROM A VERTICAL TASTING

I recently attended a 20-year vertical tasting (one involving the same wine from several vintages in a row) of Beringer's Private Reserve Cabernet Sauvignon. This is Beringer's flagship wine, one that is made to age. It was originally a single-vineyard wine, but from 1981 on, this Cab represents a blend of wines made from several vineyards and selected lots of those vineyards.

These notes were written in 2001; already I know I was too enthusiastic about the 1997s.

1977: This was the first release of Beringer's Private Reserve. It had a beautiful bouquet of age, but the fruit had faded so the wine was mild. It was a drought year and the vines were water stressed, resulting in low yields (a good thing) but high pHs (not a good thing for wines that will age for long periods of time).

1978: A great year. The wine is not pruney, raisiny, or overripe but is still plenty alive with good fruit and a classic Napa Valley Cabernet bouquet. Drinking beautifully at age 23 and probably could go for another 10 years.

1979: Beringer did not make a Private Reserve this year.

1980: In this year, Beringer made two Private Reserves. We tasted the one from the State Lane vineyard. It was amazingly youthful for a 21-year-old wine. This wine will go for many more years, although it's drinking beautifully now.

1981: This was the first year that Beringer went to a blend of wines from several vineyards to "allow us to create a consistent architecture," according to winemaker Ed Sbragia. The '81 was earthy, ripe, full bodied, and still quite alive at this tasting.

1982: Lots of rain in September during harvest, resulting in wines that were awkward when young. They're still awkward now. They'll never improve.

1983: A nice, pretty wine that has aged well and drinks at its peak right now [2001]. If you have this wine in your cellar, you'd be wise to drink it up.

1984: A fruity aroma, good depth, and firm structure keep this wine young. It needs more time yet to fulfill the promise of its concentrated fruit.

1985: This was a cool year, producing wines that age well. The Beringer Private Reserve is delicious but still tight, with plenty of tannin yet unresolved, plenty of acid, a low pH, and plenty of years left to improve still more.

1986: A tightly wound wine, not yielding much to the nose or the palate as yet. But you can tell there's intensity lurking beneath the surface. This wine is still tannic. It will take many more years before it opens like a rose to show its perfection.

1987: Another classic, balanced wine that's not yet showing a lot of fruit, but what it does show is typical Napa Valley Cabernet. It will surely open up in another few years.

1988: A problematic year that shows in the wine. Very little rain that winter, so the vines were water stressed. A small crop that never developed intensity. Irregular ripening didn't help. The wine reflects the defects.

1989: Drinking beautifully now, but not a wine for the long, long haul. Rains at harvest decimated the whites, but these reds held up fine.

1990: A great year, a great wine. Near perfect integration of fruit, acid, alcohol, tannins, and other phenolics. Beautifully balanced upon release, beautifully balanced now, and will be beautifully balanced for many years to come.

1991: A cool summer and long, cool fall gave these grapes extra-long hang time on the vine, resulting in extreme maturity of flavors. As you sip this wine, it reveals layers and layers of flavor. But the structure that would make it a long ager isn't there, and it may not last more than another few years before decline (famous last words).

1992: The tannins are still hard and rough. The fruit is submerged within a tight structure. Seems like it should age and open up with another 5 years of cellar time.

1993: All kinds of yumminess: coffee, chocolate, vanilla fudge on the nose; a rich brocade of fruit flavors on the palate. All this suggests drinking it now while it overwhelms you with sensuality rather than age it much longer.

1994: A great year. A beautiful aroma and intense depth of fruit hung on a firm structure. Gravelly tannins. Plenty of acid. One to age until 2014.

1995: Pretty, light, not concentrated, and tasty now. Time will only fade its fresh fruit. One to drink now while you're waiting for the 1990 and 1994 to mature.

1996: Juicy, fruity, and lush. Not at all tannic. A pretty wine to drink now or age for a few more years, but not one for the long haul.

1997: A truly great year, and maybe the greatest year of the vertical. Top quality and huge yields. A nose of spice and incense, plus oak. Massive, sweet fruit. Good acid structure. Lucky are those who will drink this wine in 25 years!

don't seem overly acidic. And the alcohol, at a modest 10 percent, is not perceived at all. These factors fall away and reveal the succulent core of rich, honeyed fruit. And after many years of aging, such wines take on incredible bouquet.

Aging Sparkling Wine

A word should be said here about cellar aging of sparkling wine. To make sense of the subject, it's important to know how sparkling wine is made. It begins with the vinification of still white wines, usually Chardonnay or Pinot Noir. The Pinot is made as a white wine by gentle crushing of the berries and immediate collection of the juice so that the red pigment in the skins doesn't color the juice. In California, the berries are picked slightly unripe so that the acids are high and the sugars are low, yielding a crisp, still wine with modest alcohol. The alcohol in the still wine must be of low concentration because it will be refermented in the bottle, creating even more alcohol. The very cool climate of Champagne is perfect for making sparkling wine because the grapes can spend a long time on the vine and reach maturity, with all the complex flavors that implies, while the acids stay high and the sugars stay low naturally.

The Chardonnay and Pinot Noir for sparkling wine are usually vinified separately, then kept in stainless steel tanks with no oak contact. These wines — and there can be a great number of different lots, depending on the variety, the place they are grown, and even the year the wine was made — are then assembled into a nonvintage mixture that the winemaker believes will make the best sparkling wine. In California, most sparkling wine is nonvintage, but the better bottles are given a vintage year.

In fine years in Champagne, producers may declare a vintage and date their wine with the year in which the grapes were fermented. Even though the wine may be entirely from one year, it is still almost always a blend of different *cépages* of the same variety or several varieties of grape. It may be a Brut, which is usually a mixture of Chardonnay and Pinot Noir with perhaps some minor additions of other varieties, such as Pinot Meunier; it may be a Blanc de Noirs, made entirely from Pinot Noir; or it may be a Blanc de

Blancs, made entirely from Chardonnay fruit. This still wine is then put into a sparkling wine bottle made of extra-sturdy glass to prevent shattering under the great pressure that will build up in the bottle. Into the *assemblage* (as the final mixture of still wines is called) goes a dose of sugar, yeast, and perhaps a bit of diammonium phosphate (also known as DAP) to act as yeast food to keep the yeast active longer in the bottle. The bottle is then given a crown cap, like the caps on soft drink bottles.

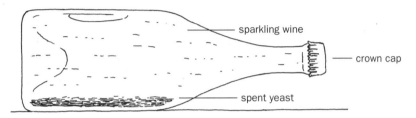

Aging sparkling wine

So, inside the sparkling wine bottle, the yeast finds itself in the presence of sugar and a nitrogen source (the DAP) and proceeds to go to town, converting the sugar into alcohol and releasing carbon dioxide, until the fermentation in the bottle is complete. What you have then is a bottle of wine, spent yeast, and carbon dioxide under intense pressure dissolved in the liquid. Good sparkling wine is then laid down for some time on its side — "on the yeast," as the saying goes.

In France, wine can't be sold as Champagne unless it spends at least nine months on the yeast. Many sparkling wines of quality are laid down on the yeast for much longer than that, however. Iron Horse Vineyards, a quality sparkling wine house in Sonoma County, released its 1992 "Late Disgorged" wine in 2001. The bottles had lain on their sides for eight years. The wine was then *disgorged,* a process whereby the spent yeast is swirled down into the neck of the bottle; the neck and the yeast therein is frozen into a solid ice plug; the crown cap is pulled off and the plug disgorged; the wine is topped up with a dose of a little sugar dissolved in clear wine to take the acidic edge off the wine; and the bottle is given a cork and a wire cage hood, then labeled.

During the time that Champagne has lain quietly on its side, however, much has been happening within the bottle. For one thing, the yeast cells have finished their work. They die off and fall to the bottom of the bottle (that is, along one side of the bottle positioned horizontally). There, these cells go through a process called *autolysis,* which means "self-destruction." Autolysis liberates enzymes and proteins that inhibit oxidation of the wine and gives it interesting flavors. As Maynard Amerine says about the process, "Enzymes from yeast autolysis account for the desirable changes that occur during bottle aging." By desirable changes, he's talking about the richness, toastiness, and brioche character that sparkling wines achieve when given long time on the yeast. The enzyme appears to be beta-fructofurfuranosidase (let's call it beta-f). Enzymes are catalysts that cause changes in other compounds without themselves being destroyed. Inside that bottle of sparkling wine, the beta-f enzyme is involved in the synthesis of beta-ethyl fructoside, an alcohol that then forms an acetal that imparts character to Champagne and sparkling wines. Of course, you remember all this from your courses in organic chemistry, right?

At a recent "Pink Tuesday," which are occasional public relations events held in San Francisco at which Laurent-Perrier Champagne treats folks involved in the arts to some of its sparkling wines, I cornered Francois Peltereau-Villeneuve, vice president and general manager of Laurent-Perrier, Inc. I asked him whether sparkling wines continue to improve after they are disgorged and the yeast removed. In other words, does cellar time improve sparkling wines?

"Improve?" he said in his Gallic accent. "Technically, no. When Champagne [or sparkling wine] is put on the market, it is ready to be drunk. Aging won't improve it, but it will evolve." And how does it evolve? "Toward oxidation," he said. "Temperature and light are the key factors. In a good wine cellar that's cold, with no light, it will oxidize more slowly than if it's in a warm place with light. This oxidation happens through the action of the air that seeps through the cork over time. Oxidized wine has aromas of candied fruit."

So, I asked, you argue against laying Champagne down? Even Laurent-Perrier? "Honestly, I don't lay Laurent-Perrier wines down for long. I like them after they've spent about a year in the cellar. Our flagship wine, Grand Siècle, can be laid down for maybe one and a half years. Realize, Champagne is a blend. It has to be fresh, without too much age."

Well, then, why all the talk about the grand old Champagnes like Bollinger and Krug that have seen years of cellar time — not only on the yeast but also after disgorgement? "Old Champagnes lose their *mousse* [sparkle]," he said. "The color of a rosé changes from light pink to an orangey copper. Oxidation occurs. I think that great Champagne has intrinsic quality — that is, the wine when put on the market has good structure and delightful character. Long cellar aging only compromises that." That's true, but not always.

In the case of the great wines, like Krug, bottle age may improve them. According to Dan Isenhart at The Wine Club in Santa Ana, California:

> There are a great many Champagnes on the market, but I don't hesitate for a moment to assert that Krug is, indeed, the best! Theirs is a full-bodied, powerful style with great intensity and seamless balance. This is a wine that ages magnificently while developing many subtle aromatic and taste gradations. The 1985 Krug is just starting to come around [this was written in 2002] and drink very well, but still has many years of life. It has enticing aromas of apricot, lime, and quince, with hints of hazelnut, butterscotch, honeysuckle, and freshly buttered popcorn. This is an extraordinarily multifaceted and, dare I say, diaphanous bottle of wine.

Well, he's a wine salesman, and yet his opinion is not without merit. Krug is the exception that proves the rule, however.

Most Champagnes and sparkling wines — the mainstays of the business — are nonvintage wines, assembled from cuvées of several years as well as several vineyards and varieties. These wines are ready to drink on release and will last for several years in the cellar before beginning their descent into oxidation. Prestige cuvées — the top of the line products of the Champagne houses — are often (but not always) vintage wines. Although these prestige cuvées cost more and are made from the finest lots of the most well balanced wines, and although the vintage date on the bottle suggests that giving them a long rest in the cellar would be advantageous, more than a few years usually does not add quality. The changes that occur are due primarily to oxidation. And so, keep your sparkling wines in that portion of your cellar reserved for wines that will be drunk soon.

THE NOSE KNOWS

When smelling wine, keep a nostril open for objectionable smells. Young white wines often have a smell that is exactly like calamine lotion. Usually this will dissipate if the wine is given a couple of years in the cellar, so I believe it's a fermentation smell.

Many sensitive noses object to the presence of the waste products of *Brettanomyces* yeast, an odd yeast that floats around the environments of wineries and can negatively impact a wine. Regarding a very Bretty wine, a friend of mine said, "They should just burn down the winery and start over." He meant that this rogue yeast had so infected the winery that all the wines smelled heavily of *Brettanomyces,* and that Brett is hard to get rid of once it gets into the winery's works. This yeast gives a "mousy" smell to the wine. I count myself fortunate that I'm not very sensitive to Brett unless it's very obvious. In my opinion, the less Brett the better, although an amount somewhere below the sensory threshold probably adds a bit of complexity to a wine.

Then there is the smell of a *corked* wine. This smell comes from 2,4,6-trichloranisole (or TCA), a substance produced by the action of certain microorganisms in the cork working on the wine. It's a musty smell, very much like old, decayed, wet cardboard and entirely unpleasant. If you identify it once, you'll always know it. I recently ordered a bottle of wine at my favorite Italian restaurant in San Francisco and it was corked — and strongly so. I called the waiter over and said, "I believe this wine is corked." The waiter smelled it and said, "It seems fine to me." At which point I realized I was dealing with an ignoramus, at least when it came to recognizing a corked wine. I said, "Please take the glass to your manager and have him smell it." The waiter did, and soon the manager was tableside. "The wine is corked," he said. "Please make another choice." Sometimes managers will do this just to

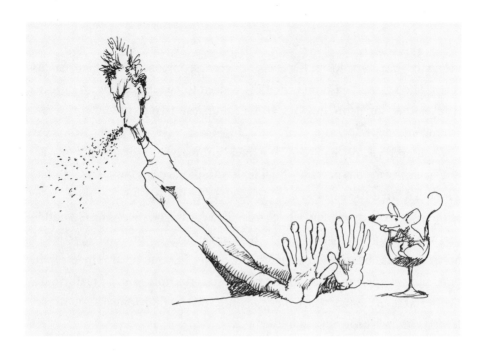

please the customer, whether the wine is spoiled or not, but I prefer to believe that he knew a corked wine when he smelled one, and later gave the waiter a chance to spend a few minutes with a glass of the corked wine, smelling it so that he could remember that smell.

Because of problems with corked wines, some wineries are getting away from traditional corks made from the bark of the cork oak tree. Some use "technical corks," which are made from ground-up cork bonded with a chemical agent into the shape of a cork, but these also have in some cases been the source of the corked characteristic. Studies differ, but traditional corks and technical corks generally have a 1 to 5 percent rate of corkiness. There was a time some years ago when up to 20 percent of wines were developing corkiness, an obviously unacceptable rate of spoilage. Other wineries use plastic corks, made from a synthetic polymer material, but in studies at the Australian Wine Research Institute, these were the most porous in terms of allowing air into the bottle, producing unacceptable oxidation and early decline of wine quality. Screwcaps let the least amount of air into the bottles, but "after 18 months, a rubber-like aroma had developed in wine sealed with the screw-cap closure," according to the Australian Wine Research Institute.

Wines that are going to age for years, or decades, obviously need high-quality corks. The received wisdom is that corks need to be replaced every 25 years. It takes that long for the wine to seep into the tissues of the cork bark, advancing by a fraction of 1 millimeter a year; at 25 years, the cork is wet through and has lost its ability to expand properly and should be replaced. But, as in much that pertains to wine, few things are hard and fast. I've had wines that were 15 years old and older with barely a half inch of the bottom of the cork soaked through, while I've pulled corks from five-year-old bottles that were completely wet through. If you plan to age wines for 20 years or more, it would be good to have a hand corker in your cellar. These can be purchased at any wine shop. Don't purchase corks until you are ready to use them, and then get the most expensive ones you can find: long ones with very few pits or dark brown holes in them.

cork with just ½ inch soaked by wine

cork almost wet through — needs replacement

Evaluating a cork

Recorking is as simple as removing the foil from the top of the bottle (you don't have to remove it from the entire neck) and carefully withdrawing the old cork. The new cork should be bobbing in hot water that's been boiled and just removed from the stove. Set the hand corker on top of the bottle, put the cork into it, close the handles, and push down the driver to seat the cork in the neck. The wine in the bottle should be exposed to air for as short a time as possible and not shaken or greatly disturbed during the recorking. If there's *ullage* (that is, the level of wine is farther down in the neck than when you put the wine in the cellar), consider adding a bit of very good, similar (but not aged) wine so that the bottom of the cork comes to rest about a half inch above the level of the wine in the neck. You could, if you wish, put a drop of paste on the foil circle you removed and put it back, but that's a bit fussy unless you store your wine with the top of the bottle facing out and the vintage year is embossed on the top of the foil.

WHY RED WINES IMPROVE MOST

"But what about those bottles of Champagne that were found at the bottom of the Baltic Sea recently?" you may ask. These bottles, going on 100 years old, were still good. And that shows you that bottles kept near freezing in the dark without being moved will last for decades. But why, when they are at their peak of quality within a few years of release? In layman's terms, young wines that will stain your teeth, show rich, bright, deep ruby red color, and have teeth-gritting tannins will last and last in good cellar conditions.

Most of the sought-after changes in wine quality happen with red wines, especially big, robust red wines. This is because of the phenolic compounds in the wine. These substances are found primarily in the skins and seeds, although a small proportion are found in the juice vacuoles in the pulp. They include tannins, anthocyanins, flavonols, catechins, and several others. These phenolics are very diverse in molecular structure, and wine scientists measure the total phenolic content in a wine in units designated *au,* for "absorption units." Stay with me as we get into some organic chemistry, because herein lies the secret to knowing which wines will age well and which won't.

According to T. C. Somers of the Australian Wine Research Institute, "Light red wines, suitable for marketing within a few months of vintage, have phenolic indices in the range of 20 to 30 au. New wines of this type may have bright color but generally have low astringency [due to the absence of tannin] and are susceptible to oxidative deterioration during long-term storage. They generally come from regions where yields per hectare [a hectare is 2.2 acres] are high.

"Robust red wines, having deeper color and phenolic indices above 40 au, require more prolonged maturation for development of full flavors and acceptable tannin finish. Astringent properties [given by tannins] in these wines decline over time as a consequence of changing phenolic composition, and the wine becomes smooth and mellow to the palate. Wines of high phenolic content, which may become premium aged wines, are associated with relatively low yields from selected cultivars [*cultivar* is shorthand for cultivated variety]."

Some big red wines start life with a pure deep ruby or distinct bluish red cast to their color. You are seeing the anthocyanins in a young wine. The color indicates the acidity, or the pH, of a wine. Young red wines with a low pH (that is, with high acidity) have a rich ruby color. Low pH in the case of wine is defined as between 3.2 and 3.5. In wines with higher pHs (about 3.6 or 3.7), the anthocyanins take on a bluish cast. If the pH rises too high (to near 4.0), the wine begins to take on a muddy or brownish cast. Interestingly, some of the forms of anthocyanins in wine are named for flowers; for instance, the color of Syrah wine is due to anthocyanins called *delphinidin*, *petunidin, malvidin,* and *peonidin* (with reference to delphiniums, petunias, malvas, and peonies).

As big red wines age, the amount of anthocyanins as single molecules (monomers) decreases as they bond with tannin to form long chains of linked molecules (polymers). The color of the wine shifts away from a blue tint toward crimson and pure red. The most rapid changes in color occur within the first two years after fermentation, when the wine is normally being stored in oak barrels. During this maturing phase, the wine has some contact with air through the barrel and the bung, which is the stopper in the hole of the barrel through which wine is inserted or pumped out. After bottling, the wine enters the aging phase, when more changes in the phenolics take place.

In wines that won't age well, the problem is usually that the phenolics are out of balance. When there's not enough tannin for the anthocyanins to bond with, the monomeric anthocyanins disintegrate into bitter compounds. In wines that will age well, the anthocyanins link up with tannins, forming polymers known as *complex anthocyanins*. As time goes by, the monomer anthocyanins and astringent tannins link up into longer and longer molecules. Scientists have found that the molecular weight of tannin pigments in young red wine averages about 1,000, increasing to 2,000 at

5 years and 4,000 in wines aged 20 years. This is because the phenolic tannins link up to form larger and heavier molecules, and they sometimes deposit out on the sides or bottom of the bottle as a stain on the glass or a sludgy gook — hence the need to decant old wines.

As these astringent tannins link up, they become less astringent and the wine becomes progressively smoother. "Such wines may then improve in the bottle for up to 40 years under favorable cellar conditions," T. C. Somers says. "Longevity and long-term resistance to oxidative deterioration are generally associated with deep color and high total phenolics in young wine."

The anthocyanins do not only lend pigment — they also contribute greatly to the flavor of a wine when linked with tannin as complex anthocyanin. By the end of 2 years, 70 percent of the monomer anthocyanins are gone, either disintegrated or linked to tannins. By 8 years, they're all gone. Between 10 and 15 years of age, wine becomes chemically very stable, and fewer further changes occur in the flavor profile. Eventually, however, the wine will lose its brightness, and its flavors will dissipate. The point here is that young wines with high levels of anthocyanins and tannins are good

AGE-WORTHY CALIFORNIA CABERNET

Movie director Francis Ford Coppola, who, with his wife, Eleanor, owns Niebaum-Coppola winery in Rutherford in the Napa Valley, recently held a tasting of old and well-aged Inglenook Cabernet Sauvignons. Niebaum-Coppola is the former Inglenook Estate, developed originally in the nineteenth century by ship captain Gustav Niebaum.

Before Coppola bought the property, Inglenook was making large quantities of mediocre wines, but through the early and middle years of the twentieth century, it made serious bottles of wine from its estate-grown Cabernet in Rutherford. The tasting included wines from 1959, 1958, 1943, 1941, 1934, and 1933 and afforded the guests a chance to settle once and for all the question of the ageability of California Cabs. I was fortunate to attend. Here are my notes:

1959: The rim shows red rather than brownish and dull red. The nose reveals tobacco and aged leather. Flavors are still bright, although the fruit is fading. A great wine.

1958: The year I graduated from high school, fergoshsakes. Amazingly, fresh fruity aromas gush from the glass. The style is elegant, the mouthfeel creamy, and the flavors of sweet fruit still fresh after all these years.

candidates for long cellar aging. I spoke with Leo McCloskey, who, with his wife, Susan Arrhenius, runs Enologix, a firm in Sonoma, California, that has been analyzing complex anthocyanins in wines for years in order to give winemakers a prediction of how good their wines will be on release. In fact, McCloskey first identified complex anthocyanins in 1989 using high field carbon-13 nuclear magnetic resonance and molecular modeling programs. "Somers (of Australia) thought the secret to great wine was red pigment tannin polymers, just as today Dr. Roger Boulton (of the University of California at Davis) has a theory of co-pigmentation," McCloskey says, "but they have it wrong. The real secret is the complex anthocyanins produced when anthocyanins react with tannins. Anthocyanins are highly reactive. Alone in a wine

1943: The nose has a hint of cigar box but otherwise is shy and subdued. The color of the wine is a pure ruby. Fruit flavors are subdued but still there. Not a great deal of life left in this wine, but it certainly isn't dead yet.

1941: This wine, the 1941 Inglenook Estate Cab, has been considered one of the all-time great California Cabernet wines, and one can see why. The nose is pretty, the ruby color clear and pure, the rim still reddish brick with no browning. Although age has dimmed the fruit, it has only made the wine more elegant. The great plush flavors fill the whole palate, front to back and side to side. When young, this must have seemed the complete, everything wine.

1934: Again, an amazingly clean and pure wine with glints of red in the brickish rim. The flavor is silky smooth, yet with some fruity punch left to it. The fruit that's there is succulent and lovely.

1933: Just about everybody at the tasting agreed that this wine was the treasure of them all. Made the year Prohibition ended, it's still celebrating 70 years later! A fabulous, suggestive, intriguing nose — not pushy, very relaxed, but smells of faded roses, old silk clothes, and memories of perfumes from long ago. Fine color, still ruby red on the rim. In the mouth, lush, silken fruit, yet with great restraint, like a person of great accomplishment who has the relaxed and confident attitude of someone who has nothing to prove. Shows the terroir of this Rutherford estate, a silk thread of great strength that winds through all these wines and ties them together. One of the greatest wines I've ever tasted.

without tannin, they degrade predictably — 50 percent will degrade in about 24 months. So rosé, which is basically tannin-free, can be observed to turn from fuchsia to brown in 24 months at room temperature."

Without tannins to react to and link up with, the degraded anthocyanins not only fail to increase wine quality, they can decrease it. In the presence of tannins, such as in a robust red wine, the anthocyanins react with them to form the complex anthocyanins that give wine good flavor, aroma, and color and allow it to age well.

Cabernet Sauvignons from great producers in northern California — Robert Mondavi, Joseph Phelps, Clos du Val, Chateau St. Jean, Arrowood, and many, many others — have enormous ability to age. I prefer them at about 12 to 14 years old, when they still have the fruit of youth on the palate, they've become chemically stable, and they've developed a pretty bouquet of bottle age. On the other hand, some producers of very tannic wines, such as Mayacamas Vineyards in California, perhaps go overboard on tannin extraction in their wines. I've had some Mayacamas Cabs made in the 1970s that still haven't relaxed, although they probably will by and by. Let's just hope the fruit hasn't dried out by then, leaving only oak and alcohol to carry the day.

Besides phenolics that impart color, such as anthocyanins, wines contain colorless or pale-yellow phenolics (tannins, mostly) extracted from seeds and stems. As much as 5 grams per liter of total phenolics may be present in a young red wine, but typically only a fifth of these are highly colored anthocyanins. However, anthocyanins themselves can exist in both colored and colorless forms, which are readily convertible from one form to the other depending on pH. (The lower the pH, the more acidic and crisp the wine; the higher the pH, the more flabby and "fat" the wine.) The crucial fact is that the lower the pH of the wine, the more the anthocyanins exist in colored forms. As pH rises, more and more colored anthocyanins are converted into colorless forms, which muddy the final color of the wine. Thus, young red wines of superior quality have lower pHs and more highly colored anthocyanins than do wines destined for an early death.

But there's the rub: The cooler the climate, the less tannin is produced in the grape skins, and thus less is available to combine with anthocyanins. On the other hand, the cooler the climate, the lower the pH will be. In very favored areas of the world, the factors come into balance. The climate allows the grapes to produce abundant tannin in their skins, yet with a pH low enough to promote an abundance of colored anthocyanins. From these regions come world-class wines destined for a long and happy life in the cellar. In France, that's Bordeaux. In North America, that happens most consistently in coastal locations, especially in Sonoma and Napa Counties. Other places on the West Coast are capable of brilliance, but with less regularity and more dependence on nature's beneficence.

To sum up, wines with higher pHs and more of their anthocyanins in colorless forms appear dull in color, while wines with lower pHs look brighter, with a rich and saturated color, and have greater clarity. Because of its influence on anthocyanins, low pH plays a major role in the ability of a wine to age well. At higher pHs, early oxidation and browning of wine in the cellar is common. Wines of high pH are also more susceptible to microbial spoilage than are wines with a lower pH. In the final analysis, color density of a wine, created by the ionization of anthocyanins caused by low pH, correlates with organoleptic quality (meaning flavor and aroma). If pH isn't mentioned on the label, you can find it by calling or e-mailing the winery, or you can test it yourself if you have a pH meter; paper pH strips aren't accurate enough for this purpose. Perhaps a more basic question comes into play here: What causes certain grapes to produce long-lived wines, while other grape varieties don't? Paul Draper, a longtime wine guru at Ridge Vineyards in Cupertino, California, explains: "First is the quality and distinctiveness of the growing site, and the suitability of the grape variety to that site. Second is the amount of fruit the vines are asked to carry. Third is vine age. A great site, low yields, and vines whose average age is 30 or 40 years will produce age-worthy wines every few years." By "every few years," he means in years of great vintages.

He's opinionated about how long certain wines will age, too. "Virtually all contemporary whites are fully developed within three to five years from the vintage. All good red wines should improve, or at least maintain full quality, for five years from vintage. Those with firm acidity and the tannins from grape seed contact during fermentation and maceration have the basics for at least some further aging," Draper says. He then goes on to talk about great bottles of wine he's had — a 32-year-old Pinot Noir from Burgundy, a 30-year-old Ridge 'Monte Bello' Cabernet Sauvignon he made in 1971, a 10-year-old Ridge 'Lytton Springs' Zinfandel he made in 1991, and so on. In essence, he's saying that most wines in most years need some bottle age, but not a great deal. Red wines of great balance and longevity from great vineyards in great years have a long life ahead of them, with improvement possible through several decades.

We assess the quality of wine through taste and smell, with smell being the predominant sense. Besides the scent of a wine, the taste of a wine is some combination of sweet, sour, salty, bitter, and umami. All the rest of a wine's flavor comes from its smell as its fumes waft up from the throat through the back of the nose. The five tastes (*umami* is a new one — it's the flavor of "yummy") are thus wrapped in layers of sensory delight or disgust because of our perceptions through the olfactory nerves in the nose.

Because white wines don't have the pigmented anthocyanins of the reds, most are ready to drink not long after bottling, usually within just a few years. Free-run juice — that is, the juice that runs from a hopper full of grapes before pressing — is light and pleasant but does not contain many phenolics. Press juice contains more phenolics, but not nearly as much as red wine. Red wines absorb more phenolics from the skins and seeds.

THE ROLE OF CLIMATE

Maybe now we can answer the question: Why do great French wines — Bordeaux and Burgundies, for instance — have such long cellar life?

The answer is primarily climate. It's cool in Bordeaux and cooler in Burgundy. In most years, this keeps the acidity up (and the pH down), which results in those rich, bright wines with pigmented anthocyanins and sturdy tannins ready to link up and create layered flavors. Such wines can last for decades and decades. In the Rhône Valley south of Burgundy, great wines are made, but they may not have the average staying power of the more northerly reds. The regions of Bordeaux and Burgundy are on the 45th parallel — the same latitude as Halifax, Nova Scotia; Bangor, Maine; and the Willamette Valley in western Oregon, an up-and-coming wine region. (See pages 234–235 for maps of prime wine-growing regions.)

Some regions of coastal California, from Mendocino in the north to Monterey Bay in the central part of the coast, are also cool, owing to the influence of the cold Alaskan waters that descend along the coast. It's not generally known to those who haven't visited California that the ocean is far too cold for swimming until you get south of Cambria, halfway between Los Angeles and San Francisco. Surfers wear wet suits north of there. The great wine regions of Sonoma and Napa Counties lie along this cool coastal strip. While days may be hot during the growing season, most nights are cool.

Ocean fog makes nightly incursions into these regions, cooling down the grapes and keeping acid levels elevated.

Because of the hot days, however, sugar levels can soar before the grapes reach maturity. If the vineyardist picks the grapes at a sugar level that will produce a desired 12.5 percent alcohol, mature flavors won't be there and the wines may be too simple. If the vineyardist waits for the grapes to mature, with all of the complex flavors that result, then the wines may become too alcoholic. That's not only bad for the consumer — wine shouldn't make one fall face down in the soup — but also for the winemaker, for the government imposes extra taxes as alcohol reaches levels above 14 percent. It's the California tradeoff.

Sometimes, as in 1991, nature solves the problem by lowering the heat during the summer and early fall so the grapes get extra hang time without a rise in sugar. And sometimes winemakers use technology to remove some of the excess alcohol.

One common technique to de-alcoholize wine involves a spinning cone. The cone is smooth, with a wide base and a narrow top. Wine is bubbled out through the tip and runs down the cone. Since the cone is spinning, the wine forms a film over the surface of the cone. The cone is then heated enough to drive off some of the alcohol fraction, and the wine with reduced alcohol is collected at the bottom.

The spinning cone can also be used to concentrate wines by removing water. Some châteaux in Bordeaux tried this in 1995 when the vintage produced light, watery wines. They concentrated the wine all right, but since it was not particularly good wine to begin with, the result was concentrated poor-quality wine — worse than what they started with. In 1996, though, things got back to normal and Bordeaux had a great year.

A simpler method to lower alcohol is to add water to the wine until the alcohol level reaches the desired percentage level. The water hose is low-tech, but it works. It, of course, also dilutes the wine.

The cool coastal regions of California, and the cool climates in Oregon and Washington, are blessed by nature with just the right conditions to produce balanced wines in most years. As soon as you get a few valleys inland

from the ocean, the marine influence is lost, the climate is very hot during the growing season, and wines end up with high pHs and flabby structure.

Parts of South Africa and Australia also have the Mediterranean climate because of cool ocean breezes, and they produce predictably good wines as a result. So for those of us looking to cellar wine, it's important to know the climate of the region where the wine comes from. When balanced wine goes into the cellar, balanced wine will come out.

PERSONAL TASTE

Finally, it comes down to your personal evaluation of the wine. The characteristics that follow will help you decide whether a wine is worth cellaring.

• **Note the color.** Is it deep and rich with a spark of clarity and fire? Look at the rim (tilt the glass above a pure white, well-lighted surface and evaluate the color where the wine thins out nearest the rim). If the wine is young, it

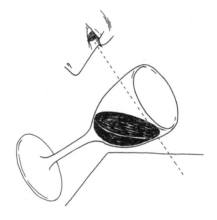

How to look at the rim

should be ruby red with perhaps a slight bluish cast to the color. You may find that the bluish cast isn't present, which indicates low pH and high quality, but all the other factors listed below are present, in which case the wine will probably be a good candidate for cellaring.

• **Think about where the wine came from and the reputation of the producer.** If the wine is from a well-respected producer in one of the best

regions, say from the Bordeaux commune of Pauillac, for example, or from the Napa Valley or Sonoma County, that's a plus.

• **Smell the wine.** Is there a distinct aroma of the fruit used to make the wine? That's a plus but not a determining factor. Avoid wines with repugnant smells. If the smell of toasted oak is dominant, that's a minus. Wines that are over-oaky when young will only become more so with age as the fruit flavors become more tenuous. The *nose* of the wine, as its smell is called, should be clean, slightly fruity, or even shy, and pleasant. If it's sharp at all, that's a sign that the wine may contain higher than desired levels of alcohol. Check the bottle. The law requires the label to state the amount of alcohol (although the label may not always be exactly correct). If it's prickly and sharp in the nose, it's alcoholic; that should indicate that the wine may not age well, as the alcohol will not go away even as the fruit fades, rendering the wine even hotter. (*Hot* is the winespeak term for an overly alcoholic wine.)

• **Take a small sip of the wine but don't swallow it immediately.** First, lean your head forward and down and draw some air through the wine, then straighten up and chew the wine, keeping the back of your nasal passage open — as though you were saying "yum-yum-yum" as you chew. Are there delicious bright fruity flavors? The more concentrated and rich the flavors, the better, as long as they are in balance with the alcohol, tannins, and oak in a way that suggests a strong, sturdy structure.

• **Take another sip and evaluate it for its tannic structure.** Rub your tongue along the inside of your lower front teeth. Do they feel gritty at all? That's a sign of a very tannic wine. Another sign is a strong astringency, such as you get from a sip of cold tea — the puckery feeling that makes you want to purse your lips. Your cellar-worthy wine will have tannin, but it should be well integrated into the structure rather than stick out as a salient feature of the wine. Another way of putting it is that age-worthy wines will have pronounced but rounded, rather than sharp, tannins.

• **Evaluate the oak with a third sip.** Oak may give a vanilla smell and slight vanilla flavor to the wine, along with woody aromas. Oak, like perfume, should be just an accent rather than a feature. If the oak gives a pickle-like smell or taste, that's not a good sign. It can mean several things, from microbial infection in the barrels to poorly-aged wood, all of them bad. Aromas of pickle juice or vinegar mean the wine may be contaminated by acetobacteria.

• **Now take another sip and notice the entrance, the middle, and the finish of the wine.** The *entrance* is the first impression it gives, usually its fruitiness (plums, cherries, currants, etc.). The *middle* is the fullness of the flavor where all the elements marry — fruit, soy, spice, tannin, etc. — into an overall impression. Here's where you'll get the most flavor from your wine. The *finish* occurs after you swallow your sip. Do the flavors dissipate rapidly, giving a finish that's short and clipped? Not a good sign. Rather, you want the finish to keep unveiling layers of flavor as you enjoy the remnants of the sip — the longer the better.

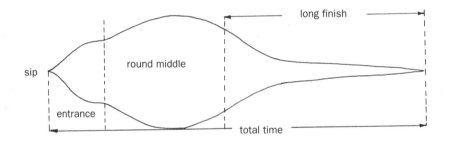

Graphic depiction of taste

• **Finally, assess how much pure pleasure the wine has given you.** Use a 10-point scale. The closer the wine gets to 10, the more cellar-worthy it is if the other elements are in line. I've had wines of great youthful pleasure that haven't aged well at all. The more integrated the elements, the better. The sturdier the structure, the better. (Structure is given by tannins, robust flavor, and texture — a sturdy mouthful.) The presence of good tannins, great color, and plenty of fruit are all there in an age-worthy wine. If you know the pH — it's sometimes listed on the label — the better you can assess a wine's age-worthiness. One accoutrement of a serious wine cellar might be a pH meter. Anything below 3.5 is great. From 3.5 to 3.7 is a maybe. Anything above 3.7 should probably not be considered for long cellar aging. Litmus paper test strips aren't accurate enough to determine wine pH.

• **Finally, look at the track record of the wine.** Is it known for its ability to age? Does it come from a great vineyard (which usually means one of positive drainage — one with soil that percolates easily so the vine roots don't stand in rainwater — yet with enough subsurface water that the vine roots never quite lose contact with moisture)? Are the vines old? Two of my favorite Zinfandels, which age beautifully, are from the Pagani Ranch in Kenwood (the fruit is sold to Ridge and St. Francis, both of which vineyard-designate the wine on the label) with gorgeous old knotty, twisted, head-trained vines over 100 years old, and Scherrer Vineyard 'Old and Mature Vines' Zin from the Alexander Valley in northern Sonoma County.

Once you have identified wines for cellaring, what should you expect? Expect that the purplish hues of youth will turn to crimson between two and (at most) five years of age. After that, a brilliant but rich ruby red color will be sustained for many years. When the wine begins to decline, the rim will be brick red, then brownish red, or — in the case of the very finest wines — a pale and fragile rose-petal red of fine clarity. At its peak, the wine will be most complex and most balanced. Then it will reveal that fabulous bouquet of age comprising chocolate, cedar, roses, tobacco, leather, faint perfume, forest floor, and so much more.

PORTS AND SHERRIES

Ports and sherries are special cases. Once sherry is bottled, it doesn't continue to improve. But before it's bottled, it is assembled from many barrels of varying ages, so that good sherries contain some relatively new wine and some very old wine, and lots in between.

Port is fortified wine. That means that when the wine was still fermenting, enough distilled spirits were added to kill the yeast while plenty of residual sugar was left. Thus, ports tend to be sweet. One can't make a generalization about aging port in the wine cellar because there are many different kinds of port. Ports without a harvest date on the label are ready to be drunk when purchased, as they don't change significantly in the bottle. Only vintage ports improve with bottle age. Let's run down the types of ports to see why this is so.

Vintage Port

Vintage port spends two years in wooden casks, then it is bottled. It will mature in the bottle for many years, even decades, revealing its harmony and complexity as it gets old. Great vintage port will reach its peak at around 20 years or so and hold its character and quality for decades.

At Oxford University, students finish their meals in the dining halls with a glass of port. When vintages are declared in Oporto and the wine released for sale, the university's stewards stock the wine cellar with new port. It stays there for 50 years. So the port that Oxford students drink with their meals in 2002 went into storage 50 years ago or thereabouts. A friend of mine who went to Oxford used to come over to my house to share a bottle of vintage port on a yearly basis.

Port comes in a dark bottle to keep light from damaging it. You may sometimes see the word *quinta* on a bottle of what looks like vintage port. Quinta means "estate" and indicates that the wine came from the estate named on the label, but in years when a vintage is declared, these fine wines tend to disappear into the blend that is marketed by shippers such as Dow, Warre, Graham, and Cockburn. So *quinta* on the label is an indication of a good, estate-bottled wine, usually from a year when a vintage has not been declared.

Vintage port has a high level of tannins that protect the wine and allow it to develop in the bottle. Port should always be stored on its side to keep the cork moist. Try not to move your cellared port once it has been laid down. As port ages, it *throws a crust* — that is, lots of gunk deposits on the glass, and crunchy bits fall to the bottom. Jiggling and moving the port may loosen particles from the crust that are difficult to remove from suspension, rendering the wine slightly cloudy.

When it comes time to drink, port demands to be decanted. Carefully set it upright for a day before drawing the cork. Very old ports may have fragile corks because of their age and the sugars that bind the cork to the inside of the neck and cause it to stick. Real port aficionados have a set of iron port tongs. These are heated to red-hot and then clamped around the neck of the bottle just below the bottom of the cork. After 10 seconds or so, the tongs are pulled away. Crushed ice wrapped in a cloth is clamped around the neck, which causes the glass to break with a slight clink. The broken top is removed, the freshly cut lip wiped carefully so that any tiny shards of glass are wiped away, and the wine decanted, leaving the crust behind.

A vintage is declared for port only in exceptional years, typically at an average of three years per decade. When buying port for long-term cellaring, look carefully at the label to make sure it's a true vintage port. Why? Because several other types of port — late-bottled vintage port and vintage character port, for instance — have trickily similar names. Real vintage port will be designated by using the words *vintage port* on the label.

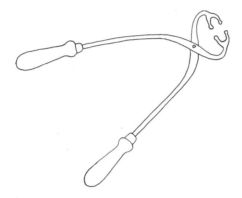

Iron port tongs

Below are the other types of port, most of which will not improve much in the cellar and can be drunk as soon as you wish after purchase. The rule of thumb is that if a bottle is vintage dated, it can profit from some aging, up to a decade, with the exception of vintage port, which will improve for half a century.

Other Kinds of Port

Vintage ports are expensive and certainly worthy of as much cellar time as you can give them. Some of the alternatives, especially the traditional late-bottled vintage ports (sometimes referred to as LBVs) and crusted ports, can give you something of the experience of a vintage port while you're waiting and at much less cost.

• **Late-bottled vintage port.** It is vintage dated and was made the year indicated on the bottle, but despite its name, it is *not* vintage port. Before bottling, late-bottled vintage port spends 4 to 6 years in wooden casks, giving it greater color maturation than vintage port. Late-bottled vintage ports are wines of intense color and abundant tannin (from those 6 years in oak). However, they have a young and fruity character that reveals a slightly oxidative element in their bouquets because during their long stay in wooden casks, much more oxygen can reach the wine than it can in the bottle. Traditional late-bottled vintage ports are not filtered and may improve with some cellar age. The more common style of these ports is filtered; fruitiness is their charm, and they are meant to be drunk within a few years of purchase.

• **White port.** While the grape varieties called Touriga Nacionale, Tinta Amarela, Tinta Barroca, Tinta Roriz, Touriga Francesa, and Tinto Cão are predominant in red ports, the white style is made from Malvasia Fina, Donselinho, Gouveio, Codega, and Rabigato grapes, among small amounts of others. White port is strongly fortified, reaching about 20 percent alcohol, and doesn't improve much with age.

• **Ruby port.** A blended wine with a bright, ruby-red color that is young, full-bodied, and fruity. It's made as a blend from several different harvests. It's not for long cellaring.

• **Vintage character.** A blend of young ports of superior quality, with an average age of three to four years. These wines may have some of the complex, full-bodied, and intensely fruity character of vintage port, but most will not. Think of them as premium ruby ports. They are not harvest dated and will not improve in the bottle.

• **Crusted port.** The name is a recent invention of British shippers. In essence, they are wines assembled from several vintages that are not filtered and will improve in the bottle for years and throw a crust, like vintage port.

• **Tawny port.** Tawny port is an amber-colored port made from a blend of wines that have matured in cask. Its maturation time in these oak casks, about three years, is shorter than that for ruby port. Owing to oxidation, its color changes from red to orange with glints of amber. A tawny port is a fine, delicate, and luscious wine meant to be drunk sooner rather than later.

- **Tawny with an indication of age.** Tawnies may be labeled 10, 20, 30, or 40 years old or more. The age on the label is the average age of the components from which the final blend is made. The color is amber from the long maturation in oak casks, and these ports have complex aromas and a refined character. They come ready aged and won't improve much in the bottle.

- **Harvest port.** This term indicates port from a single year's harvest, which must be stated on the label. Harvest ports are matured in wood and bottled according to the needs of the market. They go through at least seven years of barrel aging, which gives them a deep golden color and a soft, delicate, deep, and complex flavor.

- **Colheita.** The name refers to a single harvest or vintage, but colheitas are not vintage ports. Think of them as aged tawny ports from a single year, which must be stated on the label. Many are aged in casks for more than seven years, giving them the mature color associated with tawnies. Colheitas are generally richer than harvest ports.

Some interesting if fussy old traditions adhere to the serving of the port at the table. Traditionally, the person with the highest status at the table is served first. This may work in Europe, but it may cause fistfights to break out among Americans. Someone must be served first, however, so you decide who it will be. The decanter is then passed, always held with the right hand, by the first person served to the person on his or her left. And so the decanter goes clockwise, from right to left, around the table.

Vintage port should be consumed the day it's opened, as its quality will deteriorate after that. All other types of port can be stoppered and kept in a cool, dark place, where they will last for days. Vintage and late-bottled vintage port are served at room temperature. Other ports can be served slightly chilled but never with ice. The exception is a cocktail known to fans of rock 'n' roll as White Port and Lemon Juice (also called WPLJ), a song from the mid-1950s. To make this drink, combine equal parts of white port and tonic water, a slice of lemon, and ice in an old-fashioned glass. New Yorkers will recognize WPLJ as the call letters of a radio station that was once WABC-FM. I think the change to WPLJ is the single coolest thing any radio station has ever done.

SPANISH WINES

Spain is a wine country that's often overlooked in the pursuit of the famous châteaux and domaines of France and the Supertuscans and big Barolos of Italy. Rioja, Ribera del Duero, Navarra, Penedès, and Prioratare are all regions well worth exploring. Spanish wines of high quality are marvelous agers and cost far less than many similar wines.

In fact, 2001 was one of the great years for wine in Spain — maybe the greatest. Winemakers sometimes hype a vintage with comments like these, but I got my information from a Spanish enologist who says that late frosts cut yields 20 to 60 percent in the spring of 2001. Such natural crop thinning improves the grapes that remain. It was a hot, dry summer, and the berries stayed small and intensely flavored. As a result, the wines show great concentration and aromatics, superb depth of color, and silky tannins — exactly what you're looking for to stock your cellar. Other sources agree that 2001 is among the very greatest of the great vintages in Spain.

THE PEAK OF MATURITY

Wines that are age-worthy should be allowed to reach their plateaus of maturity. That is, a fine red wine will slowly increase in quality over a number of years, perhaps going through a dumb stage where the wine seems closed in, but finally emerging into a wine of smooth complexity, beautiful bouquet, and rich in associations. Wines will hold this state of maturity for a number of years and then slowly decline. When they decline, the color browns, the nose begins to disappear, and the flavors thin. This is called *drying out,* a winemaker's term for a wine that is losing its fruit, thinning in color, and lessening in bouquet. When a wine reaches its very old age, whenever that occurs, it takes on a thin, tea-like, tawny color, and its most prominent flavor is the taste of the acid no longer submerged under rich layers of fruit.

How long it takes a wine to reach its highest level of quality and how long it will maintain that level depend on the individual wine. But we can make educated guesses. Let's assume that all the wines we describe in the box on pages 90–98 will be age-worthy wines with great balance. Again, balance is an equality among the fruit, acid, alcohol, and phenolic compounds in a wine, in which no one component dominates. If a wine is all fruit and no structure, it won't be a candidate for the long haul. If a wine is very acidic, it will remain so and will become obnoxiously so as it ages. If a wine is highly alcoholic (*hot* in the winemaker's parlance), it will always be hot. If a wine is so ruggedly tannic that it overpowers the fruit, you will find that by the time these hard tannins soften, the fruit may have disappeared. If the wine is so over-oaked that it smells like a sawmill, the oak will remain after the fruit subsides, making it even more oaky. Balance, a rich red young color, bright acidity, and smooth tannins are the keys to ageability.

I'll let wine writer Dan Berger of the *Los Angeles Times* sum it up: "Just buy the best stuff, the stuff that tastes the best, and assume it'll age great."

GENERAL GUIDELINES FOR AGE-WORTHY WINES

Here's a general discussion of French wines listed by their appellations and varieties, and wines from other places listed by their grape varieties. Use this as a rough guide to the length of time for cellaring, but with the understanding that the guidelines are general and that individual wines may differ. By using this guide and your knowledge of the role of color, flavor, and fragrance (see pages 69–76), you should be able to figure out a cellar time that will bring your wines to their peak of quality.

French Wines by Appellation and Variety

- **BEAUJOLAIS.** Beaujolais is the wine they rush to Paris in early November each year as the first taste of the new vintage. (And now they run it to New York, London, and who knows where else.) But this has given folks the impression that Beaujolais is best drunk about as soon as it's bought. Most is, especially those wines marked Beaujolais Nouveau, but wines designated Beaujolais-Villages can last for a couple of years, while wines with place names — Brouilly, Chénas, Chiroubles, Fleurie, Juliénas, Moulin-à-Vent, Morgon, Régnié, and St-Amour — can age for 4 or 5 years. Of these, Chénas, Juliénas, Morgon, and Moulin-à-Vent can last for up to 10 years, if they're from a great vintage. But remember that Beaujolais is a quaffing wine; it's great for rinsing the peanut butter off the roof of your mouth, but it's not usually a wine to be aged and discussed.

- **BORDEAUX.** The best Bordeaux from the greatest vintages will outlive us all, and they are very expensive. Certainly these are wines to cellar and leave to your children or your grandchildren. But most Bordeaux, even great growths, don't have the characteristics for that kind of aging in most years. Figure that Bordeaux reds, made from Cabernet Sauvignon, Merlot, Cabernet Franc, Malbec, Petit Verdot, and maybe a smattering of others, will increase in maturity and quality for about 10 years in good vintages and 5 years in poor ones and then level off. Wines of the lesser vintages will start to decline after a few years at those levels, while solid wines from good years will maintain their quality for another decade. Top-quality Bordeaux whites from good years, usually made from Sauvignon Blanc and Semillon, don't need a decade to reach maturity but will certainly be at their peak about then. Sweet dessert wines like Sauternes and Barsac are incomparable in great years and will last for decades. They are excellent in good years and will last for a couple of decades, but they are still delicious in lesser years, when they will need to be drunk up by the time they are 10.

- **BURGUNDY.** Because one of the most appealing things about red Burgundy is its lovely fruit, and because Pinot Noir doesn't have the muscular structure and phenolic stuffing of Bordeaux, most red Burgundies of the first rank are best drunk as soon as they reach their peak at about 10 to 12 years. They can continue on that high plateau for half a decade more before beginning their decline. However, top-quality Burgundies, especially from the northern region of Côte de Nuits, from great years can go on at their peak of quality for decades. Poor years will see the wines develop, reach their peak at about 6 to 8 years, and then begin a slow decline. Burgundies from the Côte de Beaune show a similar development and plateau before decline as those of the Côte de Nuits, but the timescale is usually a bit shorter. White Burgundies from good years are perfect at about 10 years old. When the year isn't so good, figure 3 to 5 years of age to bring them to their peak.

- **CABERNET FRANC.** We're speaking here of Cabernet Franc from California. As one of the Bordeaux varieties, Cabernet Franc (pronounced "fronc," as in "honk if you love franc") is a sturdy red wine that needs bottle age to soften its tannins. Not as well muscled as Cabernet Sauvignon, it reaches a satisfactory maturity in about 8 to 10 years and then, in its best examples, can last for a decade or more. Give a Cabernet Franc from an ordinary year at least 8 years.

- **CABERNET SAUVIGNON.** This variety is the champion ager among grape varieties. Top-quality West Coast Cabernets, such as Robert Mondavi Reserve, Phelps Insignia, Château Montelena, and Clos du Val, will reach their peak about 10 to 12 years from the vintage year and will generally hold that quality for another decade. Some very tight, tannic wines like Diamond Creek and Mayacamas will take longer to reach full maturity and will age for longer periods. Good but ordinary Cabs are made with less tannin, more forward fruit, and soft acid structure for shorter aging and will drink well in 3 to 5 years, then last another 5 years or more. Cabernets from Australia are generally juicy and soft when young and mature in about 4 to 6 years, and they should be drunk within 5 years after that. Cabernets from northern Italy have great staying power, on a par with good California Cabs.

- **CHABLIS.** In this cool region of northeastern France, partway between Champagne and Burgundy, Chardonnay grapes yield a dry, flinty, steely wine with plenty of acid and lean mineral character. The French call the special taste of Chablis *gunflint*. Wines from other countries that are labeled Chablis are not truly Chablis and are usually white jug wine. True Chablis is one of the most food friendly wines in the world. Wine labeled simply as "Chablis" will age nicely for 6 or 8 years. A premier cru ("first growth") will reach maturity in 10 years, and a grand cru ("grand growth") will take 12 to 15 years to reach its peak and then stay at that level for several decades. The winemakers of Chablis have mostly retired their oak barrels and now use stainless steel for storage before bottling, as oak influences and obscures that mineral, flinty character of this fine wine.

- **CHAMPAGNE AND SPARKLING WINE.** The received wisdom about non-vintage Champagne is to cellar it for 2 years, then drink. Actually, 1 year in the cellar should do it, as these wines are meant to be drunk when sold. Vintage Champagnes are likewise excellent soon after they're purchased, but they may benefit from more cellar time if you have the "English" palate — that is, you like your wines a bit oxidized. Sparkling wines from places other than Champagne, such as French Crémant, U.S. sparkling wine, German Sekt, and Italian Spumante, are meant for consumption soon after release, with a maximum cellar time of 2 years.

Non-French Wines by Grape Variety

- **CHARBONO.** A California grape that may be the same as Dolcetto (discussed below).

- **CHARDONNAY.** A chameleon grape that is made in any number of styles. Some are fat and buttery and ready to drink on release. Some are big and oaky, with soft acids from malolactic fermentation. Some are lean and citrusy, with enough acid to see them through 5 or 6 years or more. You first need to determine which kind your Chardonnay is, then decide whether to age it, whereupon it will deepen in color and acquire a slightly oxidized flavor, or to enjoy its fresh fruitiness right then and there. The great French Chardonnays from Chablis and Burgundy have the steel and backbone to last for many, many years without losing quality. However, Chardonnay is usually at its best about 3 to 5 years after release.

- **CHENIN BLANC.** The fabled home of this wine is the Loire Valley between Saumur and Vouvray. In great years, the top producers of Chenin Blanc can yield late-harvest wines of deep sweetness and very high acidity. The extreme acidity means that these whites can be cellared for decades before they are ready to drink. Not all Vouvrays or Saumur-Anjou-Tours Chenins are of this quality, however. Most Chenin Blanc from this region is perfectly nice wine that has not seen oak and doesn't need much aging. Chenin is the staple white wine of South Africa and Argentina; it's planted nearly everywhere grapes can grow, and a lot comes from California. Most goes into low-cost white wines. A few producers, such as Chappelet, Chalone, and Girard, make Chenin in a more robust style.

- **DOLCETTO.** A grape widely planted in the Piedmont region of Italy, in Argentina (where it's called Bonardo), in France (where it has been called Charbonneau), and in California, Dolcetto was probably brought to these places by Italian immigrants in the late nineteenth century, along with Barbera and other varieties. Although in some areas it's a low-acid wine, Dolcetto seems to have more firmness in California than elsewhere. It contains high levels of anthocyanins in its skins and a pH low enough for these to bond with tannins to form complex anthocyanins. And so, in California at least, Dolcetto (or Charbono) will improve with age for a decade and then spend 5 or 10 years at its peak before declining. If there's too little acid in the grapes, some winemakers add a blend of tartaric, citric, and malic acids to bring the total acids and pH to desired levels.

- **GEWÜRZTRAMINER.** Gewürztraminers from Alsace are generally fairly dry affairs with an exceptionally appealing aroma and interesting flavor. These wines in good years can last for many years in the cellar, as their acidity keeps them stable. Figure about 5 or 6 years before they reach maturity, and then another 8 to 10 years of age beyond that before they start to decline. In California, Gewürztraminer is usually made with 2 percent residual sugar, and the vine's floral character is almost overwhelmingly cloying. Give these babies a good cellaring of 10 to 12 years and then see if they've learned to behave themselves.

- **LOIRE.** See the entry for Chenin Blanc concerning the region's whites. Among the reds, Cabernet Franc is the vine of choice. Its best expression is probably given in Bourgueil along the Loire River. Chinon and Saumur also produce medium-bodied Cabernet Francs that reach maturity in about 5 years and may last at that level for a decade or more in the best years. They are characterized by a cedary, "pencil shavings" aroma.

- **MERLOT.** In very special places and in very great years, Merlot, one of the Bordeaux varieties, stands right up there with Cabernet Sauvignon for ageability. Château Pétrus, for an example, is 95 percent Merlot and the most expensive bottle of Bordeaux you can buy. In less rarified realms, however, Merlot is more like a softer sister to Cabernet Sauvignon. Whereas Cabs can age for decades, Merlot may take 8 to 10 years to reach maturity, hang in there for a decade, then decline. Run-of-the-mill Merlot will take about half that time, if that. But you don't want to cellar run-of-the-mill wine, do you? In 2002, I opened a bottle of 1991 Dry Creek Vineyard Estate Merlot; it was 11 years old and from a great year, and it was one of the best California red wines I've ever had.

• **NEBBIOLO.** Nebbiolo is one of those grapes that does extremely well on its home turf, which is the Piedmont region of northwestern Italy, and far less well elsewhere. Nebbiolo yields the classic Barolos and Barbarescos. These wines are stuffed to the gills with wondrous flavors of black fruits (cherries, currants, blackberries, and plums among them), briar, and minerals, and they have an extractive depth that can border on bitter when young. On the nose, Nebbiolo gives tar and potpourri, licorice and dark plums. Because of their incredible depth of flavors, high acidity, and prominent tannins, these wines, especially in good years from good producers, can take a decade to reach maturity and then hold their quality for many years. They are worth the wait for they eventually resolve into complex but harmonious wines. Know your producers, though, since there is a trend in Piedmont to make wines that are ready to drink in far less time than the classics.

• **PINOT NOIR.** This feminine grape can make magnificent, long-lasting wines in the great estates of Burgundy (such as Romanée-Conti and Chambertin), but most affordable Pinot Noirs, especially those from California and Oregon, reach drinking age in about 3 to 5 years. The best of them from great vintages will continue to improve for another 6 to 8 years. Great years and knowledgeable producers on North America's West Coast — especially the Russian River Valley appellation of Sonoma County, the Carneros appellation that straddles southern Napa and Sonoma Counties, the cool valleys near Santa Barbara, and Oregon's

Willamette Valley — can combine to produce long-lasting wines, but be sure to taste a bottle at 6 years, 8 years, and 10 years to check development.

- **RHÔNE.** The Rhône Valley of France, south of Burgundy, has more heat and sun and consequently bigger, though not necessarily longer-lasting, wines. There are a number of Rhône appellations, such as Côte Rôtie, Châteauneuf-du-Pape, St-Joseph, and Gigondas, that produce fine red wine. The rule here is that the bigger the wine, the longer it will probably last in the cellar. Gigondas can be a lighter style of red, while the best Côte Rôties can be enormous, powerful wines that take 10 or 15 years to reach full flower. Know your appellations through tasting. A well-cellared Côte Rôtie, such as Guigal's 'Brune et Blonde,' can be a peak experience.

- **RIESLING.** There are two places in the world where the white Riesling grape yields wines with high acid structure and, sometimes, residual sugar that can carry them through decades in the cellar. The first is a roughly contiguous region that runs from Alsace in France along the Rhine River toward the north. The cold climate and slate-based soils produce a rich but steely wine with crisp acids. With enough time, they yield a gorgeous, lightly perfumed, beautifully integrated wine of great breeding and style. German Rheingaus are made in sweet styles that can last for decades, but increasingly Germans are demanding drier Rieslings and winemakers are cooperating. The second area is in the Finger Lakes region of upstate New York; wines produced by German-trained winemakers, such as Hermann Wiemer, cellar well. The Finger Lakes is still getting its Riesling act together, but the best examples have something of the character of German Rieslings. Rieslings produced in California and the Pacific Northwest have been floral, fruity wines of little consequence compared to those produced in colder climates. Winemakers there have been trying to capture the steel of fine Riesling, but the climate may not cooperate. Progress continues, however.

- **SANGIOVESE.** *Sangiovese,* which translates to 'Jupiter's blood,' is the base grape for Tuscany's Chianti and Montepulciano and is used as the sole variety for Brunello di Montalcino. It's widely grown elsewhere in Italy, especially in central Italy, where it gives light red wines for early drinking. In Tuscany, its wines are well structured but often faint of fruit, and so in recent years producers have been blending the richly fruity Cabernet Sauvignon into the Sangiovese, making the so-called Supertuscans. Fine Chianti, Montepulciano, Montalcino, and Supertuscans are similar in that they take about a decade to reach maturity but soon begin declining after that. Sangiovese is being tried in California, and I tasted one notable example that has the stuffing and structure of an Italian wine (from Villa Ragazzi, made from fruit grown on one lonely acre in the Pope Valley), but most are innocuous, simple wines.

- **SAUVIGNON BLANC.** Along with Semillon, Sauvignon Blanc is the white grape of Bordeaux and the variety behind the Loire Valley's Sancerre and Pouilly-Fumé. In California, it's widely grown and sometimes called Fumé Blanc. It's making a showing in New Zealand and is widely planted in South Africa. Other wine-producing regions also grow this vigorous vine. While Sauvignon Blanc can last for years in the cellar because of its high acidity, that high acidity is often accompanied by objectionable herba- ceousness. Newer styles of this variety are riper, richer, and slightly more alcoholic. Give this wine 3 to 5 years to reach maturity and a similar time after that for peak drinking. Fine bottles from great years may go longer, but why wait?

- **SEMILLON.** Semillon, whether in Bordeaux or Australia, is seldom a wine for great aging (with some notable exceptions, such as Lindemans Hunter Semillon, that can last for 15 years or more), but when paired with Sauvignon Blanc and infected with noble rot *(Botrytis cinerea),* it can yield fine dessert wines. In fact, the finest dessert wine in the world, Château d'Yquem, is a botrytized mixture of these two varieties. Yquem and other fine Sauternes and Barsacs can age for decades, improving all the while.

- **SYRAH/SHIRAZ.** I've already discussed this grape in describing the reds of Rhône's Côte Rôtie (see page 96), but it is widely grown in Australia and increasingly in the United States. Shiraz, as the Aussies spell it, tends to mature faster and last less long than its counterparts in France (the jury is still out on California Syrah's ability to age since it has only recently been widely planted), but the finest can go for a decade or two, especially Penfold's flagship wine, the Grange. In general, 5 or 6 years will bring your California or Pacific Northwest Syrah to a fine maturity. As for how long it can last, it's anyone's guess.

- **ZINFANDEL.** Of course, we're talking about red Zinfandel, not the sweet pink stuff. Rough tannins in fine Zinfandel, California's own grape, generally resolve in about 7 to 9 years, stay at their peak for a few years, then gently decline. Very great Zinfandel vintages, such as 1999, can see that peak of quality extend for many years. However, one of Zinfandel's charms is the lush fruit it shows in relative youth. The older Zin gets, the more it resembles a nondescript old red wine. By 20 years, you'd be hard-pressed to tell a Zin from a Cabernet Sauvignon. Ordinary Zinfandels will be drinking well from 4 to 7 years; great ones can go far beyond that.

CHAPTER 4

Cellar Size and Function

The size of your wine cellar depends on these seven factors: (1) how much wine you drink on a regular basis; (2) whether you will age wine for business reasons and for gifts; (3) how large a collection you want; (4) whether you will age wine for eventual sale; (5) whether your cellar will house wine for a friend or friends; (6) whether you want a simple place to store wine or an elaborate wine cellar with all the accoutrements; and (7) whether you are building a cellar to leave as a bequest to your heirs.

Let's look at these factors one by one.

How much wine do you drink? I'm assuming moderate drinking habits here, where wine is an accompaniment to dinner and occasionally a lunch, in a household with two adults. Given that there will be many meals eaten at restaurants, at friends' houses, and on business trips, it's probably about right to think of 240 bottles per year — about two bottles every three days for two people, or one-third of a bottle (250 mL, or about 8½ oz) per person per day. Because there are about five 5-ounce glasses of wine in a bottle, that's slightly less than two glasses of wine per day — the perfect amount for responsible drinkers who want to maximize the health benefits of wine. And because you're being so disciplined about those scant two glasses, go ahead and have a third glass on odd occasions. Still, let's figure you'll consume 240 bottles per year.

That works out to about twelve cases of wine per year. This means properly aged wine, however, so there's much more than the current year's drinking in the cellar. Some of the bottles in the cellar will hardly need to age at all, some will age for a few years, some for up to a decade, and some will be laid down for the long haul — possibly several decades. (So, if you're 60 years old, better get those bottles of Château Latour and Warre's vintage port laid down now and hope for the best.) Let's say that the average length of time you'll cellar a bottle of wine is eight years; some will age less, some will age more, but eight years on the average. Twelve cases a year for eight years is ninety-six cases. Aw heck, let's say an even one hundred cases of wine.

Wines that cost less than $10 are made to be drunk the night they're purchased. They're usually not built to age. By the time you're paying $12 to $15 a bottle for wine, most will benefit from some time in the cellar. It's not always true that the most expensive bottles of wine will age the longest, but it is often true, so wines that are very cellar-worthy are often $15 to $30 a bottle

THE EFFECTS OF WINE ON HEALTH

"There has been an enormous outpouring of scientific papers linking a favorable effect of drinking [wine] on a variety of disease states. These include atherosclerotic vascular disease, including cardiovascular mortality, stroke incidence, peripheral vascular disease, and diabetes; hypertension, cancer, peptic ulcer, upper respiratory infections, gallstones, kidney stones, age-related macular degeneration, bone density, and quality of life.

"Consumption of alcohol in moderation has health benefits. Wine contains components that enhance those health benefits."

— ALFRED A. DELORIMIER, M.D.
"The Effects of Wine on Health." *Bulletin of the Society of Medical Friends of Wine* 42:7 (2001)

and way on up from there. If the average cost of a wine in your cellar is, say, $18 a bottle, then that's $216 a case, and if you have a one-hundred-case cellar, that's wine worth a total of $21,600, a hefty sum, which is why I wrote *From Vines to Wines* (Storey, 1999). Half of my cellar is wine I made myself; the other half is wine I bought. That's still a large investment, but even if I have $12,000 worth of commercial wine in my cellar, that's just $1,200 worth of wine a year. If you're a regular wine drinker who buys wine from a retailer, I'll bet you spend at least $1,200 a year on wine.

Having a cellar helps you keep costs down. First of all, you may be buying the wine at a futures price, which is usually less than you'll pay after the wine is released and is in the stores. Second, you may be getting a case discount, which is usually 10 percent. That's $20 saved when you buy a $200 case of wine. Third, if you were going to go to a wine shop and buy a 10-year-old bottle of Clos du Val, or another good Napa Valley Cab, you'd be paying an enormous premium for the bottle age. But when you have a wine cellar, that wine accrues value you don't have to pay for.

How much wine do you need for business reasons and for gifts? A well-aged bottle of wine at its peak of quality makes an exciting gift or can add flair to a business lunch. Just make sure that the recipient isn't a teetotaler or a recovering alcoholic. Such bottles also make fine gifts for employees, friends, and family members at holidays. But don't cast your pearls before swine. Make sure that the recipient will fully appreciate what a wonderful gift a bottle of 12-year-old Cos d'Estournel really is. I recently spent some time with friends of my wife's family who visited us here in Sonoma County from Wisconsin. When they were leaving, I offered to help them pick out any wine they wanted from a good retail shop — my treat. They declined the offer because they knew just what they wanted: the same white Zinfandel they bought at home. Why buy them a fancy bottle of wine if they wouldn't appreciate it?

Let's say you want to have three cases of wine a year for gifts at birthdays and holidays; for bringing a bottle to a fine restaurant to share (most restaurants here in the Wine Country allow this and charge "corkage" of anywhere from $5 to $10 a bottle for the privilege of bringing your own wine, although it's often waived if you then buy a bottle off the wine list); and for bringing to private dinner parties and when visiting friends. So, we'll add these three cases and need a cellar that holds 103 cases.

How large a collection do you want? Some folks simply like to collect wine, knowing full well they won't drink it all. Perhaps they love wine and can't help themselves, so they buy more than they will drink just to have it, like trophies. Much of the maniacal pricing of cult wines in California and the productions of the *garagistes* in France comes from the knowledge that there are trophy hunters who will pay enormous prices for wines simply because they're scarce. Although I don't go down that road, I do occasionally run across bottles that I can't resist. Although I always plan to drink them, somewhere inside the realist in me knows I may never get around to it. But that's what irresistibility is all about. You will have to determine how much irresistible wine you'll be buying each year, above and beyond the basic 103 cases mentioned so far. Be realistic. I would say I personally buy about three cases of such wines a year. They may not be expensive, they may be from any-where, but what they have in common is that they intrigue me. So I buy them. And what the heck — you can't take it with you. Now we're up to 106 cases.

Do you want to age wine for eventual sale? There are brokers who will sell your private cellar, as long as you can convince them — usually by open-ing a few bottles for them at random — that the cellar has been maintained properly. And there are online wine auction houses that will put your bottles up for sale, again as long as you can convince them that your wine has been cellared properly. There's really no trick to selling well-aged wine, but — and this is a big but — the wine has to be of such pedigree that it will be highly valued after aging.

In 1994, I laid down a bottle of 1992 Napa Ridge Cabernet Sauvignon for which I paid about $8. I opened it in 2002 and to my delight, but not absolute surprise, it was perfect. Smooth, rich fruit, wonderful bouquet of age, as lovely as it will ever be. I laid it down because Napa Ridge wines kept win-ning tastings that I attended, beating wines that cost two, three, and four times as much — and not only Cabernet, but Pinot Noirs, too. I knew this good thing wouldn't last long and I was right. The winemaker soon moved on, the company got sued over its use of the word "Napa" in its title because the fruit did not all come from Napa County, and the wines turned back into ordinary $8 wines. However, if I tried to sell a bottle of 1992 Napa Ridge

Cabernet Sauvignon in the aged-wine marketplace, I doubt if it would bring its original $8. Nobody wants Napa Ridge. (Too bad for them.)

What sells as aged wines are the grand crus of the world: the Premier Crus of Bordeaux; the Grand crus of Burgundy; the flagship wines of the great California producers, such as Phelps' Insignia, Heitz 'Martha's Vineyard,' and Robert Mondavi's Cabernet Sauvignon Reserve; the cult wines, like Staglin and Dalla Valle 'Maya'; and other scarce but well-known wines with tons of cachet. One of my friends is Tom Dehlinger of Sebastopol, California. He's been making Pinot Noir from his cool-climate estate grapes for many years. When I moved about two miles from his winery in 1985, he was selling his Pinots for about $8 a bottle. A bottle of his 1985 Pinot Noir today would sell for well over $100. That's because wine afficionados know Dehlinger's wines: They are scarce and almost unobtainable, they are always fine wines, and they have cachet.

Do you want to age wines for future sale, as an investment? If you do, my advice is to not tie your nest egg up in it. Use extra cash. Buy a wine from a great château or fine winery in great years. I'm going to suppose that you don't plan to age wine for resale. If you do, add the number of cases here. But for our purposes, we're still at 106.

Do you want to house wine for a friend or friends? For many years, my wine cellar was at my friend Peter's house. He had an insulated room where he kept his wine, and a side room where I and another friend kept our wine. My cellar grew by leaps and bounds because I moved from Sebastopol to Kenwood, which then put my wine cellar about 20 miles away from my house. Getting wine from it meant arranging to get the keys from Peter, driving there and back (which took about an hour), and spending time fiddling around in the cellar. Now my wine cellar is at home and it's much handier and much more useful to me. Before, there were many nights I'd simply drop in at a local winery or supermarket for a bottle of wine for dinner instead of hauling all the way over to Peter's. However, when your wine-loving friends hear that you have a wine cellar, be prepared to decide whether you will store some of their wine in it, because they will surely ask. I am going to assume that your cellar will be for your personal use and keep our count at 106 cases, but if you would be inclined to store wine for friends, add ten or fifteen cases here.

Do you want a simple place to store wine, or an elaborate wine cellar with all the accoutrements? Now we're talking about the actual physical size of your wine cellar, rather than a case count. A simple insulated room with shelving for 106 cases of wine may take up less space than you might imagine. But as long as you're creating a wine cellar, you might want to make it into a nice place to be. We'll get into racks and accoutrements in later chapters, but you might want a table with chairs, and a bookshelf to hold your wine books and your cellar book. If you're managing your cellar by computer, you might want an inexpensive, dedicated computer, monitor, and keyboard in there. From time to time you'll have a memorable bottle that has been a big hit or was drunk on a memorable occasion, and you'll want to save the bottle. You'll need some space for that, too.

Obviously, you can expand or contract your wine cellar as you see fit, but the bare minimum to store, say, 110 cases of wine will be 580 cubic feet of space for the wine and that much again for you to walk around in and for any equipment you have. That's 1,160 cubic feet. That's 129 cubic yards. If your cellar is 7 feet high by 18 feet long and 8 feet deep, that's 112 cubic yards. You could fit your 106 cases in a space that big along one wall of your house's cellar, with as much room to work in there as you have shelf space.

Are you building a cellar to leave as a bequest to your heirs? If you're 28 years old, you may not be thinking this way, but if you are 60, well, then, 20 years out brings you to 80. Thirty more years brings you to 90, and you probably won't be guzzling wine the way you once did. Or maybe you will, on the theory that by the time you're 90, you might as well start drinking and smoking cigarettes again. But seriously, at some point you will exit this vale of tears, most likely leaving a bunch of wine in your cellar to your heirs.

To intentionally collect wine with the idea of leaving it to your heirs is another thing entirely, and really, very commendable. The old person who plants a tree today does it for his or her heirs to enjoy after he's gone. The port you lay down now may outlive you. But I'm going on the assumption that your heirs will get any wine left in your cellar upon your death, unless you are careful enough to drink the last bottle on your deathbed, and that

CHRISTMAS BOXES

I began my wine cellar with three empty cardboard wine cases. They were under my kitchen counter. The first case was reserved for wines that I thought needed 3 to 5 years of aging. The second for wines that I thought needed 6 to 10 years. The third was for wines I thought might benefit from 11 to 15 years of aging. When I'd visit a wine shop or market and find an interesting bottle, I'd bring it home and place it on its side in the appropriate case. When a case became full, I'd close the top, circle it with strong strapping tape, and write the year it was to be opened on all sides of the box.

Of course, when the boxes are ready, I no longer remember what I put in them. So every box, especially the long agers, is like a vinous Christmas present. Sometimes my choices have been wrong, and the wine has lost its charm. Sometimes they've been exactly right, and the wine has mellowed into a lovely drink with a fascinating bouquet. And sometimes I misjudged a wine and didn't age it long enough. But the latter result is no problem, really. If a wine still is youthful and full of young fruit flavors, that's no hardship. The only problem comes from aging wines into decline. I'm still opening boxes that I wrapped up in the 1980s and have found very few wines that are past their optimum point.

I've learned an immense amount about how wines age from doing these "Christmas boxes." I still make up a box now and then from odd bottles in my cellar but only for fun. I've moved beyond the Christmas box stage into organizing my cellar so that it does on a grand scale, and with the ability to see and reach bottles, what the Christmas box idea did on a small scale.

If you are just starting out, however, you might want to make up some Christmas boxes to see after a number of years how well your guesses as to ageability turn out. I really look forward to opening them.

you are not going to consciously fill it with goodies for them. If you do plan the gift of a cellar full of legacies, add them now. But for our purposes, we're still at 106 cases, and that's where we shall remain.

Those 106 cases translate to 1,272 bottles of wine — not an inconsiderable amount. The question now becomes, How do you organize this amount of wine so that your cellar yields a perfectly aged wine at its peak of quality every time you want one?

ORGANIZING THE CELLAR

There are any number of ways to organize your wine cellar, but all the good ways have one thing in common: They include access to wines that are ready to drink. Whether sparkling, white, sweet, rosé, feminine like Pinot Noir, masculine and red like Cabernet, or powerful like Barolo, all are at the point where their quality is maximized.

All the other wines in your cellar are aging their way toward that divine time when they can be moved to the ready-to-drink section. This is what they were made for. This is why the vines worked so hard to perfect their fruit. It's what the winemaker had in mind. It's what the winery hoped would happen to its product, knowing full well that only a tiny fraction of its production would be aged properly. And you can count yourself among the train of laborers that began in the vineyard and ended in your cellar, for it takes time and money to operate a wine cellar — although you get the payoff because you get to drink it.

Attempts to organize wine by kind (for example, white, red, dessert, or sparkling) or by provenance have pitfalls. A California Chardonnay and a German Mosel are both white wines, but Great Danes and Chihuahuas are both dogs, and both cases exemplify very different creatures. But trying to organize a wine cellar by region is a task with no end. To simply have a bin for "French wine" is meaningless: There's Chablis and there's Châteauneuf-du-Pape, and the two are as dissimilar as they can be. If you had a place for California wines, you'd surely have to break it down into more meaningful components. For example, you'd have to have a place for wines of the regions east of San Diego, the central coast by Santa Barbara, the Santa Lucia foothills by Paso Robles, Monterey County, the Santa Cruz Mountains, Contra Costa County, and Sonoma, Napa, and Mendocino Counties. And within Sonoma County, you have very different regions: the area around Cloverdale in the northern part of the county is much hotter than that around Petaluma in the south. The Sonoma Valley runs from the town of Sonoma to Santa Rosa — it's cool at its southern end and warm at its northernmost end. The Russian River Valley is very different from Carneros. Coastal California (and Oregon and Washington, for that matter) is not like the rest of the continental United States; I can drive west from my house on a 100-degree day and about a half hour later have to put on a sweater because it's only 60 degrees at the coast.

So, by the time you had your cellar organized by place, you'd have a thousand compartments. Organizing the wine by provenance therefore isn't feasible. The ideal situation is not to have a bin for every place, but a place for some of just about everything that's ready to drink. Therefore, if you're having fish tonight, you might choose a perfectly aged bottle of Sauvignon Blanc from the Loire Valley of France. With beef, you might pull out a 14-year-old Chalk Hill Cabernet. With lamb, how about a 1996 Williams Selyem 'Rochioli Vineyard' Pinot Noir, or a 1989 Charmes-Chambertin? Whatever, but there they are, laid out in front of you in the ready-to-drink area of your wine cellar.

CELLAR LAYOUT

Organization starts with cellar layout. Mine, for example, has three compartments, each behind large insulated doors. Because my house is built back into a hillside, the cinder-block wall in the back of the basement is against the ground, and the ground is always about 58°F to 60°F six feet down — the perfect cellar temperature. So I built my cellar against the cinder-block wall. Looking at it when it's closed and locked, you see three sets of double doors that are insulated on the inside. The doors reach from the floor to the ceiling, with more insulation at each side and on the ceiling behind the doors. The cinder-block wall is left "as is" in order to flood the space with cool derived from the cinder block and the soil behind it, except for a sheet of plastic taped against the lower portion of the wall as a moisture barrier so that cardboard cases don't touch cold walls that can be damp in the winter, leading to mold.

Behind each set of doors is an upper and lower shelf. The upper shelf of the far left compartment is my ready-to-drink space, filled with open racks. The bottom shelf of the left compartment and the top and bottom shelves of the center and right compartments all hold cases somewhere in the aging process. Each shelf holds eighteen cases, so I have room for ninety cases in the five shelves that are available in the three compartments, plus space for 120 bottles in the ready-to-drink area, which gives me my 100-case wine cellar.

It's important not to fill up your wine cellar, especially not right away or even soon after it's built. It took me 10 years to fill my 100-case cellar at the rate of about ten cases per year. It's quite all right if there's plenty of empty space, ready to receive new boxes to replace those that have reached ready-to-drink status. When you think about it, a first-year 100-case wine cellar

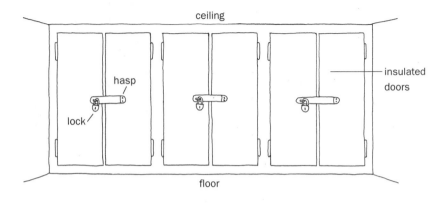

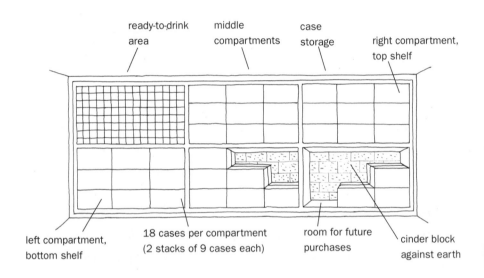

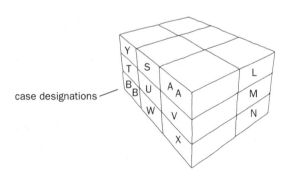

My wine cellar from the outside (top) and the interior (middle). Also, how my eighteen cases per compartment are arranged and letter-designated (bottom).

should probably only have about ten cases of wine; a second-year cellar, twenty; a third-year cellar, thirty; and so on. If you fill your cellar all at once, all that wine will be coming of age over just a few years. You won't have room to add cases each year. So don't rush things; it's counterproductive.

In addition to the wines that need aging, you'll have wines in there for drinking young, while you're waiting for the agers to come around. After a decade or so, you will find that your cellar is giving you well-aged wine on a regular basis, even as you put in young wine on a regular basis. It takes that decade for much of the wine to move through the cellaring process and reach the ready-to-drink area. When that happens, your cellar will be fully functioning.

The Ready-to-Drink Area

Because you want to be able to see your wines at a glance, it makes sense to have the ready-to-drink area made from open racks. I'll give you ideas and building plans for racks in chapters 5 and 6. I place the bottles into the racks bottom first, so that they lay horizontally with the foil capsules pointing at me as I peruse the racks. Many wineries identify themselves on the foil capsules, even indicating the vintage year, which helps immensely in knowing what you have without having to look up your wines in a cellar book.

This ready-to-drink rack can, however, be organized for the way you will use it. Wines can be graded fairly easily from lightest, crispest, and most lemony to darkest, deepest, and most concentrated. So as wines are brought over from long-term storage into the ready-to-drink racks, they can be placed in their approximate locations based on richness. It makes no difference whether you have the lightest wines on the left or right side, but be consistent. Because we read left to right, I organize my racks with the lightest wines on the left, and they get richer and heavier as we move to the right along the horizontal rows. I make no distinction for concentration in the vertical files, but one could certainly do that, with the lightest of the wines in that file on top and the heaviest on the bottom. Unless you've actually tasted and remember all the wines, however, these placements will be approximate guesses, so it may not be worth trying to organize the vertical files for richness.

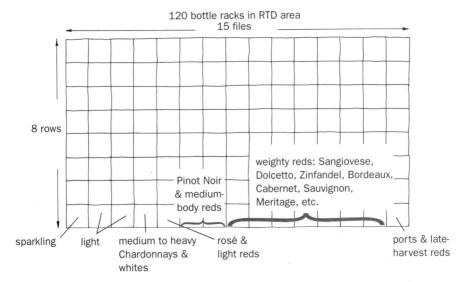

Ready-to-drink (RTD) area organized from lightest to darkest wines

I consider sparkling wines to be the lightest wines of all, and I keep them on the far left of the ready-to-drink files. As for port, I consider it to be the richest wine in the cellar, and it goes in the files to the far right. Between these are arrayed, from left to right, the whites and then the reds. Again, the wines are arranged, left to right, by degree of richness, rather than by variety or place of origin, because that's how I use them. I'll see what we're having for dinner and then make a selection based on richness to match the food.

So, to the right of the sparkling wines come Chenin Blanc, Muscadet, Verdicchio, Trebbiano, Sylvaner, Gewürztraminer, Semillon, Riesling, Sauvignon Blanc, Müller-Thurgau, Fiano, Arneis, Pinot Blanc, Vermentino, Albarino, Pinot Gris, Marsanne, Roussanne, Viognier, Greco, and Pinot Grigio, and then the Chardonnays from Chablis, Burgundy, and California, in roughly that order, from left to right. On the right side of the whites are the Muscats and dessert wines, such as botrytized wines, and late-harvest whites, like Sauternes and Vin de Paille. Of course, many whites (and reds) are blends labeled primarily by château or domaine, and these go in a spot where I think their richness warrants. So the white Bordeaux of Château La Louvière, for instance, a mixture of Sauvignon Blanc and Semillon, goes somewhere between those varieties.

Where the whites end, the reds begin. I'd say about one-fourth of the ready-to-drink wines are white, three-fourths red (and that holds true for the rest of the cellar, too). You may want more whites than I do — it's all based on your preference. For reds, I go left to right with Cinsault, Grignolino, Trousseau, Grenache, Pinot Meunier, Mondeuse, Tempranillo, Barbera, Petit Verdot, Carignane, Gamay, Pinot Noir, Montepulciano, Dolcetto, Sangiovese, Merlot, Malbec, Mourvèdre, Syrah, Aglianico, Cabernet Franc, Zinfandel, Nebbiolo, and Cabernet Sauvignon, ending with late-harvest reds, sherries, and ports on the far right side of the ready-to-drink racks. Because so many wines are blends (like the Châteauneuf-du-Papes, made from some or all of the thirteen allowed varieties) or are labeled by château or domaine only (how, without a good reference work, can one know what exactly is in Château Figeac, for instance — one or more of the five Bordeaux varieties, for sure, but which, and in what proportions?), it behooves one to know the expected richness of a wine.

But remember, this isn't brain surgery. Wines can be "out of place" without much penalty. Just try to know something about the wines you are cellaring and their approximate richness when they come out of long-term storage to take their place in the ready-to-drink racks. Asking the wine shop owner or some knowledgeable person is one good way. Experiencing a wine for yourself is an even better way. That's one good reason for keeping a cellar book and taking notes. By the time you see your wine again, you may have forgotten that "this is a blockbuster."

Another good rule of thumb is to err on the side of youth when cellaring wines. It may seem like a great idea to keep a medium-priced Cabernet Sauvignon for 17 years, but you may be unpleasantly surprised by the dried-out fruit and the generally thin and acerbic acidity of the wine after that time. Remember that long cellaring is for the big boys: wines with low pH, solid acidity, layers of fruit, dark color, a profound richness on the palate, and a fine balance among all the components.

What about the rest of the wine cellar? How do I organize things coherently so that the wines move easily and inexorably toward their apotheosis in the ready-to-drink bins?

The Aging Area

Originally, my theory was that cases closest to the ready-to-drink area would take the shortest amount of time before they're opened and placed in the ready-to-drink bins. As I move toward the center and right compartments, the cases would need more aging before they reach ready-to-drink status. But how do I organize them? Remember my Christmas boxes? The same idea can be applied to the cases of wine that are aging.

I have two kinds of cases in my arrangement. The first kind is labeled with the year it's to be opened; these are Christmas boxes, and I don't keep a record of what's in them. They're just for fun. I put one or two of them into the cellar each year for the pleasure of opening them some day in the far future and surprising myself with the wines I've selected. As before, these Christmas boxes hold wines that I think will all be perfectly aged in the year I've indicated on the box. I do record where they are in the cellar, however, so that I can find them easily. The second kind of case is labeled with a letter or letters; for these, I record where they are and what's in them. You may decide to forgo Christmas boxes and simply keep track of all of your wines.

Like wines go with like wines into the same case. For instance, 1997 was a great year for California Cabernets. I collected quite a number of individual bottles as well as a few whole cases of '97s — by whole cases, I mean twelve bottles of the same wine, as opposed to a mishmash of different bottles. Individual bottles are placed in a case until it's full. I have several different cases open at the same time, each acquiring bottles as I find them in stores or from mail-order wine clubs. One case is for wines that I think will not need great age to reach their peak but will be in fine shape at about 6 to 8 years old; another comprises wines that I think will be ripe at 12 to 14 years; and finally, one is a case of primos that I will let go longer if the vintage turns out as expected.

These cases are marked on most of their sides so that I can retrieve them easily. For instance, I have a case of 1997 Tudal Cabernet from Napa Valley that I think will be ripe at about 12 to 14 years. I've marked this with an A. I put it on the top shelf of the right-hand compartment.

The Cellar Book

My cellar book is a loose-leaf binder. The initial page is a diagram of the compartments and their shelves, so I can see at a glance exactly where all my wine is located. For instance, the first page shows that the left-hand compartment, bottom shelf, contains eighteen cases labeled N, O, P, Q, R, S, T, U, V, W, X, Y, Z, AA, and BB, Open in 2005, Open in 2006, and Open in 2006. That's fifteen cases labeled by letters and three Christmas boxes. The middle compartment top shelf contains cases GGG through UUU, plus Open in 2005, Open in 2006, and Open in 2007. And so on through the shelves.

The Christmas boxes need no further mention, but the cases labeled with letters each get a page of their own to list their contents, make notes, change contents, and so on. When I started the notebook, each shelf was given a file divider with tab and twenty-five blank loose-leaf pages for case descriptions. It's important that the notebook be loose-leaf because over the years pages will come out, be changed, or be added.

As an example, one file divider is marked RIGHT COMPARTMENT, TOP SHELF. In that section, one of the pages is marked CASE A and labeled "1997 Tudal Cabernet Sauvignon. Try in 2007." I figure this wine will be ready in about 2011, but it's a smart idea to try a bottle at 10 years just to see

First page of my cellar book

how it's aging. I'll make a note to try another bottle in 2009 when I take a bottle out of the case in 2007. Using this method, I can see at a glance when I need to taste a sample from a whole case. I know the case is on the top shelf of the right-hand compartment. Each shelf has two layers of nine cases each, so I don't have to move much wine to find the case.

When I try a sample bottle from a case to check progress, I make an organoleptic note. Here's one from a bottle of 1994 Dehlinger Bordeaux Blend that I recently sampled from a whole case that I'd purchased: "Tried 1/12/02. Fruit still youngish, very concentrated; deep crimson rim. Smooth tannins. Not much bouquet of age yet. Try again in 2005."

Whenever I take a bottle from a whole case of wine, I make a hatch mark in my cellar book. So when I take the first bottle to try in 2007, I'll make one hatch mark. In 2009, I'll make another. If a third sample in 2011 shows the wine is ready to move to the ready-to-drink area, I'll know at a glance that I have nine bottles left. It will be no hardship to have nine bottles of 14-year-old Tudal Napa Valley Cab to drink that year.

Another way to keep track of how many bottles are left in a whole case of the same wine is to make two parallel lines and then make vertical marks to create a dozen little boxes in a row. As you take out a bottle, X a box. If you add different wines to the case to keep it full, note them.

Mixed cases are another story. Most likely you won't be sampling wines when a case is made up of individual bottles. Make your best guess as to

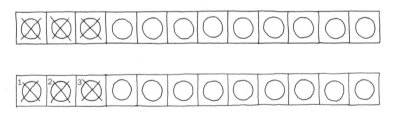

1. 1998 Jordan Cabernet
2. 1999 St. Francis Cabernet
3. 1997 Barnett Cabernet

Grid to keep track of departing/arriving wines. Cross out bottles as you use them; as you add new bottles, annotate the grid with their names.

which wines will become ready to drink at about the same time and fill a box with them. Tape the box shut and mark it with a letter or letters. These cases can be organized by year, so they contain twelve different wines from the same vintage that you think will all be ready about the same time, or they can contain wines from several years close together. I use a lettering system for these cases as well. Right now, I have some cases marked CCC and DDD, and so on, as I've used up all the single-letter and double-letter tags on other cases. When my cases marked A and B and DD and GG, for example, are emptied and taken to the ready-to-drink racks, those letters will be freed up to use again.

Here's a typical case of individual bottles — an actual case from my cellar book:

CASE DD
1 bottle 1999 Williams Selyem 'Sonoma Coast' Pinot Noir
2 bottles 1999 Williams Selyem 'Russian River Valley' Pinot Noir
1 bottle 1999 Château St. Martin Languedoc
1 bottle 1995 Pepi Sangiovese
1 bottle 2000 Robert Stemmler 'Sonoma County' Pinot Noir
1 bottle 2000 Robert Stemmler 'Carneros' Pinot Noir
1 bottle 1999 Norton Malbec
1 bottle 1999 Domaine d'Aphillanthes Côtes du Rhône Villages
1 bottle 1998 T-bar-T Ranch Sangiovese
1 bottle 1998 Norton Sangiovese
1 bottle 1998 Cooper Mountain (Oregon) Pinot Noir

My guess is that those Williams Selyem Pinot Noirs will be ready when they're about six years old, in 2005. By that time, the Cooper Mountain will be seven, and the Stemmlers will be five. That 1995 Pepi Sangiovese will be a decade old, which could be good because Pepi's Sangiovese is always made with sturdy structure, if fleshy fruit. The French Languedoc and Côtes du Rhône Villages probably won't improve much past the six years of aging they'll get, as they are not extraordinary wines (but one never really knows,

ALWAYS STORE WINE ON ITS SIDE

Whether you're filling an open case or storing wine for the long term, always keep the cork in contact with the wine by placing the case so the bottles are horizontal. This keeps the corks swollen and the closure tight. Stand older bottles that will need decanting upright a day before you're going to open them so that the sediment falls to the bottom.

and that's much of the fun), and the others . . . well, I'm guessing. But it'll be fun to drink these wines in 2005 when they go to the ready-to-drink racks.

You can see the importance of filling your individual cases with bottles you think will mature at the same time. That saves you the trouble of switching and swapping bottles from case to case, and from case to ready-to-drink racks, leaving empty spots in your cases that require lots of record keeping, especially if the empty spots are filled with other wines.

I find it easy to keep three cases or more open and not yet filled or logged into the cellar book. Wines that will mature at the same time go into the same case, and as a case is filled, it's logged into the cellar book, assigned a letter (or number or symbol or whatever you want to use to identify it; I use letters and that seems to work for me), taped up, and stored on one of the shelves in one of the compartments. The location of the case is then noted on the first page of the cellar book, where all the cases are listed.

The cellar needs yearly maintenance to keep things up-to-date. I usually do this task sometime in January. It involves looking over the cases to see which contain wines that are ready to move into the ready-to-drink racks. If there are Christmas boxes for that year, I'll open at least one of them (saving the others for later in the year).

When I find a case that's ready to open and distribute into the ready-to-drink racks, I remove that page from the cellar book. If it contains organoleptic notes that I want to keep, I transcribe those notes to history pages in the back of the book. Here's a note I transcribed after the case from which the bottle I mentioned was taken out of storage and the bottles placed in the ready-to-drink racks: "1991 Dry Creek Vineyards Estate Merlot: Fabulously silky smooth and rich, beautiful nose of ancient cedar and leather and incense, lingering finish. Exceptional wine from a year that had an extraordinarily long hang time for the fruit." I don't want to forget a wine that great. Only unforgettable wines have their notes transcribed to the history section.

The page for that case was removed and destroyed, and the letter value it had been given is noted to be ready for re-use. After all the cases that have reached ready-to-drink status in the new year are placed in the racks and their pages removed, the front page showing the location of all the cases in the cellar starts looking like a hen has been scratching around in it; thus, part of my yearly maintenance is to redo the first page. It's not a big chore, and it keeps things neat and intelligible.

In theory, as they age, cases move from right to left in the cellar, getting closer in physical proximity to the ready-to-drink racks. In practice, that involves a lot of schlepping of cases, so I find that cases tend to stay where they are first placed, except maybe the ones closest to hand. That makes sense, since I can easily peruse my cellar book and see exactly where all my cases are, no matter what stage of aging they're in.

It may happen that there's nothing that grabs you in the ready-to-drink racks some night, but you remember that you have a bottle of fine old port aging in one of your primo cases. It's late, the port is almost old enough anyway, and your friends would certainly enjoy a taste. And so you look in your cellar book and see that the port is located in case YY on the bottom shelf of the center compartment. After moving a few cases, you see YY, haul it out, open it up, and retrieve the bottle of port. Fair enough — it's your cellar, and if you want to raid it and rip a bottle untimely from its womb, that's your business. However, I would caution you to use a stick-on note or other mnemonic device to remind yourself of the fact in the morning. That bottle should be replaced with something appropriate for the case or an empty bottle for one main reason: Cardboard cases with empty spots tend to collapse under the weight of cases above them, skewing bottles this way and that. Note your replacement bottle where YY is itemized.

The above system is for do-it-yourselfers like me. I like keeping my own records, and I like keeping it simple. Yes, I could inventory everything on my computer's spreadsheet, but I like the handwritten approach. It's easy, it doesn't take much work, and it makes sense to me.

That said, there is some powerful cellaring software out there. I think the best has been developed by Robert M. Parker Jr., the wine guru who publishes *The Wine Advocate.* Parker is undoubtedly the most powerful wine critic in the world — a good word from him can send a wine price through the roof and a poor review can damage a winery's reputation. The software is called Robert Parker's Wine Advisor and Cellar Manager. The 2002 Standard Edition (the latest version as this is being written) contains Parker's notes on more than 35,000 wines reviewed in his publication from 1992 through 2001. Updates or a newer version will probably be available by the time you read this. You can enter your wines and search the resulting database by Parker rating (if any), vintage, when to drink, and so on. A new feature is a wine price database that will give you an idea of the current selling price of your wine — that is, what it would cost to replace a given bottle of wine. This might be a useful piece of software if you tend to buy wines based on Parker's ratings, largely because Parker gives estimated dates when the wines he rates will drink at their best. For the 1990 Château Margaux, for instance, he says: "Drink from January 1997 until December 2020." That's just his guess, but it's a very educated one. I'd encourage you to become wine savvy enough to make your own educated guesses — and that's best done by knowing what you like and cellaring enough wine to get the hang of it.

I think that for the price of a pen and a loose-leaf notebook, you can have a simple system as outlined above that works perfectly well. But for software buffs or those with larger cellars, Parker's is about as good as you'll get. It's available from International Wine Accessories (see pages 237 and 240 for more information). You can also supplement your loose-leaf records with wine cellar entries created electronically using your computer's word processing program (see page 186). Use the record-keeping method that works best for you.

PART TWO

Building and Using the Wine Cellar

A cave dug into the cold, dark, humid, motionless earth is the perfect wine cellar. We need to re-create those conditions as closely as we can in our homes. It's not as difficult as it sounds.

CHAPTER 5

Constructing and Equipping
a Wine Cellar

My first wine cellar was simply a shelf in the basement. Thank goodness it was in the basement, for I stocked it with one of my very first attempts to make wine, an attempt that ended in disaster, as you will see.

My friend John and I drove to Newark, New Jersey, to pick up a few 40-pound boxes of Alicante Bouschet grapes from California that had arrived by rail car. I took two boxes home and fermented 80 pounds of grapes in a crock. After what seemed like a decent interval, when the fizzing had pretty much subsided, I poured the wine through cheesecloth into rinsed-out wine bottles and stoppered them with corks that I pounded in with a mallet. Then I put on labels using a glue stick and laid the bottles on the open shelves in the basement. The next day I noticed that the corks were inching their way out of the necks. Evidently, some gas was still being produced. Remembering that the French wire hoods over their Champagne corks, I got some wire, pushed the corks back in, and wired them down tight. A few days later I heard crashing in the basement and went down to find bottles exploding. The fermentation was obviously continuing, and gas would not be denied. The bottles were not meant to be placed under internal pressure, and the corks were wired on so securely that the only way out for the carbon dioxide being produced by the yeast was through the glass.

I also had an old chest freezer in that basement that had lost its Freon and was inoperative. If any other bottles exploded on me, the freezer would contain the damage. So I began to lay wine bottles on their sides in there. I didn't realize that no air movement, darkness, and humidity are the perfect conditions for mold. Soon all my handmade labels were turning greenish black.

However, I also didn't realize then that my basement had almost perfect conditions for a wine cellar. Because I heated the upper floors of the century-old farmhouse with a woodstove, the basement, sunk below ground and with half its floor bare earth, remained a fairly consistent 55°F to 60°F year-round. You often hear that a wine should be served at room temperature; that really means cellar temperature. And a cellar in much of Europe, where these notions began, stays a fairly constant 58°F year-round with some fluctuation down in winter and up in summer. A constant 58°F is exactly what a bottle of fine wine needs to age itself toward perfection.

It was also dark down in that basement, unless I switched on the light. And the bare-earth half of the cellar kept the relative humidity at about 70 percent — again, just about exactly what a bottle of wine wants to age properly. Too much humidity, and the labels mold. Too little, and the dry air sucks humidity through the cork and from the label's glue. Before I could fix up shelving for a proper wine cellar, though, a big change in my life occurred. I moved from Pennsylvania to California.

Those who live in the mild regions of California know that few houses have basements. Some of the very old farmhouses of an age consonant with my Pennsylvania house, circa 1860 to 1880, have basements, but even those are rare. Why don't California houses have basements? For several reasons, the most prominent of which is that the winters aren't cold enough to demand central heating. I currently get by on about a cord and a half of wood in a woodstove each winter, and that's in the cooler coastal part of northern California. Second, a lot of modern California was built in the past 50 years or so and built quickly. A slab is poured and a house, sometimes without insulation, is hastily erected. A builder friend of mine calls large, mansion-style California houses "big junk." Climate-controlled rooms are the answer for most California houses. But I was lucky.

My current residence is three stories built back into a north-facing hillside, with the bottom story against the earth on three sides and the north wall of the bottom story facing north at ground level. This has allowed me to construct an insulated wine cellar in the back part of the bottom story to take advantage of the earth's cool. My situation is fortunate but rare for California.

WHAT KIND OF CELLAR?

Two kinds of situations usually determine what kind of wine cellar you can have. The first is a house with a basement that's excavated at least 6 feet below ground, with cellar walls of cinder block or stone against the earth. Because many readers of this book will have a basement, and because that affords the simplest situation, this is the basis for the wine cellar I'll describe in the next section. You should be able to construct two insulated walls in the cellar area, with the other two sides being existing foundation block, poured concrete, or stone walls providing natural cooling from the earth.

The second situation is a house with no basement or just a shallow crawl space underneath. In this case, you have four options: (1) you can excavate a wine cellar separate from the house; (2) you can install an insulated room with refrigeration and possibly a humidifier to keep the room at the proper temperature and humidity; (3) you can buy a self-contained wine storage cabinet with limited, but properly climate-controlled, storage; or (4) you can rent space in a commercial wine storage locker. (See chapter 6 for discussions of options 3 and 4.)

Let's look at these situations, starting with a house that has a basement excavated down into the earth — a fairly typical situation in much of the United States. In this case, you or your builder can create a wine cellar that keeps a proper temperature and humidity fairly easily.

BUILDING A BASEMENT WINE CELLAR

The following plan is for a bare-bones wine cellar; nothing fancy, but it will function just as well as a fancier one. You can fancy it up as much as you wish, adding knotty pine paneling, expensive racking, tile flooring, cooling units, and so on as your inclination and budget warrant. Believe me, you can spend several fortunes doing a wine cellar. One company, for instance, sells limestone slabs cut from limestone bedrock beneath the famous Burgundy region of Corton, where Charlemagne grew grapes, that you can use to panel your cellar walls or cover the floor. But the cellar that I plan out and describe here is a simple, insulated room that takes its cooling from the earth.

The first thing you have to do is to determine the size of the wine cellar. In chapter 4, we discussed a cellar that's 18 feet wide by 8 feet deep, with a 7- or 8-foot ceiling, which is adequate for holding just more than one hundred cases. If you have a cellar wall that's 18 feet wide, you may only need one newly built wall to enclose the cellar space. It would be built 8 feet out from

the 18-foot foundation wall, enclosing a room with 144 square feet of floor space. However, the likelihood of having a foundation wall exactly 18 feet is slim, and you'll probably have to build two walls. I'd suggest that the wall with the door be 14½ feet long and the other wall be 10 feet long, yielding about 144 square feet of floor space. Or you could build two walls, each 12 feet in length, again giving you 144 square feet. Any of these dimensions will work. Just try for a cellar with 144 square feet of floor space that fits well in your existing basement.

Choose a part of the basement that's dry. Places where water seeps through walls or pools on the floor are not good for a wine cellar, as humidity will get high enough to cause the wine labels to molder. Either seal the walls to stop seepage, or build the wine cellar in a dry part of the basement. If water runs across the floor into the area where you want to put the cellar but doesn't come into that area through the walls or floor, you can keep water from flowing into the cellar area by making a small berm of concrete to direct flow to a drain or to a sump pump.

If you've never built anything before, the wine cellar will be a good project to practice on. It can be purely functional rather than beautiful, and it's about as simple a project as you can dream up. However, be aware that standard board size does not reflect the actual dimensions of the wood. A 2x4 isn't 2 inches by 4 inches; it's 1½ by 3½ inches. Likewise, a 2x8 is actually 1½ by 7½ inches (or sometimes 7 5/16). So if you're planning out this project on paper before you build it, be aware of proper sizing.

I once built an outhouse; it was a beautiful thing with five sides, a four-sided roof with a slope, a picture window, stained glass, tongue-and-groove flooring, and a two-holed slab of solid oak for the throne. I'd never built anything before and couldn't figure out why nothing fit. There were all these gaps everywhere. My wife called it the worst piece of building she'd ever seen. I never thought to check the size of the building materials. I just assumed that a 2x4 was indeed 2 inches by 4 inches. Silly me.

I'm trying to describe this project clearly for those who have no building experience, so don't mind me if I'm being technically basic. I want this project to be doable by even an unskilled novice like I was.

It goes without saying that good safety practices are essential for any building project. Read, understand, and follow manufacturer's instructions before using power tools. And always wear safety glasses. Ear protection is also recommended.

Following are lists of the materials and tools you'll need. The amount of material you'll need will depend on the size of the room you'll build. Plan the job by drawing it out on paper to determine how much of each item you'll have to buy. That will help you estimate cost, too.

Note: The instructions that follow assume that the basement floor is concrete. If it isn't, consider pouring a concrete slab.

Before You Start

Before you begin construction, do the following:

• **Consider interior *and* exterior dimensions.** The 144 square feet of floor space in the wine cellar is the *interior* dimension. The walls will be 8½ inches thick; that thickness is made up of 2x8 studs (that are actually 1½ by 7½ inches) with ½ inch drywall (or *sheetrock* or *wallboard*, as it's also called) on the exterior and interior faces of the new walls.

• **Seal walls.** To prevent water seepage into the wine cellar during wet spells and heavy rains, seal the existing cellar walls with waterproof sealer. If existing cellar walls never show any signs of moisture, you can eliminate this step.

• **Vent the cooling-unit exhaust.** If you are going to have a cooling unit in the cellar, you might want to vent the exhaust from the cooling unit to the outside through the window-well casement.

• **Seal windows.** If there's a window-well casement in one of the existing foundation walls that will be inside the wine cellar, seal it up. First, make sure that the glass and metal are intact; you don't want mice climbing through any cracks or holes in the glass. Pack the casement with insulation, and then, using masonry bolts, cover the opening with a piece of plywood.

The lists of materials and tools on the following pages are appropriate for the simplest possible wine cellar built by a do-it-yourselfer. Don't hesitate to get creative if you want something fancier.

MATERIALS

___ 2x8 pressure-treated hemlock or Douglas fir, for soleplate, top plates, and studs against foundation walls

___ Duct tape

___ Non-water-based elastomeric adhesive caulk (optional)

___ Four or six ½" wedge bolts

___ Hex nuts for wedge bolts

___ 2x4s, for nailers, header

___ 2½" flathead wood screws, for top plate (optional)

___ 8x8, for corner (optional)

___ Prehung door

___ Metal or oak threshold (if not part of prehung door)

___ #30 felt

___ Waterproofing compound

___ 2" finishing nails

___ 8d common nails, for studs and rigid foam insulation

___ ¾" interior grade plywood, for header

___ Fiberglass insulation

___ 16d common nails, for header

___ Shims, for doorjamb, drywall

___ Doorknob, lock, striker plate

___ Weather stripping

___ Electrical supplies, as needed

___ 6- or 8-mil clear polyethylene plastic sheeting

___ Rigid foam insulation

___ ⅝" drywall, ¾" interior grade plywood sheeting, or tongue-and-groove paneling, for walls and ceiling

___ Screws, for applying drywall to studs and joists
     1⅝" screws, for ceiling; 1⅜" screws, for walls

___ Drywall tape

___ Drywall plaster

___ Paint, if drywall is used for walls

___ Stain, if plywood is used for walls

___ Door molding, either 1x3 or 1x4 stock

TOOLS

___ Tape measure

___ Chalk line

___ Pencils

___ 6-foot level

___ Framing/combination square

___ Caulk gun (optional)

___ Crescent wrench, to use on wedge bolts

___ Rubber gloves, for handling pressure-treated wood

___ Disposable brush, for treating ends of pressure-treated wood

___ Dust mask

___ Sawhorses

___ Ripsaw

___ Drill and bits, including ½" bit, ⅜" masonry bit, and Phillips-head screwdriver bit for drywall screws

___ Hammer

___ Ramset or concrete cartridge nail gun, for soleplate (optional)

___ Plumb bob

___ Wood chisel

___ Staple gun

___ Handsaw, for cutting rigid insulation

___ Utility knife/linoleum knife

___ Jigsaw

CONSTRUCTION TIP

Pressure-treated wood contains arsenic and other nasty compounds. *Always* wear rubber gloves and a dust mask when working with pressure-treated wood. And seal the cut ends of pressure-treated wood with copper green or copper clear.

Measure and Mark the Walls

Begin by measuring and marking the lengths of the new walls on the floor. You can do this by snapping a chalk line or by making a pencil mark, using a straight board or the level as a straightedge. These lines define the edge of the

THE 3-4-5 METHOD

The Pythagorean theorem states that the sum of the squares of two sides of a right angle equal the square of the hypotenuse. The square of 3 is 9. The square of 4 is 16. Nine and 16 equal 25. The square root of 25 is 5. So, measure 3 feet along the existing foundation wall from where the chalk line begins, then measure 4 feet out along the chalk line. Using a tape measure, measure the length of a line from the end of the 4-foot mark to the end of the 3-foot mark. It should be exactly 5 feet if you've made an accurate right angle. If it's more or less than 5 feet, adjust the 4-foot line slightly until its position is exactly 5 feet from the end of the 3-foot mark; that way, you'll know the right angle is true. If the room is big enough, you can expand the triangle using the 6-8-10 method. It's the same proportions as the 3-4-5 method, but the larger triangle gives you double the accuracy. It sounds complicated in words, but it's simple when you do it.

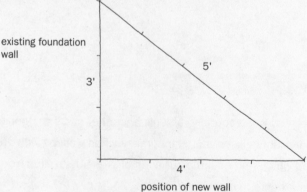

existing foundation wall

3'

5'

4'

position of new wall

inside wall of the wine cellar. Use the framing square to make sure the lines are perpendicular to each of the existing foundation walls; double-check them with the 3-4-5 method (see box on page 130).

Cut and Position the Soleplates

Prop a pressure-treated 2x8 on sawhorses, and with the ripsaw cut it to the desired length. One soleplate will run the full length of its wall and the other will butt up against it, so measure accordingly.

Lay the soleplates flat, as shown, positioning them so they come together at what will be the corner of the new walls.

Use the framing square and the 3-4-5 method to ensure that the soleplates come together at a perfect 90-degree angle. Any deviation from a true right angle will throw off everything else later, so make sure it's correct before continuing to the next step.

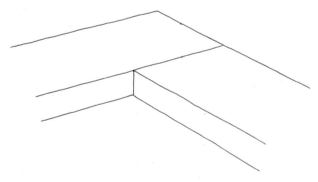

Soleplates meeting at corner

You may want to duct tape the soleplates securely in place before you drill in order to keep them in position. You can also use a non-water-based elastomeric adhesive caulk between the soleplate and concrete floor for extra grip. But don't try to save time or cut corners by using only the adhesive to secure the soleplates. If you do, like the walls at Jericho the new walls will come tumbling down.

Lay Out the Vertical Studs

Before bolting the soleplates to the concrete floor, determine where the vertical studs will be placed. This allows you to position the wedge bolts so they won't interfere with placement of the studs.

A stud is needed at the end of each soleplate where it meets the foundation wall.

See the illustrations under Construct a Corner (page 136) for a preview of how the corner where the soleplates meet will be handled. When the cor-

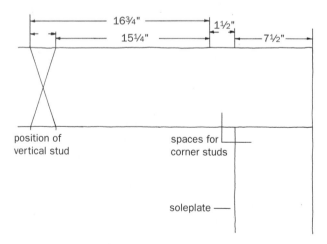

Laying out the corner and vertical studs

ner assembly is constructed, you'll place studs every 16 inches on center along the soleplates, except where the door will go (see Determine Door Placement below). You'll be cutting insulation later, so keeping studs at a uniform distance will simplify that task and save you time.

Start at the corner where the soleplates come together, allowing room for framing of the corner, and begin measuring and marking. Use the framing square and mark off 15¼ inches and then 16¾ inches. (The 1½ inches between will accommodate the actual width of the 2x8.) Draw a line from corner to corner of the rectangle thus formed. The stud will be centered over the x where the lines intersect.

Continue marking thus down the length of each soleplate.

Determine Door Placement

Decide now where the door will go so that you don't inadvertently bolt the soleplate to the floor within what will be the rough opening that you'll cut for the door.

Door widths vary, but let's assume you're going to have a 32-inch-wide door in a prehung frame (see page 140). A good rule of thumb is that the width of the rough opening is 2¼ inches wider than the prehung door frame (in this case 34¼ inches). In addition, two 2x8 studs will be used on each side of the door frame (6 inches total; 1½ inches for each stud), running from soleplate to top plate, for a total width of 40¼ inches. Mark out rough door placement. You'll need to cut one soleplate so as to leave a 34¼" rough opening. Use wedge bolts if necessary to secure cut ends to the concrete floor.

CAUTION

Before drilling, determine whether any pipes lie under or within the concrete floor, and plan accordingly to avoid them. Also, do not secure wedge bolts within the 40¼ inches reserved for the prehung door and frame.

Bolt the Soleplates to the Floor

For a short wall of 6 feet or less, you'll need to place two ½-inch wedge bolts, at least 4 inches and at most 12 inches from each end of the soleplate. For a longer wall, secure the soleplate in three places: at least 4 inches and at most 12 inches from each end and in the middle.

Using a ½-inch drill bit, drill through the soleplate. When you hit concrete, change to a ⅜-inch masonry bit and drill 2 inches more. Don't go deeper than 2 inches or you risk punching through the concrete slab. If you punch through the slab, moisture from the soil underneath can creep up through the drilled hole, eventually rotting the soleplate, studs, and drywall. Place the wedge bolt in the drilled hole, and with a hammer tap it down firmly into place. Under pressure of the hammer, the flared bottom of the wedge bolt bites into the concrete, anchoring the bolt securely.

Secure a nut to the top of each wedge bolt until it's snug against the pressure-treated wood. This further anchors the wedge bolt to the soleplate and, thus, to the concrete floor.

Other options: There are other ways to secure the soleplate to the concrete floor. A handheld ramset can be struck with a hammer to drive nails through the soleplate into the concrete floor. Or you can rent a nail gun, which uses a bullet-like cartridge to shoot nails through the soleplate into the concrete. It's your choice.

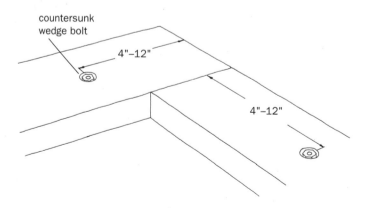

Soleplates are anchored to the concrete floor with wedge bolts.

Inspect the Ceiling

The joists in the ceiling must be exposed so you can secure the top plates. (A *top plate* is a 2x8 that will be laid parallel to the soleplate and secured to the ceiling joists.) If the ceiling is open and you can see the floor joists that support the room above the basement, fine. If, however, you see drywall, ceiling tiles, light fixtures, or anything else up there, remove them.

Draw Plumb Lines

Next you need to draw plumb lines on the existing foundation walls and on the ceiling joists or nailers.

Foundation wall: Cut a pressure-treated 2x8 so it fits against the foundation wall from the top of the soleplate to the bottom of the floor joist above it. Place the level against the 2x8 and adjust the 2x8 until it's plumb. Then make pencil marks at top and bottom, and snap a chalk line against the foundation wall. This line defines where the *outside* edge of an upright 2x8 pressure-treated stud will rest on the soleplate; the stud will be toe-nailed into the soleplate and the top plate (see page 141).

Use the 2x8 and level to do the same on the other foundation wall.

Ceiling joist or nailer: Mark a spot on a ceiling joist or nailer that is plumb, above the outside edge of the soleplate where it meets the foundation wall. To determine this spot, hang a plumb bob so the point of the bob meets the outside edge of the soleplate, or use the 2x8 and level as before. This mark defines where the *outside* edge of the top plate must be to be exactly

---

ABOUT PLUMB BOBS

It's interesting (to me at least) that the word *plumb* is spelled with a *b*. That's because the plumb bob was originally made of lead, and the Latin for lead is *plumbum*. Lines are plumb when they are perfectly vertical, as determined by a pointed weight hung from a line, usually made of brass. Just shows you how old certain building techniques are.

---

parallel to and directly above the soleplate, and ensures that the walls will be perfectly vertical, not toed in or out, from the foundation to the corner where the new walls meet.

Do the same for the other top plate.

Attach Nailers

With the ceiling joists exposed, you may discover that one of the top plates must run parallel to the ceiling joists and that there's nothing to nail to. In this case, nail pieces of 2x4 between the joists every 24 inches, so that the bottoms of the 2x4s are flush with the bottoms of the joists. These are the *nailers* for the top plate for that wall. Because the other wall will be perpendicular to this wall, you'll be able to nail its top plate directly to the joists.

Mark, Position, and Secure the Top Plates

Using the same 2x8 you used to find plumb against the foundation walls, find the spot on the ceiling that is plumb above the *outside* corner where the two soleplates meet. To do this, hold the level against the 2x8 on either side of the corner, or use a plumb·bob. Make pencil marks above the corner, then snap chalk lines across the joists or nailers on the ceiling. These lines define the position of the *outside* edges of the top plates.

Cut two untreated 2x8 studs to length. Nail or screw the top plates in place, being sure to keep the outside edge of each top plate on the chalk line. This will help ensure that the walls are true, not toed in or toed out.

Construct a Corner

In addition to the vertical studs you've planned for, you'll also need a sturdy corner upright where the two new walls come together. Because the new walls will be at right angles to each

other, the studs along one wall will be perpendicular to the studs along the
other wall. There are two ways to handle this corner. Both methods give you
places to nail the drywall to at the inside and outside corners of the two new
walls.

Option 1: Where the two soleplates come together at the corner of the
new walls, you can use an 8x8. You'll be able to nail drywall to the 8x8 to

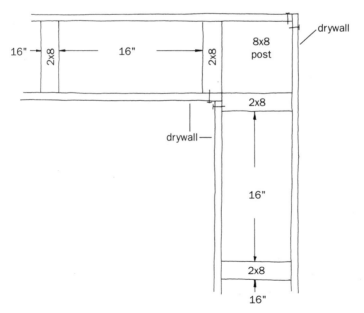

*Constructing a corner, option 1. Note that the 2x8 studs that are flush
with the 8x8 post are needed as nailers for the interior drywall.*

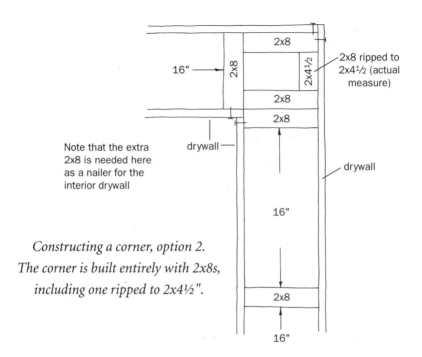

2x8

16"

2x8

2x4½

2x8 ripped to
2x4½ (actual
measure)

2x8

2x8

drywall

drywall

Note that the extra
2x8 is needed here
as a nailer for the
interior drywall

16"

Constructing a corner, option 2.
The corner is built entirely with 2x8s,
including one ripped to 2x4½".

2x8

16"

finish the outer surface of the new walls, but inside the wine cellar, there will be nothing in the corner to nail to. To remedy this, set 2x8 studs flush against the two "interior" sides of the 8x8.

Option 2: Construct a corner from four 2x8 studs and one 2x8 that you rip to 4½ inches wide.

Purchase a Prehung Door

Hanging a door in a door frame that you've built yourself is sort of an art, and unless you have done it several times and feel sure of yourself, take my advice and buy a prehung door. You'll save yourself a lot of aggravation and work. The ideal wine cellar door is a simple flat door made of plywood and prehung in a ready-made *jamb,* or door frame.

Measure the distance between the top of the soleplate and the bottom of the top plate before you go shopping. You'll need this measurement to determine whether the door you choose will fit.

Choose a door with a threshold already in place. You can buy insulated doors, but that seems like overkill to me. Wood is a fine insulator, and a solid wood door should afford you a sufficient R factor (resistance to heat transfer) to prevent warmth from flooding into the wine cellar. (Don't get a door with glass in it; remember the goal is to keep the wine cellar as cool and as dark as possible.) If you are concerned, you can always insulate the interior surface of the door with rigid insulation.

CONSTRUCTION TIP

It's a good idea to buy the prehung door *before* you make a rough opening so that you can put the frame in place before you start nailing. It's a lot easier to check for proper fit before the nails go in.

If you can't locate a prehung door with threshold, you can buy a metal or oak threshold at a building-supply store. If you choose an oak threshold, put #30 felt under it as a moisture barrier. If you need to screw or nail the oak threshold to the concrete floor, apply waterproofing compound to the spot on the felt where the nails will go. This will prevent moisture from the floor from creeping up into the oak and rotting it.

Once you find a door that seems promising, inquire about the height of the "rough opening" the door frame will fit into, and write down the dimension. Compare this against the measurement of the distance between the concrete floor and top plate. Make sure that you have plenty of room to accommodate the height of the pre-hung door.

The standard size of a prehung door with threshold is 81 to 81¼ inches. A good rule of thumb for the height of the rough opening is that it be about 1 inch higher than the height of the prehung door frame — including the threshold — in this case, 82 inches. That extra space will be taken up by the framing of the prehung door (or the jamb you install yourself if you go that route).

Rather than struggling with the entire prehung door, remove the door from the frame. Place the frame in the rough opening that you cut in the soleplate (see page 133) so the door will swing toward you rather than away from you and into the wine cellar. That way you'll have more room to maneuver in the wine cellar.

Hold the frame in place with a single finishing nail that is partially driven in or with a piece of duct tape. Good carpenters know that you don't nail stuff down tight until you're sure everything fits.

Create the Rough Opening for the Door Frame

You've already established where the door frame will be placed and how wide and high the rough opening will be (see page 133) — in this case, 34¼ inches and 82 inches, respectively.

You've already cut out the width of the rough opening in the soleplate, removing the pressure-treated wood where the door will go. As before, treat cut ends of pressure-treated wood with copper green or copper clear.

Two pairs of 2x8 studs will be placed on either side of the opening. The *king studs,* farthest from the opening, run from the soleplate to the top plate; the *trimmer studs,* closest to the opening, run from the soleplate to 82 inches

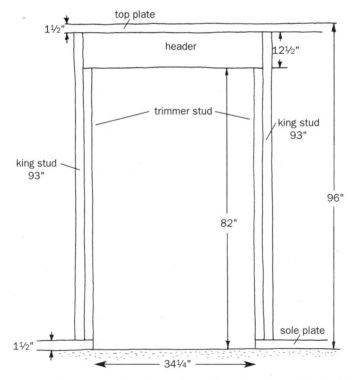

Rough opening for prehung door, jamb, and threshold

---

above the concrete floor. The trimmer studs will thus be cut to 80½ inches and the king studs to 93 inches.

Cut king and trimmer studs to length. Position king and trimmer studs as shown, and check fit and straightness, ensuring that all are plumb.

Using 8d nails, toe-nail the bottom of the king studs, check plumb, then toe-nail the top. It never hurts to check your work at each step. Place the trimmer studs flush against the king studs and toe-nail the trimmer studs to the soleplate. Now nail the trimmer studs to the king studs, being careful not to knock the king studs out of place. You might want to hammer in a few nails from the trimmer side and a few from the king side for added stability.

CONSTRUCTION TIP

Toe-nailing is a technique in which you attach one piece of wood to another by driving nails at a 45-degree angle through a vertical piece and into a horizontal piece. Use 2½-inch 8d nails angled through the studs about 1¼ inches away from the soleplate or top plate. You want the nail point to come through the center of the stud and then enter the soleplate or top plate. If the wood of the studs splits, pre-drill holes for the nails in the studs only, not in the soleplates or top plates. Let the nails find their way into the plates so that they're firm and snug.

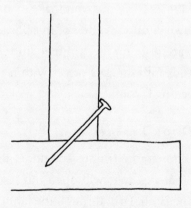

Make the Door Header

The *header* is a horizontal frame that will rest on the trimmer studs above the rough door opening (see illustration on page 140). It should fill the space from the top of the trimmer studs to the bottom of the top plate; amend the dimensions that follow to suit the requirements of your basement.

In this example, the top of each trimmer stud is 82 inches above the floor, and the 1½-inch top plate is nailed to joists that are 96 inches above the floor. The space that the header must fill, therefore, is the difference between 82 inches and 94½ inches (measuring from the top of the trimmer studs to the bottom of the top plate), or 12½ inches. The distance between the king studs is the 34¼ inches of the rough opening plus 3 inches for the two 1½-inch trimmer studs, or 37¼ inches. The depth of the header is the depth of the 2x8 king studs, or 7½ inches. Thus, the header must be 12½ inches high by 37¼ inches wide by 7½ inches deep.

There are many ways to make the header, but in all cases it should be insulated so that warm air doesn't seep into the wine cellar. The easiest way, in my opinion, is to saw ¾-inch interior plywood into two pieces, each 12½x37¼ inches. (In the case of plywood, ¾-inch stock is actually ¾ of an inch in thickness.) The two pieces of plywood will take up 1½ inches of the 7½ inches of depth needed in the header, leaving 6 inches between the plywood pieces to be made up. The simplest way to do this is to cut scrap 2x4s into six pieces, each exactly 6 inches long. Screw one of the plywood pieces to the six pieces of scrap, then turn it over and screw the other piece of plywood to the open ends of the 2x4s, so that you make a box 7½ inches wide. Place the separators as shown. Stuff the center of this box as full of fiberglass insulation as you can, place it up on the trimmer studs, and hammer 16d nails through the king studs into the 2x4 pieces within the header to hold it in place. The rough opening is complete.

Position the Door Frame

Place the prehung door frame (minus the door) into the rough opening, again making sure that the door will open out toward you. Use shims to square and plumb the jamb. Drill through the jamb into the trimmer studs and nail the jamb in place using finishing nails. Make sure it's nailed in securely enough to tolerate some slamming. Doorstops (those thin pieces of wood that the door rests against when closed) are already in place in prehung doors. Hang the door on the hinges.

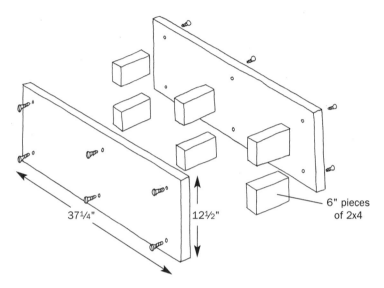

37¼" 12½" 6" pieces of 2x4

Constructing header, exploded view

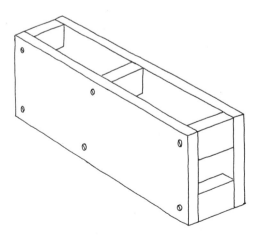

Completed header

If the threshold is sturdy and feels secure, you may not have to anchor it to the concrete floor. If the threshold is wood and not part of the prehung door, however, put #30 felt under it and secure it with the ramset or nail gun. Then weather-strip the door all the way around so that the cool air in the wine cellar doesn't leak out.

You will have to buy the hardware for the door, except for the hinges. The doorknob with lock and striker plate are easy to install. If you need to chisel out some wood from the trimmer stud to accept the tongue of the door lock, use a wood chisel. Mark the position of the striker plate through the metal opening, then use the chisel to pry the wood out about 1 inch deep. Try not to tear up the stud any more than is necessary.

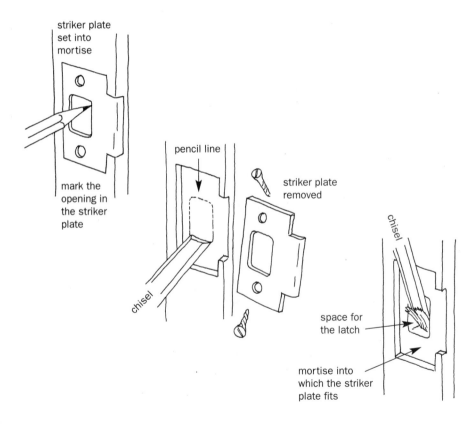

Using a wood chisel and hammer, chisel out wood from the trimmer stud to accept the tongue of the door latch.

CONSTRUCTING A DOOR JAMB

If you're making the door jamb yourself, cut 1x8 pieces and nail them to the trimmer studs and across the bottom of the header to make the jamb. Measure carefully and leave ⅛-inch of space all around to accommodate the weather stripping. Cut the doorstops to length, and nail the doorstops to the sides and the top. (They're usually made from 1¼x⁵⁄₁₆ inch stock.)

Cut and notch the door and the jamb to receive the hinges, and install. Install threshold and weather stripping. Hang the door, making sure that it's level, clears the jamb easily, and doesn't tend to swing open or shut, which would indicate that it's improperly hung. If you've never hung a door before, I'd suggest getting some advice from a pro.

Cut and Secure the Studs

Choose pressure-treated hemlock or pressure-treated Douglas fir for the vertical studs that will be snug against the foundation wall, because the foundation can sweat and rot wood. If you don't want to use pressure-treated wood, use cedar or redwood shims, or #30 felt strips, between the stud and the foundation. Use untreated 2x8 hemlock or Douglas fir for all other studs. Cut studs to length and set them in place on 16-inch centers as marked. You may need to adjust the placement of one or two studs to accommodate the door opening, cooling unit, or whatever else goes through the wall.

Starting at the bottom, toe-nail a stud to the soleplate, then use the level to make sure it is perpendicular before toe-nailing it to the top plate.

Call an Electrician

Arrange for an electrician to install electrical service for fluorescent lighting, which is cooler than heat-producing incandescent bulbs; wall switches; a bench light for decanting; power for cooling units; and a couple of extra three-prong outlets.

A COOLING PRIMER

"Ah," you might think, "but wouldn't the wine cellar be a perfect place to put a regular room air conditioner? Wouldn't that be a lot cheaper than a specific wine cellar cooling unit?" Well, no. First of all, we're designing this wine cellar to be cooled by the earth outside the foundation walls. You don't need to have the room aggressively cold. Second, if you want to cool the room with an electrical cooling unit, room air conditioners aren't the best choice. The fan will run constantly, even when the compressor is off, unless you rig it up to a timer of some kind.

In humid areas of the country, the moisture that's taken out of the air in the wine cellar may freeze on the coils of the air conditioner, causing it to labor and possibly overheat while preventing it from cooling the wine cellar. And the unit shudders and shakes when the compressor goes on and off, as anyone who's tried to sleep in a room with one can attest — and wine doesn't need constant daily jarring. Thus, a room air conditioner isn't the tool for the job; a cooling unit designed for a wine cellar is.

But in my book, the best tool of all is the earth. Even if the temperature climbs to the low 60°F range, it won't harm the wine as long as the change comes gradually as the seasons change.

Install the Vapor Barrier

When the electrical service is installed, you'll need to install a vapor barrier on the ceiling and around the joists, as well as in the walls and across the header. Choose 6- or 8-mil clear polyethylene plastic sheeting that is large enough to cover the joists, as well as the flooring above them, and long enough to wrap around three sides of the studs. You can put it up with a staple gun. The vapor barrier will go behind the insulation and around three sides of each joist or stud.

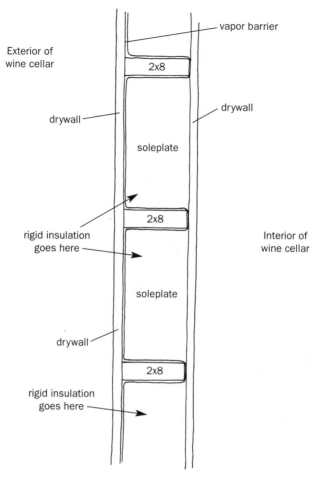

Installed vapor barrier

To make installing the vapor barrier easier when doing the walls, you might temporarily tack up, with nails driven in just far enough to hold it in place, a sheet of plywood on the outside of the studs. The plywood will give you something to stretch the vapor barrier against so that the fit is neat and tight. Leave plenty of nail and nail head showing so that you can easily remove the nails and move the plywood as you continue to install the vapor barrier.

Install the Insulation

When the vapor barrier is in place, install rigid foam insulation (sometimes called *open-cell styrene board*) on top of the vapor barrier inside the wine cellar. It comes in 1-inch, 1½-inch, and 2-inch thicknesses. Each inch of insulation gives you an *R factor* of 7.2. (The R factor is a measure of resistance to the passage of heat through the material.) You will have 7½ inches of space in the walls to work with, so if you pack the spaces between the studs and the joists with 7½ inches of rigid insulation, you'll have an R factor of 54, which is ideal. You will probably do fine with something less than that, unless your basement gets ungodly hot for some reason. So, I suggest using three panels of 2-inch rigid insulation (R factor, 43.2), depending on whether your basement stays cool or gets warm from a furnace, for instance. That will leave an air space in the walls, which itself will provide some resistance to heat passage.

The insulation is easy to cut out with a handsaw or a jigsaw. Use a sharp utility knife or linoleum knife to notch out for pipes, electrical wires or conduit, joist braces, and so on.

To prevent the rigid insulation from falling forward, leaving a gap at the top of the walls, and to prevent it from falling down from the ceiling before you put up ceiling tiles or drywall, lightly tack a few 8d nails here and there at the edges of the insulation to hold it in place. Ceiling insulation is as important as insulation in the walls and should be placed between the ceiling joists to the same R value as the walls.

Finish the Walls

Once the insulation is in place, you can finish the walls by putting up drywall, plywood, or paneling. If you choose drywall, do the ceiling first. When you do the walls, use ½-inch shims or spacers to keep the drywall just off the concrete floor until you nail it on; then remove the shims or spacers. The space prevents the drywall from absorbing moisture from the concrete floor, which can cause it to disintegrate.

Use screws to attach ⅝-inch drywall or ¾-inch interior plywood to the studs outside and inside the new walls. Pre-drill holes and use screws to prevent any possible jarring of the soleplate, as might occur when hammering.

If the soleplate is wedge bolted securely, however, hammering shouldn't be a problem.

Building-supply stores sell tape that goes over the joints between sheets of drywall and plaster "mud" that coats the tape to make it invisible. There's a practical art to putting up drywall, which isn't hard to learn, but you should ask someone at the store or a friend with experience in installing it to give you a few tips. After screwing it to the studs, tape and mud the drywall.

Add Finishing Touches

When the drywall or plywood is installed and finished, you can paint it to fit your decor. Plywood for the walls should be ¾-inch interior grade and given a natural stain but no sealant. Why no sealant? Sealant isn't needed because the walls already have a vapor barrier, and sealing the surface will create a space where moisture can't escape and may cause a musty odor. If you've used tongue-and-groove paneling, remember to nail in the grooves before inserting the tongue of the next panel.

You can add molding to finish the edges of the walls at top and bottom and in the corner where the two new walls meet. If you want the molding to be the same color as the walls or ceiling, install it before you paint. Or paint the walls, then stain the molding a natural wood color and install it to cover the rough edges where the new walls meet the ceiling, each other, or the floor. At this point, your bare-bones wine cellar is finished.

WHAT IF I HAVE NO BASEMENT?

Before describing how to build wine storage racks and shelving, let's consider situations where there is no cellar or basement in the house.

The first option is to excavate a wine cellar. This option works best if your dwelling is on a hillside, so that the wine cellar can be dug back into the hillside. It can also be dug down into level ground, but with a lot more potential trouble. An excavated wine cellar should ideally have its roof covered with 6 feet of soil in order to keep a steady 58°F to 60°F in the cellar.

An excavated cellar is expensive. If a contractor does it, you might figure about $300 per square foot. For a wine cellar that's 8 by 10 feet in area and

8 feet high, that's $25,000. That includes the excavation, a poured slab concrete floor with drain, walls, a roof, complete waterproofing all around, a door, electrical service, an exhaust vent, hardware, and shelving. If it's dug down into level ground, add a few hundred bucks for a sump and pump arrangement in case the waterproofing doesn't keep out all the rainwater.

Of course, you can do it all yourself. Scott Nearing, an acquaintance from years ago who's now deceased, dug himself a pond in his Maine backyard simply by taking a few bucketfuls of earth from the pond site every day, religiously. Three buckets a day for 10 years adds up to over 10,000 buckets of earth — and there was his pond. There's something to be said for simple persistence. If you provide the labor, the cost will be for materials only, probably around $5,000. However, consider that 6 feet of earth on the roof will weigh tons, and the roof must be strong enough to bear the load. Local building codes also will have plenty to say about how all of this will be done and often will require plans drawn up by an architectural engineer, which will up the cost.

I first became aware of the cooling power of an underground room in 1969, when I rented an old Pennsylvania Dutch farmhouse. It was built circa 1835, and behind the big stone house was a hump of earth. Five or six steps led down into the hump, where there was a door. Behind the door was a set of fourteen steps leading down to a root cellar about 12 feet long and 10 feet wide. A stone trough lined one side of the room. The farmers of those bygone days would fill the trough with water, then set their milk cans in there to cool the milk. Potatoes, beets, turnips, and such, along with apples, would keep well in the cold, damp climate of this underground cellar. The stone roof was vaulted and was a magnificent piece of work. No matter what the temperature outside, the root cellar kept itself at a steady 58°F year-round. It would have made a marvelous wine cellar.

Because the part of the farmhouse yard where the root cellar was located sloped down and away from the hilltop where the house was located, evenly spaced flagstones with earth-filled spaces between them allowed any water to percolate down through the cracks and out to the slope, where it drained away. Enough air exchanged through the door at the top of the steps to prevent mold from forming. In fact, the cellar, although probably 12 or 13 feet

---

underground, was dusty dry — another tribute to the farmers, who must have been knowledgeable stonemasons and builders.

Today, modern technology can make short work out of digging an underground wine cellar. For regular earth, a backhoe is probably sufficient, but if you have a hillside of solid rock, earth-boring machines that can drill out even hard, igneous rock will be needed. Underground mining and tunneling contractors can be found in most areas of the United States, but these services are usually conscripted for large operations, and their cost can be considerable. A tunneling contractor should work in tandem with your building engineer in excavating and installing an underground cellar.

The second option is to insulate and cool a large closet or small room in the house as a wine cellar. In this case, you'll need to insulate all four walls, the ceiling, and the floor. A cooling unit installed over the door will keep the room at a steady temperature. Install cool fluorescent lighting. Because the structure of the walls and ceiling is already there, you'll simply need to remove the sheetrock, paneling, or tiles, install rigid insulation (as much as will fit between the studs or joists), and reinstall the sheetrock and paneling. Rather than tear up the floor, it's simpler to install a second floor, one step up from the floor level, and pack rigid insulation between the floor joists, then put plywood or tongue-and-groove paneling over the second floor. If there's a window in the room, you can use it to exhaust the heat from the cooling unit to the outside, but be sure to insulate around it so that changes in temperature outside (cold as well as hot) don't make the temperature in the wine cellar fluctuate wildly. And don't let light enter the room through a window.

BUILDING DIAMOND BIN FRAMES

Diamond bins, so called because of their orientation, are a simple storage option. I recommend building a diamond bin frame and making some horizontal shelves for holding wine in case boxes. (By the way, until your wine cellar is filled with wine, these shelves could also hold your home canning jars, since the same conditions — that is, cool and dark — that are right for storing and aging wine are perfect for storing home canning jars filled with your garden's produce.)

A diamond bin, with a 14-inch interior dimension on each side, holds one case of wine of Burgundy or Bordeaux bottles. Sparkling wine bottles are larger, as of course are the larger size show bottles like magnums, and fewer will fit in a diamond. A frame 9 feet high by 18 feet wide will hold 600 bottles of wine (equal to 50 cases) in diamond bins. The edge slots of the diamond bin are just parts of diamonds; these are good for holding sparkling wine or oversized bottles. You'd need two frames of bins like this to hold your entire 100-case cellar. That's why I'd reserve the diamond bins for ready-to-drink wine and store the rest as cases. Shelving for the other 75 cases in their case boxes is straightforward. A frame of diamond bins 9 feet tall and 10 feet wide would hold 25 cases — a full quarter of your wine, and probably all the wine

MATERIALS

___ 1x12 stock or ¾" interior plywood, for top, bottom, sides

___ 8d nails, for bin frame

___ Bricks, to keep shelving off concrete floor

___ Masonry bolts (optional)

___ 13-gauge wire or nylon cord (optional)

___ 1⅝" countersunk screws (optional)

___ 1x12 stock, for bin boards, diagonals

___ 1½" finishing nails, for bin boards and diagonals

___ 1¼" finishing strips of redwood, oak, or walnut

___ Wood stain (optional)

___ ½" plywood, as backing for wine racks (optional)

___ ¾" trim, for edges of wine racks if plywood is used

TOOLS

___ Framing/combination square

___ Circular saw or handsaw and miter box

___ Hammer

that's ready to drink in your cellar and then some. So, one 9-foot by 10-foot frame of diamond bins with 14-inch interior dimensions will fit in most wine cellars. You'll have to adjust dimensions up or down as appropriate for the space you have. Now, how do we build such a frame?

Cut the Top, Bottom, and Sides

Begin by cutting the top, bottom, and two sides of the frame from 1x12 stock or ¾-inch interior-grade plywood. The top and bottom boards of the frame are 10 feet long and each of the two sides is 9 feet long. End-nail the bottom to the two sides. It's important that the sides sit on the bottom board and be flush with its edges.

Set Up the Frame

Set the frame against the wall in its permanent location. You may have to prop it with boxes or some other method to keep the sides from falling outward or inward. It's probably a good idea to slip bricks under the bottom board to keep the wood off the floor. Set the top board across the top to give the frame stability, but don't nail it down just yet.

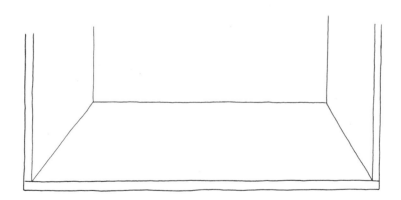

Sides nailed to bottom boards

If the floor is uneven or pitched forward a bit, the whole shebang may fall over face first when it's full of wine. To prevent this, prop the bottom board so that the frame leans back against the wall at a slight angle, or better, attach two masonry bolts to the foundation or wall behind where the frame will go and then attach the bolts to the frame in some way to keep it from toppling forward. Strong wire or nylon cord attached to the masonry bolts and then to large, sturdy screws near the top of the wine rack should do the job. Just be careful here.

Cut and Secure Diagonals and Bin Boards

When assembling the diamond bins, you'll need two kinds of boards that I designate *bin boards* and *diagonals. Bin boards* run up at 45-degree angles from left to right, and *diagonals* run down at 45-degree angles from left to right. Bin boards are all the same length (14 inches), but the length of diagonals will vary depending on their position in the frame. Your best bet is to cut and assemble each course as you work.

Circular saws can be set to cut at 45-degree angles, but I prefer a miter box, which gives you a more precise cut, although you have to do the cutting by hand. Before cutting pieces for the diamond bins, practice on a piece of scrap wood to be sure you have the exact angle you'll need to snug the bin board into the frame.

Start by toe-nailing the first bin board into the lower left corner of the frame. The edge of the bin board will be cut at a 45-degree angle to fit in the corner (see detail), making one side just slightly longer than the other. Don't worry about it. Just make sure the slightly longer side measures 14 inches.

Remember that 1-inch stock is actually ¾ inch wide. With the first bin board toe-nailed into the corner, cut your first diagonal with 45-degree edges. The slightly shorter side will be 28¾ inches long. The edge of the shorter side should touch the side of the frame exactly 19.8 inches above the top of the bottom board. The other end of the diagonal should touch the bot-

---

tom board exactly 19.8 inches from the side board. (See illustration below.) This measurement can be calculated by using the Pythagorean theorem.

Set the diagonal in place and back-nail it to the bin board so that the nail is exactly in the spot where it will penetrate into the middle of the edge of the first bin board.

Now we're ready for the next bin boards, which will be cut square across the edges instead of at 45-degree angles. The only time the bin boards will be cut at 45 degrees on the edges is when they butt into the bottom, sides, or top board. All the diagonals will be cut at 45 degrees on the edges, as they will all butt against the sides or top. Make sure each square-edged bin board is 14 inches long. Use the framing square to make sure all right angles are true.

From the nail you placed into the first diagonal (which defines the center of the first bin board), measure out exactly 7 inches on each side so that you have 14 inches of space. That's where your next bin boards will go. Toe-nail them into the first diagonal, making sure there's 14 inches of interior space between them. Measure and cut the next diagonal. Lay it in place. If you need

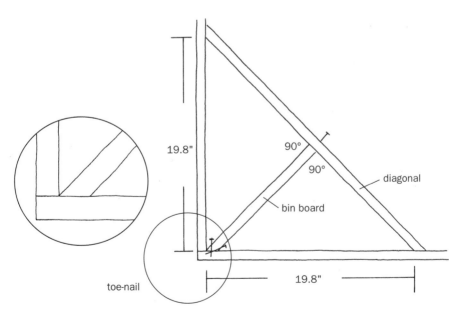

Beginning assembly of the diamond bin. Detail shows position of bin board.

CREATING PERFECT ANGLES

The Pythagorean theorem states that the sum of the squares of the sides of a right angle are equal to the square of the hypotenuse. In the diamond frame, right angles occur where the bin board meets the first diagonal. Because the sides of the triangle along the bin board and diagonal are 14 inches (interior dimension), the hypotenuse is 19.7989 inches (let's just call it 19.8 inches). Thus, our first bin along the bottom and side boards is 19.8 inches.

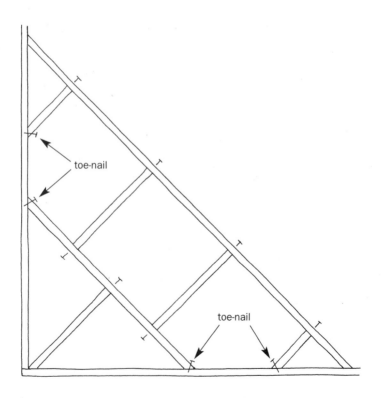

Toe-nailing and nailing successive courses for diamond bins

short little bin boards on the edges, cut and toe-nail them. Even if they won't accommodate a bottle of wine, these short bin boards will add sturdiness to the frame. Back-nail the second diagonal to the second level of bin boards.

Repeat this process until you reach the top of the frame, constantly checking your work to ensure that the interior spaces are 14 inches on a side and that right angles are true. When you reach the top course, mock the construction (tack or prop the bin boards in place without nailing securely), then lay the top board across them and trim any too-long bin boards and the last diagonal, if necessary, until the top board fits neatly and snugly. Nail the top board to the bin boards and diagonals at the top row of bins. You now have space for the equivalent of twenty-five cases of wine placed in bins so that you can easily see the tops of their capsules. They, and you, are ready to drink!

Finishing Touches

You can dress up the bins with finishing strips of redwood, oak, walnut, or other fine woods. Use finishing nails to tack them to both the diamond bins and shelving. The 1x stock you used for the bins and shelves is actually ¾ inch thick. You'll find a variety of finishing strips, but 1¼ inches is probably the best for facing these bins and shelves. You'll be nailing them to the center of the ¾-inch widths of the 1x stock, which will leave about ¼ inch of overlap on each side. If your finishing stock is lighter in color than you'd like, cut it to the desired lengths, give it a quick wood stain in whatever shade you like, let it dry, and nail it up. You can use whatever pattern suits you, but I think doing the vertical strips or the diagonals of the diamond bins first, then doing the horizontals or bin boards, looks neat and trim.

Freestanding Units and Other Cellar Options

You have options other than building a wine cellar in your basement. You may consider buying a freestanding wine storage cabinet. These have features such as Breezaire cooling units; LED temperature and humidity readouts; zoned cooling for cellar temperature (58°F), long-term storage (52–54°F), and chilling for white and sparkling wine (42–48°F); low-heat and low-intensity lighting; fine wood construction; and double-paned glass doors, among others.

FREESTANDING UNITS

The smallest freestanding units hold only twenty-four bottles, but large ones can hold the equivalent of one hundred cases or even more, enough for an adequate wine cellar. You may want to consider a medium-sized unit just for your ready-to-drink wines, placed in the kitchen or dining room, as an adjunct to your regular wine cellar in the basement. They are useful in apartments, where you don't want to build anything permanent, and they can be a pretty piece of furniture in which to prominently display your wines. Units come in tall cabinets about 6 feet high, in credenza-style cabinets about 3 feet high, and a few have front venting so that they can be built in under counters, into the setbacks under shelves, or as part of a setup of cabinets for glassware.

158

There are some drawbacks to these units, however. First, they are expensive, running to many thousands of dollars for ones holding five hundred bottles or more. Second, the cooling unit is built in, resulting in some vibration during operation, which is not ideal for long-term wine storage. In some carefully constructed models, vibration is kept to an acceptable minimum. The Silent Cellar, made by Electrolux, keeps a constant 55°F temperature without vibration because it has no motor. You'll want to ask the company that makes the cabinets about vibration levels. Third, in well-lighted rooms, glass-door models will admit some light, also not ideal for long-term storage. A little light and vibration might be fine for your ready-to-drink wines because they are out of long-term storage and available for current drinking. But these units don't do anything that a built-in wine cellar downstairs doesn't do, and your own cellar may do a better job of keeping wine in the dark and resting quietly.

WALK-IN WINE ROOMS

Complete walk-in wine cellars (commercially called *wine rooms*) are also available. They come disassembled, and you put them together yourself. All walk-in cellars are 80½ inches wide and 80½ inches tall, but they come in four depths for increasing numbers of bottles stored. The 900-bottle unit is 45½ inches deep, the 1,300-bottle unit is 61 inches deep, the 1,900-bottle unit is 88 inches deep, and the 2,600-bottle unit (that's a whopping big wine cellar) is 10 feet deep. Features include a Breezaire cooling system, natural oak exterior and mahogany interior, clear heart redwood individual bottle racking, and floor space for stacking a few additional cases of wine. These units aren't cheap — figure the cost as somewhere in the neighborhood of $2.50 per bottle if you include options like a window in the door, low-heat lighting, security lock, and furniture finish on the wood.

Manufacturers offer the builder of the home wine cellar other types of help. Premade 4x4x2-foot panels of stiff insulation bonded to a wooden, nailable panel are available as individual panels and as a kit consisting of eight panels and a Koolspace-1500 cooling unit, enough to turn a small closet into a wine cellar if racking and weather stripping are added.

Another product that can be used to insulate walls or a closet space is called Reflectix. It's a flexible roll consisting of reflective foil front and back, with three layers of polyethylene and two layers of bubble packing material between the foil layers. You nail furring strips to the walls of the closet or space you intend to use as a wine cellar, staple Reflectix to the strips, and seal all joints with special foil tape that's provided. Depending on the size of the space, you can use a Breezaire, Koolspace, or Opticool cooler for a small closet, or one of the many larger sizes of Breezaire units for a large closet or large wine cellar. Breezaire offers models that will cool spaces from 140 cubic feet up to 1,800 cubic feet and offers a 5-year limited warranty on most of its units. Our home-built basement wine cellar is slightly less than 1,000 cubic feet. It's meant to hold a fairly steady temperature without additional cooling, but if you want to keep the temperature steady between 58°F and 60°F, you'll want Breezaire's standard model that cools a room with a maximum of 1,200 cubic feet of space. This mounts into the wall of the wine cellar and vents into the basement or to the outdoors.

Other self-contained refrigeration systems are mounted on the outside wall of the wine cellar and contain a condenser and evaporator to cool and humidify air. Cool air is ducted into the wine cellar and returned to the cooling unit through a separate duct. The fans that move the air are located outside the wine cellar, which cuts down on noise and vibration where the wine is resting.

SPLIT SYSTEMS

Breezaire and other manufacturers also make what's called a *split system.* This means that the condenser is located outside the wine cellar, where its heat and vibration can't affect the wine inside. Refrigerant is pumped from the condenser into an evaporator located on a wall in the wine cellar. Air in the wine cellar is drawn into the evaporator, where it is cooled by a coil, then blown back out into the wine cellar. A pipe drains moisture (water removed from the air when it is cooled) into the room outside the wine cellar.

A variation on the split system is called a *ducted system* or, sometimes, a *split air handler system.* It operates like the split system, except there's no evaporator located within the wine cellar; cooling and moisture drainage in an evaporator, as well as the refrigerant condenser operation, occur outside the wine cellar. All you see in the wine room are air ducts that blow cool air into the wine cellar. This system operates like a central air conditioning unit

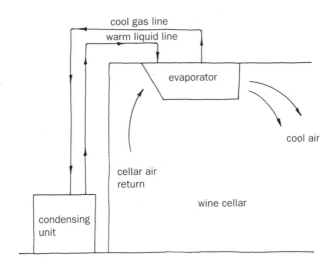

Split air system. Refrigerant is evaporated from liquid to gaseous state in the evaporator, where cellar air passes over the evaporator coils, which cool it. Refrigerant is changed back to a liquid in the condensing unit

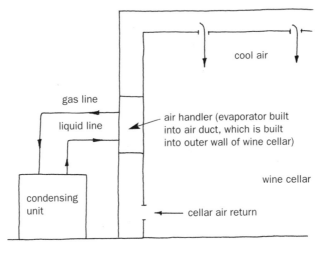

Ducted system

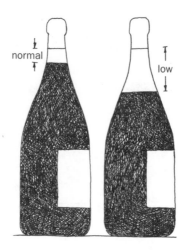

Normal vs. low ullage

and is just as quiet and vibrationless in the wine cellar, because all hardware is located outside the wine cellar.

Both self-contained cooling units and split systems are meant to keep relative humidity in the wine cellar at about 55 to 75 percent, the ideal range for stable wine aging. Humidity levels of 80 percent or more can cause mold to form and rot or discolor the wine labels. Air that's too wet can also encourage moldy cardboard wine boxes, racks, and walls. Drier air will increase the amount of ullage in the bottles and will dry out the glue beneath the label. (*Ullage* is the air space between the cork and the wine when the bottle is turned upright.) Remember that the cooler the air in the cellar, the drier it is. That's why cooling units produce moisture (water) as air is cooled. We've all seen air conditioners dripping like leaky faucets on hot, muggy days — the same thing happens when air is cooled by a wine cellar cooling unit. Most wine cellar refrigeration systems can humidify air as well as cool it. Any unit you select should maintain the relative humidity at 55 to 75 percent.

HUMIDITY- AND TEMPERATURE-CONTROL UNITS

The *waterfall refrigeration system* is an in-room humidifier that maintains proper humidity, while an air handler cooling unit keeps the temperature in the wine cellar at a steady 55°F. A water chiller located outside the wine cellar delivers cold water to a cabinet topped with a black granite pyramid, a black granite spiral, or a rotating rose-marble sphere. The cold water is emitted at the top of whichever of these waterfall shapes you choose, runs down into a collection basin, and is returned to the chiller. It seems more like a conversation piece than a necessary appliance. If your wine cellar air is too dry, humidifiers that work with cooling units are available.

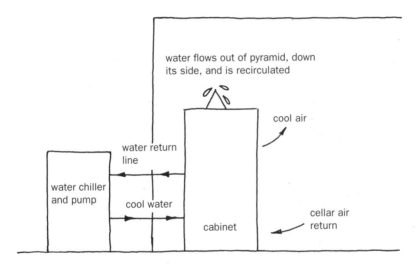

Waterfall refrigeration system. The cabinet is an air handler using chilled water to cool air in the wine cellar. The bubbling pyramid on top maintains proper humidity.

Valance Systems

Another wine cellar cooling unit is called the *valance system*. A water chiller is located outside the wine cellar and cold water is piped through an insulated hose to the valance unit mounted at the top of a wall. Cold water is circulated through tubes with fins and is then returned for more chilling. Warm air in the wine cellar rises and comes into contact with the cold water tubes and fins, is cooled, and falls down the wall below the valance unit, across the floor, and eventually back to the valance. Because there are no moving parts (no fans, no pumps, no motor) inside the wine cellar, the valance unit is quiet.

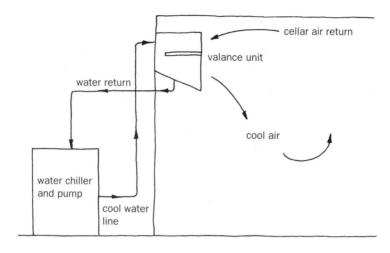

Valance system. Water is cooled in the chiller, then pumped to the valence, where it flows through tubes and then back to the chiller. The air circulates by natural convection.

MY RECOMMENDATION

I think the way to go is this: Build your wine cellar with positive insulation on the interior walls, ceiling, and door. Check the temperature and relative humidity regularly, especially if the furnace is also in the basement. The temperature will rise and fall slowly as the seasons change, but any sharp or daily rise and fall in temperature is not good. The wine itself acts as a thermal flywheel: That is, its temperature will rise or fall slowly as it absorbs or gives off heat. But if the ambient air temperature swings daily in the wine cellar, it gives the wine the jitters. Little daily tugs up or down on the air temperature may not change the wine's temperature by much, but the effect is there, expanding and contracting the wine in the bottle and slowly but surely drawing air through the cork to increase ullage and prematurely age the wine. If your insulation doesn't control swings in temperature, think about installing one of the cooling units described earlier. I think a split air handler system is by far the best way to go if you can afford it, but any of the options can work for you as long as you make sure it doesn't cause excess heat, noise, or vibration as it works, and that it keeps the relative humidity between 55 and 75 percent.

PREFABRICATED PACKING SYSTEMS

In chapter 5, I give directions for making simple diamond bins, but you can also buy prefabricated racking systems in many shapes and sizes. Manufacturers will usually give you plans for systems to fit the space you have if you send them the dimensions of your wine cellar room, then send you the racks disassembled for you to install, or they will assemble them at the factory and deliver them for you or your carpenters to install.

The most common woods are clear heart redwood or cedar. Styles include rectangular bins, bins sized to hold wooden cases, diamond bins, curved corner units to give you bottle storage along smoothly curved corners, racks that hold bottles individually, and bins to hold cardboard cases. Diamond cubes and case storage bins are the cheapest rack styles, usually running a bit over $1 per bottle stored; curved corner racks and individual bottle racks are the most expensive, costing anywhere from $2 to $4.50 a bottle, depending on design. Kits that you assemble yourself from cut pieces of wood with provided hardware can run from about 75 cents to $2 per bottle stored.

Stackable kits can be even less expensive, with prices ranging from about 50 to 75 cents per bottle. Styles include individual bottle racks, half-bottle racks, curved corner individual racks, diamond cubes, cardboard case bins, bottle bins, champagne and magnum bins, and wood case bins. They come in two heights: 32 and 46 inches. Stacking two can give you three heights: 64 inches, 78 inches, and 92 inches. Hardware for attaching the units to the wall is provided with these kits.

Modular racking is also available. Individual bottle lattice racks made of redwood hold 126 bottles at about 35 cents a bottle if you order four racks or more. Solid pine diamond bins each hold 24 bottles in four triangular compartments for about 30 cents per bottle when shipping is figured in.

As you can see, even the simplest pine diamond bins will cost more than $350 to furnish a 100-case cellar of 1,200 bottles. Individual bottle racks will cost you at least double that. A really nice racking system you'd be proud to show off could run you $3,000 with no trouble. I'm giving you the simplest and cheapest options, figuring that you'll upgrade as you see fit.

CELLAR TABLES

Racking systems also include island racks with black melamine tops for the middle of the wine cellar. These hold 216 bottles (108 individual racks in nine vertical and twelve horizontal spaces on each face). Useful, but I'd do something different for a cellar table. Let's start at the beginning, with the function of a table in the wine cellar: namely, so that you can inspect the color of a wine and for decanting.

Rather than a black melamine top, I'd find a table with a sturdy wooden top and give that top a coat of pure white paint, then top that with a urethane sealer so spills don't discolor the top and so that you can wipe them up easily. The white surface allows you to tilt the glass of wine and inspect the color of the *rim* — the edge of the wine where it thins out. The color gives you important information about the age of the wine. A rich purplish red color indicates a young wine. A rich ruby color indicates a wine in its prime. A brick or orange-red color indicates an older wine that may be losing some

quality. And a color like strong Pekoe tea or a washed-out color indicates a wine that has passed its prime and has lost its fruit flavors. If you must store wine under your table, look for one that will accept prefabricated racks of the correct size (which will depend on the table you find and on what prefabricated racks are available to fit that table) and fix them to each side of the table with metal brackets.

COMMERCIAL FACILITIES

There is one more option: storing your wine in a commercial wine storage facility. You pay for lockers by the month, and the operator keeps the lockers at the proper temperature and humidity. My experience with one of these facilities was a good one. My wine had been stored at my friend's extensive cellar for a number of years, but he sold his house and was moving to Virginia, so I had to move my wine out of his cellar. This prompted me to first sell off half my wine cellar to reduce its size and then to build a wine cellar at home.

While it was being built, I moved my wine into a commercial storage locker. This was a large air-conditioned warehouse kept at a constant 58°F. Its main purpose was as a centrally located warehouse in Sonoma County taking in shipments from wineries that were then sorted into lots destined for restaurants, wine shops, supermarkets, and trucking firms for long-distance shipping. To turn unused space into a moneymaker, the warehouse operator built bins with wooden doors and hasps on them. I had to supply the locks for the hasps. I needed two bins, each holding about twenty-four cases of wine; each bin rented for $30 a month. When my wine cellar at home was finished, I was able to stock it about half full with my remaining forty-eight cases of wine and begin to collect more wine for aging. It's always good to have space in your cellar for new wine coming in. As of this writing, I'm afraid the wine collector in me has once again pretty much filled the cellar, with only enough free space left for some eight cases.

The commercial storage cost me $60 a month, or $180 for the three months my wine was there. That's not a great deal of money, but it was $180 more than I wanted to spend. My new wine cellar, on the other hand, cost me about $800 — about what I would have paid for commercial storage for a year. My cellar is now over a year old, so it has paid for itself and then some compared to commercial storage — and I have instant access to it. I no longer have to drive a half hour to my friend's house or to the commercial storage place to snag a bottle of wine for dinner.

Commercial wine storage bins don't have individual bottle racks, so you have to move cases of wine every time you want a bottle. And unless you map out exactly where every bottle is, you'll be searching through cases looking for needles in haystacks. I consider commercial wine storage a temporary solution should you need a place to stash your wine for a little while, not a long-term solution.

HOW TO DECANT

One of the most important processes for enjoying old wine is decanting. As wines age, especially robust red wines, they throw off sediment. The older the wine, the more sediment, up to a point where everything that can precipitate out has done so. By 10 years old, most of the sediment the wine is capable of depositing will likely have precipitated out. Some is in the form of large, solid tartrate crystals, some is complexed tannin and other phenolic compounds, some is simply tiny particles of detritus, and some will form a residue on the side of the bottle that was on the bottom when it lay horizontal for its aging period, or encrust the cork. If you simply pull the cork from a bottle of old wine that has thrown off a lot of sediment, the first glass may be clear, but when you set the bottle down, the wine inside may slosh and stir up the sediment, and your next pours will be unacceptably cloudy.

Decanting is the process of getting the clear wine off the *lees,* or sediment. First, stand the bottle upright for a day before you plan to open it. Second, withdraw the cork very carefully, without shaking the bottle. Whether it's true or not, think of the bottom inch of the bottle as containing very fine sludge that will billow up in clouds of sediment if you slosh the wine, then handle it that way.

Speaking of withdrawing the cork, very old bottles of wine may have corks that crumble away as you try to withdraw them. If you have an old

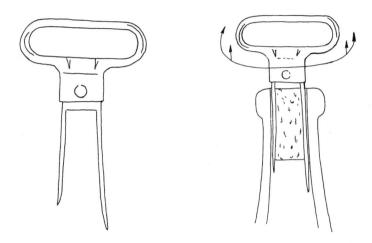

The ah-so and its use

bottle, make sure that the corkscrew is screwed into the cork as deeply as it will go, so that it grabs the entire cork (see pages 178–181 for a discussion of the best types of corkscrew). Very gently try to withdraw the cork. If you get any crumbling, or if the metal screw begins to tear out the center of the cork, stop. Unscrew that corkscrew and reach for an *ah-so,* a kind of cork remover that has two prongs, one slightly longer than the other.

Insert the ah-so as far as it will go, and gently twist it to loosen the cork, then with a twisting and pulling motion at the same time, withdraw the cork. This almost always works. If, however, the cork is just impossibly old and breaks or crumbles away, don't worry. Simply push it into the bottle and pour the wine through a fine strainer or funnel lined with cheesecloth when you decant it. If the cork floats into the neck of the bottle and stoppers it from the inside, insert a chopstick into the neck of the bottle and hold it in place as you carefully decant the wine.

I've seen folks use many methods for decanting wine. I have a friend who holds the bottle and decanter over his head so that the ceiling light in the kitchen shines through the bottle. I have another acquaintance who uses a flashlight set upright, places the decanter on one side of the light, and lets the light shine through the neck and shoulder of the bottle as he gently pours off the wine into the decanter. And I have a friend who uses a candle as a light

source. He claims the direct light of a candle flame provides the best view of the wine as it's poured, and he's probably right.

The reason for the light is so you can watch the wine as it's being poured. As you gently tilt the neck downward, clear wine will pour off into the decanter. Don't tilt the neck back up during the decanting process or the wine will slosh back in the bottle and stir up the sediment. Keep the wine coming in a slow, steady, gentle pour. You will eventually see a dark river of sediment inching up toward the neck. Keep pouring off the clear wine until the sediment is just about to flow through the neck. Then tilt the neck up and set the bottle aside. It may have an inch or two of wine left in the bottom. Don't try to salvage it; it is sludgy and will remain so. Pour it down the drain.

If you want to pour the decanted wine back into its original bottle, rinse out the remains of the sediment from the bottle and hold it upside down for a good 30 seconds until all the water has run out. Then insert a funnel into its neck and pour the clear wine from the decanter back into the bottle and stopper it. The simplest and cheapest stopper is the cork itself, its top cleaned off, turned upside down and partially pushed into the neck. But, if you are so inclined, there are beautiful bottle stoppers available in wine accoutrement catalogs. One set comes with rosewood and marble handles, with a nickel-plated body with channels that hold rubber O-rings that seat snugly into the neck. Recorkers may be topped with tiny statues of dogs (not a comment on the quality of the wine inside, one would hope), golf balls, chess figurines, and so on. I personally just use the cork that came in the bottle. I have

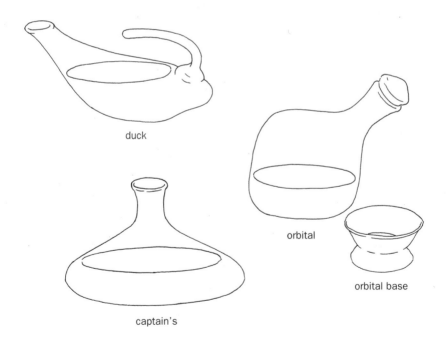

duck

orbital

orbital base

captain's

Decanter types

enough to keep track of in my life without having to look through a drawer for my rosewood bottle stopper.

The other option is to leave the wine in the decanter. Most decanters are crystal and come with a crystal stopper. Some are vaguely shaped like a duck — these are traditional in France. Some have huge, wide bottoms and are called *captain's decanters* because they were supposedly used aboard ships to hold the captain's wine and keep it from overturning or sloshing out as the

ship rolled and heaved through the waves. They also expose the most wine surface to air, allowing it to breathe. The Riedel company makes what they call an "orbital" decanter. It has a V-shaped bottom that rests in a holder. When you remove the decanter from the holder and set it on the table, it rests on the bottom portion of the V at a 45-degree angle, and if you give it a push, it rolls in a tight circle, aerating the wine inside without any danger of tipping or spilling. You can buy many styles and sizes of new decanters (usually either a size that holds one 750-mL bottle or one 1.5-L magnum), but I like to rummage through antique shops for gorgeous old cut-crystal decanters.

A glass funnel is excellent for decanting because glass is completely inert and cannot impart anything to the wine, as metal or plastic might. These are available from wine accoutrement catalogs. Glass funnels made specifically for decanting usually have a curved spout that directs the wine against the side of the decanter, minimizing splashing and aeration. (Although, unless the wine is really old, some aeration is a good thing and helps open up a wine.) French pewter decanting funnels have a curved spout and a removable screen that traps chunks of sedi-

Glass funnel

ment (or *crust,* as port sediment is called) and bits of crumbled cork.

While you're in the antique shop, look for an old-fashioned decanting cradle. This is a sturdy wire device with a crank at one end that operates a worm or gear mechanism. You set the opened bottle of wine into the wire cradle and turn the crank, and the device lowers the neck of the bottle ever so slowly. You put a decanter or pitcher or some sort of adequately sized catch basin under the neck of the bottle. Many turns of the crank lower the neck just a little at a time, so that the wine inside the bottle isn't disturbed. It's much slower and more precise than trying to do the job with a shaky hand.

Lighting for Decanting

Now we get to the reason for this discussion of decanting and our wine cellar tabletop. Place the table near easy access to an electrical outlet. Use a keyhole saw to cut a circle out of the middle of the table. Fix a light socket in the hole and screw it to the underside of the table. Purchase a size that will hold a 90-watt halogen spotlight bulb, available at any good hardware store. Make sure the wood of the tabletop is lined with the proper metal receptacle, as the bulb generates lots of heat. Attach the on-off switch to a side of the table where it's handy. When you want to decant your wine, throw the switch and

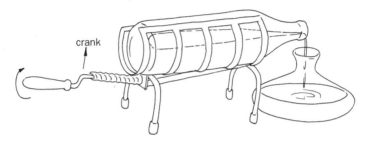

crank

Turning the handle (crank) gradually elevates the rear end of the decanting cradle

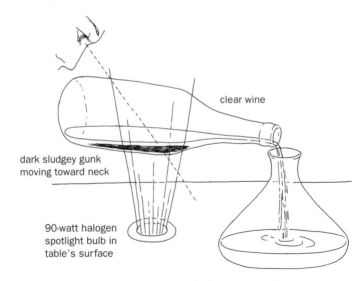

clear wine

dark sludgey gunk
moving toward neck

90-watt halogen
spotlight bulb in
table's surface

When decanting, stop pouring before any gunk gets out.
A few wispy threads of sediment are OK but not any dark sludge

the strong halogen bulb will throw up an intense beam of light through which you can watch the advance of the sediment toward the neck. Strangely, in all the wine cellars I've seen and catalogs I've pored through, I've never seen a decanting light or light stand or table offered for sale, and yet decanting is the most important thing for folks who want to age their wine properly and drink it without getting sludge in their mouths. Maybe a reader of this book with an entrepreneurial spirit will put something like what I'm suggesting on the market.

WINE GLASSES

Another important part of the wine cellar is the collection of wine glasses.

Housewares stores and wine cellar catalogs offer both glassware and hanging racks to hold the glasses upside down — a nice addition to the wine cellar. If you have deep pockets, Baccarat makes wonderful but very expensive crystal glasses with superthin stems that break easily. Waterford makes a more moderately priced Vintage Marquis line of stemware, with 19-ounce Burgundy and Bordeaux glasses and a strangely flaring 9-ounce white wine glass. Nine ounces is a bit small for my taste, and the open, flaring top doesn't hold the aroma in the glass where the nose can get at it. Personally, I don't like small wine glasses, cut-crystal glasses, colored wine glasses, or anything other than generously proportioned glasses of traditional shape with no embellishments.

The best wine glasses, I believe, are made by Riedel in a variety of sizes and shapes tailored to the wine they're meant to hold. I once went to a tasting put on by Riedel at Geyser Peak Winery in Sonoma County where we were asked to taste the same wine from a variety of glasses, including the Riedel glass supposedly tailored to the type of wine. Riedel's idea is that the right shape of glass will deliver the wine differentially to different places on the tongue — an idea I have trouble believing. In other words, wine that is fruit forward will be delivered to the receptors on the tongue that recognize fruit flavors in greater quantities than to other parts of the tongue. That's the idea, anyway.

At the tasting, I was intrigued to find that the same wine seemed to taste better when served in the Riedel glass than in other shapes. I chalked it up to the power of suggestion, but who knows? Maybe they are really on to something. Riedel has followed through with a whole line of glasses at fairly reasonable prices called the Vinum series. It includes 21-ounce Bordeaux/Cabernet Sauvignon/Merlot glasses; 13-ounce Chardonnay glasses; 25-ounce Burgundy/Pinot Noir glasses; 23-ounce Rhône/Syrah/Shiraz glasses; 13-ounce Zinfandel/Chianti glasses; 8-ounce Champagne/sparkling wine flutes; 8-ounce young white wine glasses; 14-ounce Rioja glasses; 8-ounce Sauvignon Blanc/Beaujolais glasses, and 8-ounce port glasses. The whole idea seems a bit precious to me (why not Valdiguié glasses, Charbono glasses, and Arneis glasses?), but there was that tasting where the wines did seem to taste better in their proper glasses . . .

Bordeaux-Cabernet   Sauvignon Blanc   Chardonnay-Chablis   Burgundy-Pinot Noir

Rhône-Syrah   Zinfandel-Chianti   Vintage Champagne   Young white

Assortment of Riedel glasses

Riedel also makes a less expensive Overture series of five wine glasses in their patented shapes, but they hold only one-half to two-thirds of the wine that the Vinum series holds. Go with the bigger glasses. You might want to consider Riedel's new Vinum Extreme line of five very generously proportioned glasses, which are slightly larger than the Vinum series. These are designed specifically for New World wines, they claim, although why they'd be any better for New World wines than Old World wines escapes me. The bowls are roughly diamond shaped, angling out dramatically from the stem and then narrowing at the top, creating a wide evaporation surface but a tight opening that focuses the wine's aroma and bouquet.

I think that you do need at least five different glasses for your wine: Bordeaux varieties (Cabernet Sauvignon, Merlot, Cabernet Franc, Malbec, Petit Verdot, and Méritage); Burgundy (Pinot Noir); white wine; sparkling wine; and port. The Bordeaux glasses will suffice for Rhône varieties and other red varieties. Beyond that, you and the Riedel company are on your own.

Of course, there are cheaper large glasses in the red and white shapes (red being taller, white being smaller, and Burgundy being wider) on the market, and often these have thicker stems that break less easily. They're what I use for every day. For special occasions, Riedel glasses are appropriate. Don't skimp on size. Large glasses allow the development of aroma or bouquet. But only pour an inch or so of wine in them so the wine can be vigorously swirled without sloshing out.

The slender stems of fine wine glasses are easily broken, and they're especially vulnerable in the dishwasher, where strong jets of water can knock them about and into one another. At housewares stores, at some wine shops, and in accoutrement catalogs, you'll find special vinyl-coated steel racks that cradle wine glasses and keep them from banging into anything when they're in the dishwasher. They're not expensive compared to the cost of replacing broken stemware.

Some glassware is absolutely necessary to have if you're going to enjoy wine properly. Champagne or sparkling wine should be served in straight-sided flutes, not in wide champagne cocktail glasses, for example.

Now let's take a look at corkscrews. For some reason, corkscrews are highly collectible devices, especially old or unusual ones. But here I'm going to focus on function over form. The first duty of a corkscrew is to get the cork out of the bottle as easily and reliably as possible. The best corkscrew is one with the following features. The business end is a round wire with five turns; the wire forms a helix (imagine wrapping the wire around and around down the length of a slim pencil, then withdrawing the pencil) and comes to a point on its tip; the tip follows the helix without veering off to the center; and the corkscrew has a large grip for your hand. For my money, the best corkscrew is the kind called a *waiter's corkscrew*. It has a small knife at one end for cutting the foil capsule to expose the cork and a five-turn round-wire screw. You turn the screw down into the cork, then hook a lever extension at the end of the corkscrew opposite the knife end onto the lip of the bottle. You then lift the knife end and body of the corkscrew up and the cork is easily levered out of the bottle. It sounds more complicated than it actually is.

A nice variation on the waiter's corkscrew is the Chateau Laguiole corkscrew, made in France. It performs exactly the same as a waiter's

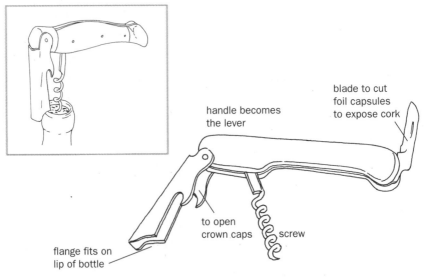

blade to cut
foil capsules
to expose cork

handle becomes
the lever

to open
crown caps   screw

flange fits on
lip of bottle

Waiter's corkscrew

corkscrew, but it is entirely handmade and first rate. And you pay for it, too; they're not cheap. The body of the corkscrew comes in natural horn, wood, or stainless steel. Every wine cellar should have a waiter's corkscrew and an ah-so, too. Other options are the bench-mounted lever-action cork pullers you see in bars. They work like a charm but are expensive and are probably overkill for individuals. But if you like them, go for it.

Don't go for corkscrews whose screw is made from a single piece of metal with flanges that encircle the metal in a helical pattern. These have two handles that rise like wings as the metal is screwed into the cork. To extract the cork, you grasp both handles and push them down. This infernal device shreds more corks than any other in my experience. There are more elaborate corkscrews, but they are no more functional than the ones I recommend.

THE FUTURE OF CORKS

There's a big debate going on about the use of corks. Too many bottles of wine are turning up *corked;* that is, contaminated with trichloranisole from an organism that grows in the cork itself and makes the wine smell like musty, rotting cardboard. What a huge disappointment to spend a lot of money on a bottle of wine only to have it be corked!

Some wineries are using screwcap closures rather than corks to avoid the problem. Many others would like to go to screwcap closures but are reluctant to give up the use of cork because they believe that corks are equated with quality in the public's mind, whereas screwcaps are equated with bulk-quality jug wines. Personally, I like the feeling of pulling a cork and the satisfying pop when it comes out.

I can tell something about the quality of the wine by the quality of the cork. Really high-quality corks have no obvious channels or flaws, they won't have absorbed more than one-half to two-thirds of an inch of wine into themselves at the interior end over 10 years, and they'll be longer than most average corks. Very-high-quality corks are becoming increasingly rare because they are expensive and can bite into a winery's profit. Perhaps one day the world wine industry will decide that corks are an obsolete technology for stoppering a bottle of wine and move wholesale to plastic corks, which I see more and more often, or screwcap closures. I suppose there are those who'll yowl, as I suppose there were those who mourned the passing of the buggy whip (that firm leather, the satisfying snap and crack of the whip, the jauntiness of it), but time marches on. However, no one will miss having a great bottle of wine spoiled by the stink of trichloranisole.

In the final analysis, I believe that the best wines will always be closed with a cork. If we can land a man on the moon, surely we can prevent cork taint.

Screwpull makes a variety of corkscrews based on its proprietary engineering design, and they all have a round-wire helix screw. There's a basic plastic model with a Teflon-coated screw, and a lever-operated model that clamps onto the top of the bottle. There's also the lever model with a stand that accommodates a bottle and holds it securely. All of the Screwpull devices work well, but they seem to be a little more complicated than necessary. A similar device, called the Rabbit Corkscrew, looks a bit like a jackrabbit's head, with the grip handles as the rabbit's ears and the corkscrew's body as its head. I stick with my waiter's corkscrew.

I see many other types of corkscrews on the market, such as a carbon dioxide cartridge device that forces the gas through a needle into the bottle, which forces the cork out — but why get so fancy? Take my advice and buy a waiter's corkscrew and an ah-so, and you'll be able to use the money you save to buy a nice bottle of wine.

AFTER THE WINE HAS BEEN OPENED

Once the wine has been opened, other accoutrements come into play. There are drip collars that fit over the lip of the bottle and prevent those last drops of wine from landing on your new white tablecloth, and there are wine servers that fit in the mouth of the bottle and form the flow of wine into a thin stream that prevents splashing and dripping. Then there are fancy coasters and chillers. Coasters can be useful if you're bringing a bottle to the table, but special chillers don't do anything that the fridge doesn't do. I do have a fondness for a nice ice bucket for sparkling wine kept tableside, however.

There are special stoppers for sparkling wine that seal the bottles so no pressure escapes. Which brings us to Thing One.

Thing One: Air is the enemy of wine. Exposure to oxygen soon transforms those subtle and tasty compounds that make wine so wonderful into blech. Now, responsible drinkers know that you maximize the health benefits of wine when you consume just one glass (or two at most) of wine with a meal. A bottle of wine holds about 25 ounces, and a glass of wine is about 5 ounces (even if the glass itself is much larger), so there's enough wine in that bottle for five glasses. After you pour your glass of wine, you then have enough wine left for four more days, or two days if you have two glasses. I'm tempted to suggest that you acquire a spouse or companion who likes wine as much as you do so that you each have two glasses of wine with dinner, and the fifth glass is used in cooking. But still, it often happens that you have wine left over, being exposed to air. So what's to be done? Can you keep the wine drinkable? The answer depends on the wine.

Young red wine improves for a day or two after being opened. Straight out of the bottle, it's usually tannic and tight. A day or so on your kitchen counter plugged with the cork will help it relax and yield up its soft fruit flavors. After three or four days, it will start to lose quality, but the fifth glass will still be drinkable if the wine is truly young.

Young white wine stores well in the fridge for a week. Just plug it with the cork and put it upright in the door compartment. After you pour a glass, put the wine back in the fridge, but let your glass warm up for 10 or 15 minutes. Cold liquids shut down your ability to taste. Sparkling wine is best finished all at once, although it too will keep in the fridge for a day or two if you use a stopper specially designed to cap sparkling wine bottles.

Here are two other low-tech methods of dealing with an opened bottle of young wine. One is to use the excess wine in your cooking. The best idea is to use the same wine in your cooking that you're going to drink with dinner. If a bottle does become oxidized enough to make it unfit for drinking, it will serve fine in a coq au vin. The other is to find small bottles with stoppers (remember Grolsch beer bottles, with the rubber and ceramic stoppers?) and fill them to near the top with the extra wine. You can also buy clear glass bottles of various sizes with screw caps at the drugstore. Those pretty glass decanters are not for storing wine. They are receptacles for clear wine that's poured off accumulated sediment. Many are designed to maximize initial air contact with wine that's meant to be finished right away. Except (there's always an exception) there is a half-bottle-sized decanter offered in wine accoutrement catalogs. This might suffice if you have half a bottle left. The main point is to fill any bottles to the brim.

Our purpose in this book, however, is to discuss well-aged wine. And it's sad but true that old and well-aged wine doesn't ordinarily keep very well once it's opened. Once a wine reaches its peak, it very quickly becomes vulnerable to oxidation and its subtlety is soon lost. Is there any way to preserve an older wine that you have left over?

We go high-tech for the answer. The VacuVin preservation system is a small pump and reusable stopper that fit over the top of the bottle and let you pump out most of the air. You remove the stopper to pour out a glass, put it back on, affix the pump, then pump out the air again. It will help keep your red wine fresh for a week.

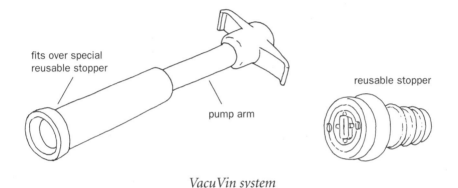

fits over special
reusable stopper

pump arm

reusable stopper

VacuVin system

Private Preserve is a canister of nitrogen with a plastic straw. You put the straw in the opened bottle and squirt in enough inert nitrogen to purge the bottle of oxygen, then recork. A more expensive outfit is The Keeper System. This is a canister of nitrogen connected to a stopper-faucet combination. You put the stopper-faucet on the opened bottle and turn on the nitrogen, which fills the bottle with inert gas and creates a modest pressure so that when you open the faucet, wine pours out. The same idea is used in the professional Winekeeper System. These units hold four or eight bottles of wine, each under nitrogen sparging and pressure. They come with separate temperature zones for white and red wines and keep each at the proper temperature. The wooden case that holds the bottles of wine is natural wood.

To my way of thinking, Private Preserve does the best job for the least money. You can check these items out in wine accessories catalogs (see page 237).

OTHER ACCOUTREMENTS

The wine cellar may need a bookcase. I keep my wine books in my office, but that's because I'm a wine writer and I use them as reference almost daily. If I had a large enough wine cellar, and my business were something other than writer, I might well keep them in the wine cellar. My wine library now includes about fifty books. In addition, you can store any handwritten cellar books you create in the bookcase.

Folks who like to decorate their wine cellar will probably want some art on a wall somewhere, if there's any free space left after racking is built and air conditioning is installed. While some of the wine catalogs offer murals and sculpted ceramic wall art with vineyard motifs, I consider such art to be on a par with the Dungeons & Dragons type of art that features wizards, beautiful maidens, trolls, and the like — prettified schlock, in other words. I see no reason why a wine cellar can't have a piece of art that simply appeals to its owner. If there's a tie to wine, fine, but if the reason the art is chosen is that it has something to do with wine, regardless of the intrinsic quality of the piece, the cart's before the horse. In a similar vein, painted floor tiles, stained-glass panels, etched glass ceiling lights, etched and painted glass doors, and so on are all available with wine and grape motifs, but these seem excessive to me. But maybe that's just me.

Other accoutrements you may find useful in the wine cellar include bottle tags. These hang on the necks of the horizontal bottles in individual racks. You can use a marker or pen to write information about the wine on the tags. The value of these fussy little tags is that you don't have to disturb the wine by pulling the bottle from its space to see what it is; all the information you'll need is on the tag. The less shaking and pulling of the wine one does, the better, although I would find the work of writing a description of every bottle in my racks on individual tags burdensome. Any information I need about a wine is stored on my computer's hard drive.

If you have room, a table and chairs are useful additions to the wine cellar, especially if the cellar is a beautiful place to spend some time. The table and chairs let you comfortably decant, update the cellar book (or use your wine cellaring software if you put a computer in the cellar), read from one of your wine reference books, or even throw a dinner party if it's not too cold for your guests.

THE LAST WORD

What it all comes down to in the end is the few pieces of equipment that you really like, and to which you return over and over again as you pursue your interest in fine wine. I always reach first for a corkscrew, probably over 100 years old, beaten from a piece of solid steel by a craftsman using forge and hammer and anvil. The thing is crafted from a single piece of metal, has acquired a patina of age, and never fails to work perfectly. To cut the foil capsule off the top of the bottle, I use my trusty Kershaw pocketknife. Other than that, all I really need is a glass and some quiet time.

CHAPTER 7

Record Keeping

The main purpose of record keeping for your wine cellar is to know at a glance, and without having to look over every shelf and bottle, what you have and where it's located. That means you need to have a map of your cellar that shows you that information.

Because bottles come and go and move around in the cellar, the map should be easy to update. Even if you don't buy a commercial wine cellar software program, a computer is a remarkably useful tool on which to create an easily updatable map. I use a combination of methods, keeping records by hand (see page 115) and using my computer's word processing program.

The map should present all the information at a glance in the most easily readable form. But what's the information for? Let's look at this logically. When you want to select a wine to accompany a meal, what do you think of first? Usually, the first criterion is the color of the wine: red or white. If you're not after a still red or white wine, you're probably after a rosé, a sparkling wine, or a dessert wine. So your major categories should be Red, White, Rosé, Sparkling, and Dessert.

Let's say you want a red with dinner. What's the next thing you want to know about that red wine? It could be where it's from: Bordeaux, Burgundy, Rhône, California, Spain, Italy, Chile, Argentina, Australia, South Africa, or wherever else. But a case could be made that the next thing you want to know is the variety: Cabernet Sauvignon, Pinot Noir, Syrah, or Sangiovese, for example. I personally think it makes the most sense to know first the color, then the variety or nature of the blend, then the place it's from. The computer file doesn't have to be a literal map of the cellar but, rather, should be a key to where everything is located so you can easily find each bottle.

After you know the color, the variety, and the provenance, you'll want to know what vintage year it is so you know whether it's ready to drink or still youthful. At that point, it's then good to know the winery, the vineyard designate (if any), and any quality marks it may have (such as *Kabinett* wine from Germany, *grand cru classé* from France, DOCG [Denominazione di Origine Controllata e Garantita] from Italy, or Reserve from the United States). If you want, you can toss in the price at this point, and then finally any comments about the wine (if you know any), such as light, medium, or heavy bodied.

Then you need to enter how many bottles you have and the location of the wine in the cellar. In my case, a wine that's been aged to drinkability would be labeled RTD and located in the ready-to-drink individual slots, where it's easy to spot because of the way the wines are laid out left to right by color and intensity (see pages 109–120). Or, if it's in case storage, it might be in "Right Bin, Bottom Shelf, Case YY," although I try to be disciplined enough not to break into the wines in case storage, which are nominally supposed to be aging their way toward the ready-to-drink section. In my system, I shorten the case location designations to, for example, RB, TS, A (meaning "right bin, top shelf, case A"); RB, BS, YY (meaning "right bin, bottom shelf, case YY"); CB, TS, MM (meaning "center bin, top shelf, case MM"), or LB, BS, SSS (meaning "left bin, bottom shelf, case SSS"). I think you can easily see how my cellar is arranged from these examples. The left bin, top shelf is all ready-to-drink wines in individual slots. The other five bins are all case storage. This is about as simple as I can make it.

So, in my cellar I have a 1995 Dry Creek Valley Cabernet Sauvignon Reserve, for which I paid $22.95 in 1998 when it was released (or when I first found it at a Healdsburg wine shop). I bought it because I tasted it at the winery and know it is a medium-bodied wine of fine concentration. So here's how it's listed in my computer program:

RED
Cabernet Sauvignon
California
1995 Dry Creek Estate Reserve $22.95   Medium   2 btl.   CB, BS, LL

All my other California Cabernets will go under the boldface headings, too, organized by oldest year first. If there's a piece of information I don't know, such as the price, I simply leave it out. Here's how my cellar book looks for five of the several hundred California Cabernets in my bins, selected from a page toward the end of the book:

1998 Chimney Rock 'Stags Leap'	$40	Heavy	3 btl.	RB, TS, Q
1998 Dry Creek Estate Reserve	$38	Medium		RB, TS, C
1998 Joseph Phelps Napa Valley		Medium	2 btl.	RB, TS, D
1999 '2480' Napa Valley Estate	$70	Heavy		RB, TS, Q
1999 Barnwood 'Santa Barbara'		Light	2 btl.	RB, TS, Q

By laying out all the Cabernets in your cellar, both in the ready-to-drink section and case storage section, you can just drop your eye down the year column on the far left to find a wine you think would be the proper age and thus good with dinner. If you need a wine with a light, medium, or heavy body, all you have to do is drop your eye down that column to find the wine in your selected age group with the body you want.

You could do all this by hand in a big ledger, but that's a lot of bookkeeping. I know — I've done it and felt like Bob Cratchett. Having a computer makes the task simple — and once you have a wine entered, you can easily move information with a couple of clicks of the mouse.

Moving a single bottle from its case to a ready-to-drink slot will involve first moving the physical bottle, then using the cut-and-paste function of the word processing program to cut the entry from its spot in the case storage section and paste it in the proper place (that is, sorted by year) in the ready-to-drink section, and deleting the "RB, TS, Q" from the tail end of the entry and substituting "RTD." If you are taking one bottle from a group of many that are the same and moving it to the ready-to-drink section (for instance, taking one of the two bottles of Joseph Phelps Napa Valley Cab in the example above), then you'd delete the *2 btl.* note (no bottle number means I have just one bottle of the wine), highlight the entry, hit the *copy* function key or choose it from the drop-down menu, and move it to the ready-to-drink section, where you'd paste the copied entry into the proper place.

As bottles are drunk from the ready-to-drink section, I delete them or, if they were particularly noteworthy and worth a little organoleptic dissection, cut them from the ready-to-drink section and paste them in a separate file I've named "Noteworthy Bottles." This file is organized by varietal and then within the varietal section by year. Here are a few examples:

NOTEWORTHY BOTTLES
Pinot Noir
1991 Williams Selyem 'Allen Vineyard' Pinot Noir. '91 was an extraordinary year with a long, cool fall that went on forever. This pinot wasn't picked until the second week in October! [*Note:* Pinot Noir is usually ready to pick in the Russian River Valley by the end of August to the middle of September.] The extra hang time gave rich, mature flavors. The wine smelled of perfume and roses, was as smooth as silk, and stuffed full of sweet black cherry flavor. Drank it with Thanksgiving dinner, 2000, and it got raves all around.

1993 Dehlinger Estate Pinot Noir. Opened a little backward, but within 20 minutes was gushing ripe pinot fruit with that Russian River cola aroma and a background smell of fresh-cut black truffles. Bouquet of age just beginning to develop. Light to medium color and body, but the flavor components were astoundingly rich, well integrated, and delicious. Opened it for Susanna's birthday dinner in 2001.

As you can see, my "Noteworthy Bottles" file becomes in effect my cellar history. I'll make note of exceptional bottles I buy at a restaurant or have at a

friend's house and add them to the file along with wines from my own cellar. Thus, not every noteworthy bottle is in my personal wine cellar. The criterion for inclusion is simply that it be worth noting.

Why do this? Well, I've thought about that and even accused myself of desperate attempts to cling to the past. But that's not it at all. First of all, as a writer it helps to have a cellar history to draw upon when describing current wines: "This is the best Rochioli Pinot Noir since that memorable vintage of 1986 when winter floodwaters washed fresh life into Rochioli's vineyard soil." That sort of thing. But even if I weren't a writer, some bottles of wine are just so wonderful they should be immortalized somewhere, in someone's cellar book. Besides, searching for descriptors to accurately describe wines will help you put your finger on the qualities of future wines when you encounter them. And that leads, as I've said before, to your knowing what you want in a wine so that you can organize your wine cellar to give it to you.

We've already taken a look at some of the wine cellar software out there, and I'm sure there's more on the way. Several computerized wine cellar software programs are available, but I recommend Robert Parker's Wine Advisor and Cellar Manager.

WHAT MAKES PARKER'S SOFTWARE SPECIAL?

For the past 20 years, Parker, a lawyer who dropped law as a profession when wine became his consuming interest, has published *The Wine Advocate* from his home in Maryland. Parker was the first wine critic to assign numbers to a wine to indicate its quality. His scale runs from 50 points to 100. But he also writes pithy and accurate descriptions of each wine he tastes. These little essays evoke the flavors and nuances of the wines, list the prices at retail without discounts, and suggest when the wines will be ready to drink, be at their peak, and will begin to decline. It's amazing that Parker can write hundreds of these reviews a year and keep them fresh and to the point without simply repeating himself. Those who know Parker say he can remember every wine he's ever reviewed — tens and tens of thousands. If so, and I have no reason to doubt them, he has a genius for wine criticism that surpasses understanding. But isn't that the nature of genius?

It's this ability to really penetrate to the heart of the wine and define it in succinct words that makes Parker's reviews so worthwhile. His entire backlog of entries for 20 years is available on his software, although unless you are buying very old wine or have cellared it yourself, his reviews of older wines won't be particularly useful. What is useful is to read his opinions as an education for yourself. You can see at a glance what he finds in wines — descriptors like "melted chocolate," "spice box," and "smoke" — although I'd be hard put to say exactly what he means by "spice box" or how the gustatory impact of melted chocolate differs from that of the unmelted kind. Still, these terms give you handles on facets of a wine's sensuousness, and those handles give you a chance to name the sensations that wine imparts. A glass of good wine is one of life's few quotidian pleasures that embraces a range of gratification from the earthy enjoyment of a rough young wine to a truly divine delight in a properly aged fine wine.

Here, for an example, is Parker on the 1997 Bacio Divino, a Napa Valley take on a Supertuscan (Supertuscans are newfangled blends of traditional Tuscan Sangiovese with Cabernet Sauvignon), from the June 2000 issue of *The Wine Advocate*:

> *This intriguing as well as innovative blend of 63 percent Cabernet Sauvignon, 20 percent Sangiovese, 9 percent Merlot and 8 percent Petite Sirah is an outstanding effort. Already evolved and delicious, the dark ruby/plum color is followed by aromas of new saddle leather, black raspberries, plum liqueur, cherries, and toasty, smoky new oak. Medium to full-bodied, with sweet tannin, an open-knit, fleshy texture, and low acidity, this California "Supertuscan look-alike" can be drunk now and over the next decade.*

You can see how one short paragraph packs a load of information. The aroma descriptors are clear. Note especially the "sweet tannin" and "open-knit, fleshy texture, and low acidity." This means that the wine is smooth, lush, and generous, not all gnarled up tight with gritty tannins and hard, unyielding fruit. It sounds like a wine to drink soon, at least within a couple of years, even though Parker gives it another decade. Sometimes those gritty tannins, high acidity, and hard, unyielding flavors in a young wine mean it is a candidate for long aging in the cellar, but deep, concentrated fruit must be there, even though tightly wound when young. In the computer business, there's a saying that's shortened to GIGO: garbage in, garbage out. The same thing holds true for a wine cellar. Age won't improve bad wine; it may, however, improve great wine.

While reading Parker can help increase your knowledge about wine, reading bad wine writing doesn't teach you much. Here's Robert Draper in the February 2002 issue of *GQ*, writing about the 1999 Bacio Divino: "The '99's fruit attack soars like a meteor shower, then seethes in the palate like a cosmic bath of nearly unplumable depths . . . like an unforgettable encounter with a raven-haired ingenue, one is left feeling exhilarated, intrigued, and ultimately covetous." Pfui! That's purple prose all right, and not because it's stained with wine. Besides saying nothing, the paragraph ought to be used in writing schools as an example of mistakes to avoid. Meteor showers don't soar, they fall to earth. Things may seethe on the palate, but not in the palate. The word is *unplumbable*, not *unplumable*. And while I may have been exhilarated and intrigued by my encounters with raven-haired ingenues, I've never been covetous. But I thank Mr. Draper for such a magnificent example of bad writing.

The point is that in your record keeping, you may want to include your personal tasting notes on bottles of wine you find exceptionally good. And to do this well, so it makes sense, you need to be able to touch all the bases that Parker has touched: what stage the wine is at when tasted ("already evolved and delicious"), the color of the wine ("dark ruby/plum color"), aromas or bouquet ("new saddle leather, black raspberries, plum liqueur, cherries, and toasty, smoky new oak"), the body or weight of the wine on the palate ("medium to full-bodied"), the tannic structure ("sweet tannins"), the texture of the wine ("open-knit, fleshy texture"), the acidity ("low acidity"), and the anticipated lifespan of the wine ("can be drunk now and over the next decade").

One could take Parker to task for not including any flavor descriptors for the wine itself, but that might be because there are only five actual tastes: sweet, salty, sour, bitter, and umami, and Parker already used the word "sweet." The rest of the taste is in the retronasal aromas that reach the olfactory nerves through the back of the throat and up into the nasal passages. That's why we say "Yum!" when we like the taste of something. If you close your nose and taste various foods, you'd be hard-pressed to distinguish warm applesauce from mashed potatoes except possibly by the texture. For you and me, though, I'll suggest that we use flavor descriptors, even though we may be getting those flavors from the aromas. Two good examples of accurate flavor descriptors for wines are found for Russian River Valley Pinot Noirs and Dry Creek Valley Zinfandels. Russian River Pinots often have a definite cola flavor among their black cherry and berry notes. Dry Creek Zins, on the other hand, often show dead-ripe red raspberry flavors along with their briary blackberry tones.

What's the purpose of recording all this information in a cellar book? First and foremost, it contributes to your education about wine and what you like, and as we saw in previous chapters, having an educated palate and definite likes and dislikes means you can develop a wine cellar that truly works for you. The act of sitting down with a glass of wine, slowly picking its nuances apart, and recording them engraves the information on your mind. It's exactly what professional wine tasters (winemakers, wine marketers, sommeliers, wine writers, and so forth) do day in and day out. Just remember, when doing this on a regular basis and tasting through a lot of wine, use a spit bucket. Alcoholism can be an occupational hazard of the wine business, and you don't want to go down that road.

Most often, however, you'll open a wine for dinner, and as you enjoy it and the dinner table becomes more convivial, the wine will air out and open up, and it will taste better and better. It doesn't take long to grab a piece of paper and a pen and spend a few minutes recording its organoleptic qualities. If you're using a notebook, write the following on the inside front cover so you don't miss the bases: (1) winery, (2) varietal, (3) vintage, (4) appellation, (5) vineyard, (6) appearance, (7) aroma or bouquet, (8) flavor, (9) finish, (10) comments, (11) date. For now, realize that recording these factors supports your prime objective: having a bottle of wine to open on any given night that is perfectly aged and ready to please the senses in that special hedonistic way that only perfect wine can do. Sometimes wine labels will give the pH, titratable acidity (TA), and even residual sugar of a wine. These numbers can be noted, too.

Shorthand charts supposedly tell you whether to "drink," "hold," or "hold or drink" your wine, along with the merits of the vintage. For some wine-growing regions, this is nonsense, since the charts are by their very nature general but wine is very specific, right down to the bottle. For instance, 1998 was supposed to be an off year for California North Coast wine. Cold weather, delayed harvests, rains — all these were supposed to have ruined the vintage. Well, that may have been true for some wines of certain varieties. However, that vintage, like most vintages, was a mixture of the great, the good, the bad, and the ugly. Rutherford Cabernets, for example, were and continue to be wonderful examples of the best that the 1998 vintage had to offer.

Vintage charts make more sense for regions where the climate doesn't vary much over a wide area and where the vines are close to the limits of the range in which they ripen reliably and well. Bordeaux and Burgundy are two good examples. The weather in the Médoc tends to be the same from top to bottom, much as it is in the eastern part of the United States. That doesn't mean that if a summer shower drops rain on Paulliac it's going to be raining in Pessac-Léognan, but it does mean that large weather systems will blanket the Médoc and surrounding areas with the same kind of weather, whether cold and rainy or bright and sunny.

In California, however, where the typical summer day is always bright and sunny, microclimates tend to dominate. For instance, at the same time it can be 105°F in Sacramento, 100°F in the Napa Valley, 90°F in the Valley of the Moon (Sonoma Valley), 78°F in Freestone, near Sebastopol in western Sonoma County, and 58°F in Bodega Bay on the Sonoma coast. That temperature differential, combined with extreme variations in elevation, disparate soil types, sheltered places versus exposed places, sunny places versus foggy places (resulting in wide variations in solar radiation), give California's wine country remarkably diverse climatic and geologic variables that grape growers can exploit to get complexity into their fruit and thus into the wine. You can see that vintage charts for Sonoma Cabernets alone won't be very useful, since there's a world of difference between a Cabernet grown in hot, dry Cloverdale and one grown on Vine Hill Road near cool-climate

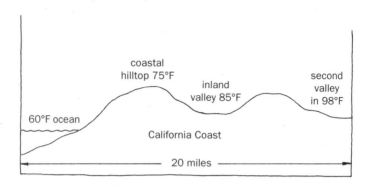

Microclimates in coastal California

Sebastopol. Climate influences the grape grower's choice of variety and, thus, which wines are made there.

So, if a vintage chart says that a given year in Bordeaux or Burgundy is a real dog, you might take the information at its word. But if a vintage chart says 1998 in California was a dog — well, nonsense.

DECIPHERING LABELS

Part of record keeping is accurately defining each wine by the information on the label. For Americans, a California label is undoubtedly the easiest to decipher, followed by the French and German. Italian labels are the most inscrutable of all. But it pays to know what every word on those labels means. Some folks soak off the labels of wine bottles that are particularly noteworthy and paste them in a cellar book after they dry. That's a bit fussy for my taste, but it's a good idea if you have the inclination because all the important information about the wine is right there along with your notes.

Let's look at several labels closely.

French Labels

Here's a French label for a white Burgundy (that would ordinarily be made from Chardonnay grapes, with, perhaps, a bit of Pinot Blanc, Pinot Gris, and Aligoté. Aligoté, though only a fraction of the total acreage, is the second most widely planted grape after Chardonnay). Corton-Charlemagne is the great

white wine produced along the slope of the hill of Corton in Burgundy. The best Corton-Charlemagnes are very expensive wines, denoted *grand cru,* which come from a band of vineyards on white chalky soil just below the hilltop. The name refers to Charles the Great, whose wife Hildegarde insisted that white grapes be planted there in order to avoid the red wine stains that she believed desecrated Charlemagne's beard. In the 1890s, Louis Latour III replanted the phylloxera-devastated grapevines of Pinot Noir and Aligoté with Chardonnay, recognizing that the soils and exposure were ideally suited to Chardonnay, thus paving the way for the Corton-Charlemagne Grand Cru.

Under the "Corton-Charlemagne" designation, the label says "Grand Cru," which means that the grapes come from these special vineyards. And under the words *Grand Cru,* the label says: "Appellation Corton-Charlemagne Contrôlée," which means, of course, that the wine comes from the vineyards entitled to the Corton-Charlemagne name and from nowhere else. A bit further down the label comes something more telling: "Mis en bouteille par Louis Latour, négociant-éleveur." This means that the wine was produced and bottled by Louis Latour, négociant and éleveur.

Maison Louis Latour is a Burgundian producer of two entities. The first is the Domaine Louis Latour, which is one of the largest owners of premier and grand cru vineyards in the Côte-d'Or. The domaine consists of 115 acres in 21 appellations in the Côte-d'Or, 90 percent of which is grand and premier cru vineyards. The crown jewel of the domaine is 24.1 acres of the

REMOVING LABELS

I've soaked off more than my share of labels (usually to get bottles for my homemade wine) and discovered that European wine labels tend to soak off easily but that American wineries tend to use stronger glue. Soak the bottles in hot water until the labels loosen; if they don't loosen, forget it and copy the label information into your cellar book. Take the wet labels and stick them while wet onto the front of your refrigerator, with the *printed side* against the fridge. If you stick the glue side against the fridge, residual glue may stick the label to the enamel, and you'll have to soak it off all over again. Because the label is flat against the enamel and vertical, the water dries off fairly rapidly, leaving a perfectly flat label for you to reglue into your book. If the back label contains interesting information, you can soak that off the bottle and paste it into your book along with the front label.

highest quality parcels of the Corton-Charlemagne vineyard. According to Robert Parker, in his definitive book *Burgundy,* "Many people consider the Corton-Charlemagne made by Latour to be the reference point for the other wines of the vintage."

The second entity of Maison Louis Latour is its role as a négociant-éleveur. The relationship between growers and négociants is a mutually beneficial symbiosis. The average vineyard holding in Burgundy is 12 acres. Due to the high overhead of producing wine, many growers cannot afford to vinify their grapes, which is where the négociant enters the picture. Throughout history, through economic ups and downs, the négociant is the only entity to support the growers. This role results in relationships and contracts with growers that go back for years and years. While many négociants produce mediocre to poor wines, the wines of Maison Latour and other négociants such as Louis Jadot and Bouchard, Père et Fils are consistently rated outstanding by trade publications. Stick to the well established and respected négociants to ensure the highest quality.

Eleveurs, on the other hand, are those who buy grapes from the vineyards and process them into wine. Elevage involves all the steps from crushing through fermentation and barrel aging to bottling. So *négociant-éleveur* means that the firm of Louis Latour negotiates for grapes and processes them into wine, then bottles the wine. The vineyards are owned by someone else. It's an important distinction, because the best wines are usually those grown, fermented, and bottled by the owner of the vineyards.

While most Bordeaux vineyards are owned by a single château, vineyards in Burgundy are often owned by a multitude of producers, each of whom uses the vineyard name for his or her wine. There are the famous Grand Cru Chambertin vineyards, for instance, of Gevry-Chambertin. The two that can legally call themselves *Chambertin* are Chambertin and Chambertin-Clos de Bèze. All the others carry the name *Chambertin* after the vineyard name; for example, Latricières-Chambertin. The grand crus comprise vineyards of approximately 245 acres. Premier crus, the next step down in quality designation, comprise 211 acres. These 456 acres are farmed by approximately 20 growers. And so you can have wine called Charmes-Chambertin from several producers, designated either as a *domaine,* such as Domaine des Varoilles, Domaine Dujac, or Domaine Pierre Gelin, or as a *name,* such as J. C. Boisset, Faiveley, or Joseph Roty.

In Bordeaux and Burgundy, the more precise the designation of the place-name, the better and more expensive the wine should be (although it may not always be). For instance, if a wine label appellation is merely "Bordeaux," that can mean the grapes could have been grown anywhere in Bordeaux's large region — even in the districts noted for poor wine. If the label specifies the wine is from "Médoc," that narrows the area to this fine-wine region. But Médoc has two parts, the lower Médoc (Bas-Médoc) and the upper Médoc (Haut-Médoc). These terms refer to the land's elevation, not to their north-south orientation. The lower Médoc is low land actually located to the north of the elevated (and thus better drained gravelly soils) of the Haut-Médoc. Thus the appellation *Haut-Médoc* designates a finer portion of the Médoc than the simple term of *Médoc.* Within the region of Haut-Médoc are some of the finest communes of Bordeaux, such as

Margaux, Pauillac, St-Estèphe, and St-Julien. So the designation of *Pauillac,* for instance, cuts the pie finer still and denotes higher quality than simply Haut-Médoc. If an estate is named, such as Chateau Prieure-Lichine in Margaux, then the pie is cut to its finest slice. In Burgundy, estates are called *domaines* and this term has the same meaning as *château.* You'll also see *premier cru* or *grand cru* ("first growth" or "great growth," respectively) referred to on certain wines in both Bordeaux and Burgundy; these terms denote vineyards that have been judged to be superior. In the Médoc, the cru may refer to the Classification of 1855. This was an attempt to classify Bordeaux wines by using a simple yardstick: the most expensive wines got the best classifications. So much time has elapsed, and so much has changed, that the 1855 classification is essentially meaningless today, except for the great growths: Chateaux Lafite-Rothschild, Latour, Margaux, Mouton-Rothschild, and Haut-Brion. They were the most expensive wines then (except for Mouton, which was added to the premier crus in 1973), and they continue to be because the income these properties generate allows for extra care and expense to be taken in the vineyard and in the winery, something nobody wants to fool with. Besides these first growths, you may also see second or third or lower growths referred to on the labels of other chateaux.

German Labels

Let's look now at a German wine label. I went by my local wine shop and picked out the first German wine I saw, a Mosel. It said at the top of the label, "Dr. Weins-Prüm," which seemed at first to me to be an attempt to squish together a few words that echo some high-quality German wines. Among the finest Mosels are those of J. J. Prüm, and there are famous "doctor" estates, such as Dr. Thanisch and Dr. Fischer. But on investigation, I discovered that the firm of Dr. F. Weins-Prüm, now owned by Herr Selbach-Weins, grows Riesling on 17 acres of the famous Wehlener Sonnenuhr vineyard across the Mosel River from the village of Wehlen. In German, *Sonnenuhr* means "sundial," and *Wehlener Sonnenuhr* means the "Sundial Vineyard" in Wehlen. It's a vineyard famous for its ability to produce ripe Riesling with an attractive, sweet character. In German wines, sugar is king, probably because it

Mosel

Saar

Ruwer

Erzeuger-Abfüllung

L A. P. Nr.

2 576 548 5 03

ALC. 8.5% BY VOL

CONTENTS 750 ML ℮

PRODUCT OF GERMANY
WHITE WINE

Dr. Weins-Prüm

Inh. Willi Weins

QUALITÄTSWEIN MIT PRÄDIKAT

2002er

Wehlener Sonnenuhr

Riesling - Kabinett

D-54470 Bernkastel-Wehlen · Uferallee 4 · Tel. / Fax 06531-2636

seems counterintuitive that vineyards so far north can produce such ripe, luscious grapes, with such magnificent character.

On this wine label, as on most German wine labels, is the word *Qualitätswein,* which means "quality wine." This doesn't mean much, because about 95 percent of all German wines carry this designation. Furthermore, it's part of the following phrase on this label: "Qualitätswein mit Prädikat," which means "quality wine with a distinction." The distinction here is the term given for its sugar content: in this case, *Kabinett.*

German wine distinctions begin with *Kabinett,* the lowest distinction, which refers to a sugar level a little sweeter than dry. Winery owners once upon a time placed wines with elevated sweetness in their personal cabinets, hence the term. As levels of residual sugar increase, wines are designated *Spätlese* ("late-picked"), *Auslesen* (the word means "selected" and refers to the process of selecting the ripest bunches for a separate fermentation), *Beerenauslesen* ("berry-selected," a process in which individual, very ripe berries have been selected for a separate fermentation, yielding wines with more residual sugar than Auslesen or Kabinett wines), and *Trockenbeerenauslesen.* *Trocken* is German for "dry," and the term usually indicates that the wine is fermented to dryness. However, in *Trockenbeerenauslesen* it means "dried berry-selected" and refers to the picking out of ultra-ripe raisins that are almost half sugar for a separate fermentation. The word also reveals the penchant of the German language for stringing words together to make new words that increase in length until they almost fall over from their own weight. By the way, German Trockenbeerenauslesen wines are the honeyed nectar of the gods and you pay dearly for the privilege of drinking them.

Getting back to our label, the wine's distinction is simply Kabinett, but it's coupled with the grape variety: "Riesling-Kabinett." I believe that the variety is put on there to reassure buyers that this wine is made from the noble Riesling grape and not from one of the lesser grapes that grow along the Mosel and in nearby areas of German wine production that don't match the Mosel for delightful drinking. German wine labels may also carry the designation "A.P.-Nr.," followed by a number. That is the testing number required by German wine laws for all Qualitätswein. You may also see the word *Erzeugerabfüllung* or *Gutsabfüllung* on a label. They both mean approximately what "estate bottled" means in English — that the wine has been bottled by the grower. Occasionally you may see the related term *Abfüller* on the label. This means "bottler" and usually denotes a winery or bottler who purchased the grapes but didn't grow them.

Italian Labels

In Italy, things can get a little confusing. Place-names sound like family names, and it can be hard to know what's what. However, let's look at a typical label. Here's one from my wine shop that has "Fonterutoli" in large letters across the top of the label. It looks like it should be the name of the winery. Under it is written, "1999 Chianti Classico." I look at the neck of the bottle and there is the Black Rooster, symbol of the Consorzio Vino Chianti Classico, an organization of classic Chianti producers dedicated to keeping and improving the quality of these wines. Further down on the main label, the next thing I read is "Denominazione di Origine Controllata e Garantita," which is fairly easily translatable as the name of origin (Chianti Classico), which is controlled and guaranteed. This is usually shortened to DOCG and is found on the capsule on the neck of the bottle. It was the mark established by the Italian wine industry in 1963 to give recognition to Italy's finest wines

and guarantee their authenticity to buyers. With few exceptions, DOCG is indeed a guarantee of wine Italians can be proud of. The acronym DOC may also be found; this simply means that the place-name is controlled but says little about quality.

Under the DOCG line on the label, in fairly large letters, is the word "Mazzei," and under that is "In Fonterutoli dal 1435." Mazzei is the winery name, and they've been making wine in Fonterutoli since 1435. A little research turned up the fact that Fonterutoli is a small castle near Siena. And so the prominent display of the Fonterutoli name suggests that the Mazzei winery is proud of its fruit from this famous place. Many labels, although not this one, also feature the word *imbottigliato,* which means "bottled."

In Europe these days, wines that are not estate wines carry the bottler's postal code. In France, this may be a number referring to the bottler's *département.* In Italy, it may be a two-letter code referring to the bottler's district. In Champagne, letter codes will appear next to the bottler's number. Knowing the meanings of these codes lets you in on some interesting information. "NM," for instance, stands for *négotiant-manipulant* and refers to one of the big Champagne houses or shippers; "RM" stands for *récoltant-manipulant* and refers to an estate grower who makes and bottles his own wine; "CM" stands for *coopérative de manipulation,* or a cooperative that has bottled the Champagne; "RC" means *récoltant-coopérateur,* which translates to a grower who sells wine made by a cooperative; and "MA" stands for *marque d'acheteur,* or a buyer's own brand, such as a wine made for a restaurant with the restaurant's name on it. "SR" and "R" are not often found on Champagne, but if they appear, they refer to a very small family-owned company or grower.

California Labels

A California wine label is a little easier for Americans to figure out. The name of the winery is usually featured. If the wine is estate bottled, the label will state that forthrightly. If it's from a particular vineyard, that will be stated. If it's a selection of fine wine culled from the run-of-the-mill wine, it may say "Reserve," but that doesn't mean more than the vintner wants it to. What is graven in stone are the appellations. "California" means the wine can come from anywhere within the Golden State. "Napa Valley" means the wine can come from anywhere within the Napa Valley. Then there are subapellations: Stags Leap, for instance, is a subappellation of Napa Valley and refers to a small section of the valley at the southeast corner.

A vineyard designation may also appear on the label. California is just now in the process of identifying specific single vineyards that consistently turn out fine or unique wines. Heitz's 'Martha's Vineyard' led the way years ago. At Stag's Leap Wine Cellars, for example, there's a separate bottling of 'Fay Vineyard.' While Europe has had centuries, even millennia, to figure out precisely which grape variety grows best on which plot of land, California viticulture has had only 30 years or so at most. Viticulture had flourished in the nineteenth century, but not far into the twentieth; Prohibition utterly devastated the wine industry. Although repeal was instituted in 1933, it took until the late 1960s and early 1970s for the California wine industry to raise its head and pick itself up, brush itself off, and get going again. Lots of mistakes were made. Cabernet Sauvignon was planted in the cool climate of

STAG'S LEAP WINE CELLARS

FAY

Cabernet Sauvignon
2000 Estate Napa Valley

WARREN WINIARSKI, PROPRIETOR

Monterey County, and the wines tasted like canned asparagus. Pinot Noir was thought of as a difficult grape because it was planted in warm regions. But among the mistakes were lots of successes. Cabernet Sauvignon was planted in Oakville and Rutherford in Napa County. Chardonnay found a home in the Carneros region and Sonoma County. Zinfandel thrived in Dry Creek Valley, and now the cool climates of the ridgetops above the fog line along the Sonoma Coast, the Russian River Valley, and cool Carneros were found to be perfect for Pinot Noir.

Then disaster struck — but the dark cloud had a bright silver lining. Vast plantings of vines were planted on AXR rootstock at the recommendation of the viticulturists at the University of California at Davis. It turned out that AXR is susceptible to destruction by the phylloxera root louse, the same bug that destroyed the wine industry in France in the 1870s. Vineyards across the Wine Country came crashing down and were ripped out wholesale, at great cost. Wine production slowed.

The silver lining was that from the early 1970s to the mid-1980s and 1990s when phylloxera struck, much was learned from the French and locally about vineyard techniques. Replantings were made on improved rootstocks with better clones of the grape varieties. Closer spacings were used. Better trellising methods were chosen. And most important, replanting encouraged vineyardists to change the variety of grapes to ones better suited to the land. These replantings are now maturing, and the quality of California wines is accelerating rapidly. If you've liked California wines before, you're going to love them even more in the future. Vineyardists and winemakers take great note of their climate and soils and are in the process of identifying subregions.

Sonoma County, for instance, has subappellations within subappellations. Green Valley, where Iron Horse makes its sparkling wine, is a subappellation of the Russian River Valley, which in turn is a subappellation of the Sonoma Coast appellation. These subappellations make perfect sense. I know, for instance, that Green Valley is a very cool climate compared to the majority of the Russian River Valley around it. I lived just one hill over from Green Valley, on Vine Hill Road, from 1985 to 1993. I soon discovered that the slough along the creek in Green Valley is much cooler than the "banana belt" on the elevated ground where Tom Dehlinger's vineyards are located. And Sonoma Coast is such a wide region that the name is almost meaningless, except as it refers to the strip of land along the Pacific Ocean from the coast inland to the western edge of the Santa Rosa plain and the Laguna de Santa Rosa, the second largest estuarian drainage region in California, second only to the Bay Area's estuarine topography that drains the watershed from the Central Valley and forms the extensive bays that surround San Francisco. (See page 236 for a map of California wine regions.)

Wines from other parts of the United States tend to have larger appellations, simply because weather patterns extend over greater areas. You have the Finger Lakes region in upstate New York, Long Island's North Fork, southeastern Pennsylvania, and so on.

USING LABEL INFORMATION

Of what use are all these label terms to the owner of a wine cellar? They're of great use. They provide a huge amount of information that you can use to gauge when your wine will be ready. A premier cru Bordeaux, you'll discover, may take a decade to reach full flower, while a wine from Languedoc may take only five years. Because of their intense sweetness, a German Trockenbeerenauslesen or a French Sauternes like Château d'Yquem will last nearly forever. A Reserve wine may have more structure and stuffing than an ordinary wine and handle more cellar time. An Italian DOCG Barolo will take a lot of cellar aging, while most DOC wines were ready to drink yesterday.

Your cellar book can be as detailed or simple as you want, but at a minimum, it should give you a record of the wines you have and where they are located. Keeping notes on wines that have made your socks roll up and down is a fine idea, if only because it cements them in your memory and gives you yardsticks against which to measure future great wines. Keeping a note on the price you paid for a wine is fun when you drink the wine a decade later and realize that you'd have to pay ten times as much for the same wine if you were to buy it similarly well aged at a wine shop.

Finally, if you are concerned about your alcohol consumption (it's easy for it to inch up, and you should face facts), you can keep a page that tracks your consumption. A simple graph listing the number of glasses of wine per day will show you at a glance if you're surpassing the level of moderation. Keeping the graph up-to-date has the salutary effect of reminding you to be moderate. After all, moderate wine drinking can prolong life, while immoderate drinking can shorten it. And a long life ensures you'll be able to drink some of those young ports when they, and you, are old.

CHAPTER 8

Consuming and Evaluating Wine

Now comes the good part. When the wine hits the taste buds, you know immediately whether you like it or not. Simple, you may think. Except the more you know about wine, the more you may come to appreciate certain facets that at first you might dismiss, ignore, or not even be aware of. In fact, isn't that the way it is with everything? The more you know about any subject that interests you, the more you come to love it.

What this means is that an uneducated palate may have a narrow range of appreciation, while an educated palate (that is, the palate of someone who knows a lot about wine or is familiar with its diverse qualities) can experience a much wider range of sensory impressions that will delight him or her. As children, we may have appreciated hamburgers, French fries, chocolate milk, and spaghetti above all other foods. This didn't mean that our sensory apparatus was faulty; we were probably more sensitive to certain tastes at that age than we are as adults. It did mean that we were neophytes in the world of food, just starting to learn, unable to appreciate the silken, savory lusciousness of a seared foie gras or the flaky delicacy of a fresh Alaskan halibut poached in white wine and charentais melon juice. Well, the same thing happens with wine. The more we know about wine, the more we can appreciate it. Our appreciation of wine broadens with education.

The question becomes, How do we get from here (wine neophytes) to there (wine-savvy aficionados)? The single greatest device we have to help us make this worthwhile journey is our own wine cellar. How wonderful to have a wine cellar! It is a device that delivers the pleasures of the palate to us easily and regularly. As we enjoy, we learn. As we learn, our enjoyment increases.

Jancis Robinson, MW, made the observation that one only knows when a wine has reached its peak after it has passed its peak. (The MW stands for "Master of Wine," an honorific that is earned through a yearlong educational process, in addition to gustatory talent). Unfortunately, it's true — it's all uphill until you discover that it's now downhill.

WHEN TO DRINK WINE

When Bordeaux and Bordeaux-variety wines decline, the fruit tends to disappear before the structure, leaving all dry bones and no flesh. With Burgundies and Burgundy-style wines, it's often just the opposite. The structure (the acids, the firmness, the phenolics, the body) disappears before the fruit, leaving a pretty wine, but one that's almost vaporous. What we want, of course, is plenty of fruit hung onto a firm body. That actually argues for drinking wines while they're younger rather than older. For every wine that's reached perfection after a couple of decades in the cellar, three will have lost fruit or structure.

If you err on the side of youth in a wine, at least you're drinking it on the way up rather than on the way down. The French do it all the time. They're known for taking the wine when it's full of fruit and exuberance. The so-called English palate likes its wines in a smooth old age, with plenty of bottle-aged bouquet. And there's no denying that wine at its well-aged best is the apex of wine-drinking pleasure. But again, for every wine that's truly peaking at a ripe old age, several other wines laid aside as candidates for long aging will be over-the-hill.

What we really need is a surefire gauge, beyond the ones we've already discussed, that will give us a strong clue to the wine's ageability. We've already seen that good strong color and phenolics in the form of anthocyanins and tannins indicate ageability. But maturity is even more important.

I've seen many wines of great concentration when they were young peter out over the long haul because the grapes got ripe before they got mature. Let's define terms and vinification procedures so it becomes clear what I'm talking about here.

Concentration and Extraction

Concentration is the intensity of flavor and color in a wine. It's an aspect of how much of the flavor and color in the grapes is extracted during vinification. The process of vinification may start out with a cold soak, in which the grapes are crushed and allowed to sit as a macerated mash of juice and skins, seeds, pulp, and possibly some stems, for a day or so. Fermentation is then allowed to proceed. Fermentation can be supplemented with whatever yeasts are naturally present *(native yeasts)* by the addition of commercial yeasts or by killing off or stunning natural yeasts with sulfites and substituting commercially-grown yeasts. In the perfect medium for growth — a warm slurry of sugary grape juice and solids — it doesn't take native or commercial yeasts long to start reproducing exponentially.

Primary fermentation then starts and soon hits a fever pitch, as the yeast rapidly converts sugar to alcohol and wreaks other mysterious changes in the *must* (the fermenting grape juice) that transmogrifies grapes into wine. A tank of must in the midst of a primary fermentation literally boils, not with heat but with carbon dioxide bubbling up from the secret heart of the fermentation — a metamorphosis echoed in Christianity by the miraculous conversion of water into wine. In wine-growing regions around the world, grapevines turn water into grape juice, and yeast completes the miracle by turning that grape juice into wine.

After the primary fermentation subsides, secondary fermentation slowly finishes the job. This process may include malolactic fermentation, which is not accomplished by yeast but by bacteria that convert malic acid (an acid that's unpleasantly harsh) into lactic acid (a softer and milkier acid).

After the secondary fermentation finishes, the must may be allowed an *extended maceration,* meaning that the finished fermentation is allowed to just sit there for a week or several weeks. The grape skins and other bits and particles of the fruit float to the top, where they're called the *cap.* More extraction (and prevention of infection of the wine by vinegar-producing bacteria and other nasties) happens when the cap of skins is under the new wine, rather than floating on top, and so the cap is submerged in one of several ways. Small batches may be *punched down* by hand several times a day. Larger vats may be subjected to *pumping over,* which means that juice is drawn out of the tank from underneath the cap, propelled through a pump, and sprayed across the top of the cap. This is rough treatment for a wine, however, and vintners are getting away from pumping over as a technique. The latest technique involves a wire mesh screen that fits the fermenting vat. It's pushed down into the vat and keeps the cap submerged at all times. It's gentle, it creates full extraction, and it doesn't require much work when it's in place. No matter how the cap is handled during the primary and secondary fermentations and the extended maceration, the fermenting vat is best protected from bacteria-carrying fruit flies and other wandering microorganisms by floating a cover or heavier-than-air gases (like carbon dioxide) on top of the must.

I've pressed out new wine from young musts that have not undergone extended macerations and found the grape skins (where most of the color, flavor, and aromatics that make great wine are located) hard to press, thick with cells that haven't burst or decomposed, and retentive of juice and flavor components. And I've let musts sit for a couple of weeks or more after the fermentation finishes, until the floating cap of skins soaks up enough new wine to get soggy and sink through the surface. When the cap *falls,* as this is called, it's the sign to press out the juice. Now the pressing is easier, as the skins are yielding and compress easily. Each pressed skin is like a thin foil of paperlike material. All the color, flavor, aromatics, phenolics, and other components that make for great wine have been extracted from the skins into the must. Now when I press, the solids become like a tight cake. The skins have yielded all their goodies to the new wine. Now this wine has great depth of flavor. That's extraction.

Concentration, on the other hand, really happens in the vineyard. Conditions are such that the grapes are small, with a high ratio of skin to juice. The weather has been such that the flavor and color of the grapes are exceptionally intense. As a result, wines from these grapes become concentrated. All that is to the good, ordinarily, but in some cases the wine is too concentrated, too intense, so stuffed with flavor and aromas that it's out of balance. Such a wine is awkward and over-the-top. It's very much akin to what a person looks for in a potential lover. If the other person is too intense, too pushy, too forward, you instinctively back off. If they're too wishy-washy, too weak, too soft, you don't find a lot to like. But if a person has that magic balance of depth and gentleness, puissance and sophistication, intellect and physicality, he or she warrants attention. Balanced wines are like that. Yes, they have concentration and extraction, but it's held in check. There's a controlled energy, a balance of complete control with complete freedom. All great art is like that, and wine is no exception.

Ripeness

Ripeness, as opposed to concentration, is understood to be a function of sugar in the grape. A grape berry becomes ripe when its sugar level reaches about 23 brix, or 23 percent sugar. The sugar level can be lower in colder regions. In parts of New York State, Germany, and northern France, grapes with 21 or 22 percent sugar may be as ripe as they'll get. A sugar content of 23 to 24 percent is considered optimum in many places in the world. In warm climates like California's Central Valley, however, grapes reaching 24 or 25 percent sugar (or more) are considered ripe.

The level of sugar in a grape is an indication of final alcohol levels, because sugar converts to alcohol, but it is not necessarily an indication of quality. Quality is indicated much more by the concept of maturity than by ripeness.

Maturity

What is maturity? Consider the maturation of a grape berry. It may show concentration from the beginning, since concentration is developed in the vineyard when berry size is small to moderate, weather conditions have allowed the berry to produce the full complement of flavor components in its skins, and these flavor compounds are captured in the wine by a full extraction. When the grape develops enough sugar, it shows ripeness, but it still may not be mature. Maturity has to do with the tannins and with subtle compounds in the grape berry that develop only when allowed sufficient hang time. *Hang time* means the length of time that the bunches of grapes hang on the vine, usually counted from *veraison* (when the grapes start to show color) to harvest. During extended hang time, beneficial changes occur.

In 1991 in California, the late summer and fall were inordinately cool. The grapes hung and hung and hung some more, without the sugars increasing very much. Vintners were fretting. The grapes weren't getting ripe! Would they ever get ripe? And still they hung — some through October into November. And although sugar levels never went through the roof, the grape flavors got magnificently, beautifully mature. In addition, the tannins that developed on the seed coats turned dark brown and ripe. Instead of being hard and astringent, they became silky and smooth. The flavors backed off from their bright intensity and became subtle, mellow, and sophisticated. Everything fell into balance, into place. As I write this, it's been 12 years since that wonderful vintage of 1991, and the 1991s show great longevity. I have Zinfandels from 1992, 1993, and 1995 that have evolved into wines indistinguishable from other old red wines. They were probably at their peak in the late 1990s. But the 1991s are perfect right now. They still taste of Zinfandel, smooth as a satin sheet but still lively. This shows that maturity is key to longevity in the cellar, even above concentration and ripeness.

How can you tell whether its grapes were mature when you taste a wine that's young and just offered for sale? This is where the California dilemma kicks in. Because of its steady, warm climate, the grapes in many years reach ripeness of sugar before they reach maturity of flavor. If you wait for them to mature, they become overly sugary, which means that they become overly alcoholic. Wines with over 15 percent alcohol aren't unusual in California, and yet wine shouldn't be blatantly and harshly alcoholic but should augment the enjoyment of food. To counteract the excess alcohol, vintners use a variety of high-tech methods. *Reverse osmosis* reduces alcohol content but reduces the quality of a wine. *Spinning cones* gently heat wine to drive off alcohol as it flows down the cone, but heating wine also reduces its quality. The more procedures used in the winery to "improve" wine, the less distinctive the wine will be.

In Europe, one finds the opposite problem: The grapes often have trouble ripening, although they become mature. You see a lot of alcohol levels at around 12 percent. And while mature flavors develop, tannins may remain stubbornly tight and hard due to cool weather.

In general, California has the advantage of reliably great weather in most years, which produces rich ripeness; Bordeaux has the advantage of long hang time in many years, and so the grapes mature well.

How can you tell whether a wine's grapes were mature when the wine is young and just released? Look for complexity in the flavor profile. Immature grapes yield simple flavors that may be pleasant enough, but they are not deep and profound. Mature flavors are kaleidoscopic in the facets they present to the palate. The tannins of mature wines are smooth rather than gritty. They offer layers of tastes; they don't give you a single impression and then quit on you. They reveal complexity and then continue that revelation through a long, long finish — meaning that after you've swallowed the sip of wine, the residual wine in the mouth continues to unfold new charms for many seconds, even up to a minute. The nuances only slowly die away. That's maturity.

Balance

In great years, rich ripeness meets great maturity, which brings us to another factor we should look for in wines that promise to develop beautifully with lengthy cellar time: balance. *Balance* means that all the wine's elements are in proportion.

Any great work of art shows proportion, that subtle sense that everything is perfectly composed, perfectly in balance, with no awkward passages. Balanced wines can be cellared for years, during which their beautiful balance improves. When a wine has harmonious balance among all its elements, time only moves them all forward together. Although time in the cellar can change the character of each of those elements, the overall proportion and harmony remain consistent and pleasing. I was talking about balance with John Williams of Frog's Leap winery in Rutherford in the Napa Valley, and he said, "Wines are like people. If they're ugly when they're young, they'll be ugly when they're old." So don't expect much from a charmless, awkward wine if you decide to cellar it. But a wine that has a fine balance of mature flavor, tannins, alcohol, body, structure, ripe fruit, and concentration — even though it may be young and tightly wound — is a candidate for long cellaring.

Rob Sinskey, who makes serious Pinot Noir from Carneros fruit, was talking about big, showy, extra-ripe wines (he called them "show wines") that appeal to wine critics, and he offered this wisdom: "Show wines are like a bad date [who] reveals everything interesting about herself in the first five minutes. But great wine is like a developing relationship, where you discover her slowly, and she reveals herself only over time."

He's right. The greatest wines I've ever had saved their best sip for the last sip, and I was sure that if there were more of it in the bottle, it would have continued to get better, more complex, more interesting, and more pleasurable with each sip. But alas, it ends at the bottom of the bottle. Wine drinkers know that going for another bottle dooms them to several disappointments. First, the new bottle, even if it's the same wine, will not be nearly as generous right out of the freshly opened bottle. The sips will be disappointing because the wine has not had time to air out and develop over the hours of the evening like the first bottle.

Also, if you try to regain that high ground you experienced at the end of the first bottle, you will surely drink too much wine, and as your central nervous system becomes more and more depressed from the alcohol, you become less and less able to appreciate the wine. And after drinking too much wine, you may go to bed in a state that leaves no room for love, or wake up with a head that feels unlovely indeed. When that wonderful bottle of wine is finished, it's finished, and that's that. Think of it as a one-night affair that worked out beautifully but that will only lead to ruin if you try to recapture it. If you need something more to drink, have something nonalcoholic. I raised five kids, and I taught them all the same thing about alcoholic beverages: When it feels good, stop drinking. It will only get worse with more input.

When I was a wastrel youth, I used to say that a bottle of wine was the size it is because that's how much wine one is supposed to drink over a day. But time has proved me wrong. A bottle of wine is the size it is because that's the amount of wine *two* people are supposed to drink over a day. A bottle contains five glasses. Two glasses are exactly the right amount for good health, good cheer, and good companionship. The fifth glass should find its way into the recipe for dinner.

DATING WINE

Appreciation of wine reaches some kind of apex when it's drunk as part of a meal rather than as a cocktail. Not that wine as a cocktail is wrong, inferior, or a misuse of the beverage. But wine glorifies food, and food enhances wine in a synergistic way. The most telling comment along these lines I ever heard came from a diner I didn't know, at a table next to mine in a restaurant in Sonoma County, California. I noticed him taking a bite of his food and obviously savoring it, and then he took a sip of wine. His eyes widened, he stared at his dinner companion with his mouth half open, and he said, "Oh, my!" That about sums it up.

What is it about wine that so pleases the human senses? Certainly grape juice, while it's a delicious drink, doesn't offer the nuance and multifaceted delights of a glass of really good wine. One can be scientific about the answer and talk about the crisp acidity of a wine that stimulates the salivary glands and the appetite and refreshes the palate between bites. But there's something else. The sheer delightful flavor of wine incorporates so many fruits other than grapes. Wine writers peg the subtle flavors of wine to blueberries, strawberries, peaches, plums, cherries, black currants, red fruits, black fruits, raspberries, and so on. I know of no other food whose character is so well defined by other foods, and diverse foods at that. Even though wine is what it is — grapes — as you sip it, hints of other fruits and foods and substances reveal themselves: chocolate, tobacco, leather, dried leaves, tea, pie spices, vanilla, and on and on.

Who wouldn't love a food or a beverage that opens up before you as you enjoy it, revealing layer upon layer of delicious flavors and aromas? Granted, it takes knowledge and a certain frame of mind to gain full value from a great wine. You need patience, because (as Rob Sinskey said) a great wine is not going to reveal all its charms immediately. And you can't force the issue by slamming a few quick glasses, because you're not going to get the result you're after in that fashion. You really have to romance the glass of wine. Let it open up slowly, of its own accord. Then approach it slowly, savoring each sip. If you rush things, you run right past the beauty. Drinking a fine wine should not be a goal-oriented exercise. It should be a very enjoyable road to

travel, where the journey matters rather than the end. We all work so hard and so intensely these days, we can thank goodness for wine that slows us down and points out some very human and correct ways of enjoying life. (See the Wine Aroma Wheel on page 233 to learn more about describing wine aromas.)

How can we personally evaluate and score the wines we so carefully age? There are all kinds of scoring systems. Most common in the United States is the 100-point scale used by Robert M. Parker Jr. in *The Wine Advocate,* by

The Wine Spectator, by *The Wine News,* and other publications. If you note these scores carefully, though, you'll see that the scales don't exactly match up. Parker's 89 points might be *The Wine Spectator's* 91 points, while *The Wine Spectator's* 91 points might be *The Wine News's* 88 points. And scoring varies from issue to issue, because how can a human being be perfectly consistent in scoring wines subjectively? All we can do is give it our best shot, unless wines are scored by using some objective scale, such as a chemical analysis of the various compounds in wine. But such analytical reductionism remains suspect in many circles because it can't take into account the profound synthesis that takes place in the human mind when all the reductive factors merge into one synergistic impression.

Besides the 100-point scale, we find *The Connoisseur's Guide* using a scale of no puffs to three puffs, *Decanter* magazine from England using a scale of no stars to five stars, and many tasting panels and other wine critics using a 20-point scale. I suggest that if you want to score wines and keep your evaluations in a cellar book, use the system you feel most comfortable with. Personally, I think it's unlikely that anyone can tell the difference between an 89-point wine and a 90-point wine. But I know I can tell the difference between a wine of three stars and one of four stars, or any other stretch of quality that covers 20 percent of the scale at each increment. I'd opt for the scale of zero to five stars because I'm sure I can be that accurate. Scales that increase by one-hundredth of the scale at a time are, I believe, prone to inaccuracy at best and can be presumptuous as well as inaccurate at worst. But that's just me. You decide.

Besides the goodies we find in wine (such as cassis, black cherry, cola, chocolate, plums) and the flavors that may or may not be meritorious depending on your personal taste (Vegemite, toast, leather, tea), there are smells and flavors that are actively bad (hydrogen sulfide, sulfur, dill pickle, corkiness, Brettanomyces, and chemicals) — and then there is oak.

I liken oak to perfume on a woman or cologne on a man. If it's below the threshold of discernment when you're talking to the person but comes as just a hint if you're in a clinch, then they've applied the scent properly. Similarly with wine, if a glass smells like oak, it's way over-the-top and that's a defect. If it arrives as just a hint of vanillin ester when you actively taste the wine, that's fine — unless the wine is one that shouldn't have seen time in an oak barrel in the first place. Some wines, such as a crisp Sauvignon Blanc, are not improved by oak. Others, such as Cabernet Sauvignon, most certainly are improved by the grace note of oak.

When tasting a group of wines, be aware that the order in which you taste them will have an effect on your scoring. If you taste a very dry white wine immediately after tasting a rich, sweet, alcoholic port, that white wine might seem washed out. Also, the first wine you taste gets the benefit of your fresh palate. By the last wine, your palate might be tired, or overwhelmed by tannin. Professional tasters recognize this problem and will go back and try the wines a second, third, or several times; each time, they cleanse the palate before starting with a sip of water, a piece of bread, a bit of cheese, or a bit of a slice of roast beef, then mix up the order in which the wines are tasted. At the end of these rounds, certain wines will recommend themselves to you more and more strongly. Now go back and try these favorites together. Try one against the other. Try them in one order, then reverse the order. And for goodness sake, have a spit bucket and use it, or you'll pass out before you finish. The point is to make sure that a wine isn't given an unfair advantage simply by the order in which you taste it.

You may find that as a case of the same wine ages, the wine will vary from bottle to bottle. One bottle of 10-year-old Merlot served with dinner tonight might seem strangely different from a bottle served with another dinner a week and a half from now. What could account for this?

I've found that when winemakers have no ready explanation for why the very same wine tastes different from two different bottles, they invariably attribute it to "bottle variation." Lots of factors could account for bottle variation. First of all,.our moods and frame of mind differ from day to day. I know I have my good days and not-so-good days, my up and happy-go-lucky days and my down-in-the-dumps, nothing-goes-right days. When I pitched baseballs to batters, there were days when I hit all my spots and days when I couldn't find the strike zone with a pair of binoculars. We bring a lot of baggage to the dinner table with us, whether mental or physical. When I have a bad cold, for example, I couldn't tell Château Lafite from a cup of coffee. Certainly, who we are on a given day can contribute to how we perceive a wine.

Then again, it could be the food we're having the wine with. A light, crisp, grassy Sauvignon Blanc may not taste particularly wonderful with a slab of pork ribs slathered with baked-on barbecue sauce, no matter how good the wine is; the flavors just don't mesh very well. And a blackberry-fruity Zinfandel may overpower a delicate piece of poached halibut. But put the Zin with the ribs and the Sauvignon Blanc with the fish, and you'll up your enjoyment of each tenfold.

And finally, there may actually be variations from bottle to bottle of the same wine. When wine is put on pallets at the winery and moved through shippers, some bottles will be on the outside of the pallet, making them more subject to temperature fluctuations of hot and cold from the air than are bottles far in the interior of the pallet, which are insulated by their neighbors. Once at the wholesaler, differing conditions will do different things to the wine. At the retailer, some wines may be stored near the heat pipes while some get the cold drafts of air through the loading dock doors. And when you get the wines home, some may be stored under slightly differing conditions — though not, it's hoped, if you've been careful to follow the suggestions in this book for constructing and using a wine cellar.

Finally, there may be further variations in the bottle. This bottle may have a bit of corkiness (trichloranisole) in its flavor given by a faulty cork, while that bottle may be perfectly sound. Some few cells of Brettanomyces might have given this bottle a little Brett, while that bottle doesn't have a trace. And the wine may develop subtle differences in flavors over time because it is alive, and, like any individual living thing, it becomes more itself with time — like a photograph developing in the chemical bath, it becomes clearer and more distinct with time, until finally, you can recognize the face. Time in the cellar will accentuate those unique facets of the wine in the bottle, and the longer wines are in the cellar, the more these subtle differences may be exaggerated. So, I'm a believer in bottle variation, even if it is sometimes a cover for a simple lack of knowledge. Wine is a biological creation, prone to change.

Despite the occasional appearance of bottle variation, most wine of the same kind (that is, wines with the same label and year, such as four bottles of 2003 Flora Springs 'Trilogy') will be similar enough that you can count on them tasting pretty much the same.

TERROIR

One flavor clue that indicates longevity of a wine is minerality. One often sees "minerals" or "liquid minerals" referred to in wines of good structure, especially those that exhibit terroir. This idea of terroir seems to be the modern Holy Grail of winemaking: Everyone seeks it but few attain it. As the word itself suggests, it's a concept first defined in France but now used ubiquitously in California. One could translate it as "earthiness," but it's more than that. *Terroir* is the unique taste of a specific place as revealed in a glass of wine. Think of the great vineyard estates of France. The owners like to think that their wines have unique tastes that can be recognized vintage to vintage by those familiar enough with their wines. These unique flavors arise not only from the soil, the French believe, but also from the entire situation of each vineyard — its clones, its climate, its latitude, its hydrology, its underlying rock structure, its natural history, its proximity to bodies of water, its exposure to the sun, the kind of birds that fly over it, the ecology of the insects, arachnids, and microorganisms that inhabit it, and who knows what else.

In other words, each vineyard is a specific place on the earth and yields wines with a specific taste unique to that place — that's terroir. Large wineries that produce tens of thousands of cases of wine for the international market are more interested in consistency of soft, accessible flavor from year to year than terroir, which can vary as the influences on the vineyard change from year to year. Besides, the large wineries tend to buy or grow grapes from many different vineyards and blend them together, which obscures any possibility of terroir. They also tend to subject their wines to such techniques as blending, acidulation, de-alcoholizing, filtering, and fining, all of which erase whatever terroir might show in the wines.

Terroir, then, can really only show in *estate wines:* that is, wines from a single vineyard. If it's the taste of a place, then there must be a specific place

to yield that taste. But conditions within a single vineyard are seldom homogeneous. Some vines may grow on elevated hilltops that are better drained and have poorer soil than the vines down in the swale, and so produce smaller clusters of smaller berries that give very different wines from the vines in the more well-watered and richer-soil bottomlands. This side of a sloping vineyard may face north, while that side of the vineyard faces south, giving very different sun exposures within the single vineyard. So, what does *terroir* mean when a single vineyard contains a variety of conditions?

Well, the grapes from such a vineyard might be harvested and fermented together, producing a blend of all the grapes from that place. And so, the mingled terroirs from that vineyard might produce a flavor that's recognizable from year to year. Or, more likely, the vintner will taste through the different lots of grapes from the various parts of the vineyard and select those that meet his or her criteria for quality, then ferment them separately and produce a final blend based on the best possible wine that can be blended from those lots. If this kind of system is followed assiduously from vintage to vintage, terroir might then show itself in the final blends. The rejected lots will be sold off to other wineries; *bulked out* is the term among vineyardists and winemakers. These bulked-out lots tend to end up in the blends of inexpensive wines that are known as *fighting varietals*. Sometimes a winery may have a second label under which it sells wine made from the lots that don't make the cut for the primary label.

As you can see, terroir is a tenuous quality at best. And yet, some wines from certain parts of the Napa Valley seem to consistently show terroir. A powerful core of Cabernet Sauvignon fruit that's enveloped by graceful and elegant nuances is a classic feature of the Stags Leap district. Cabs from Oakville and Rutherford differ from one another, even though these regions are contiguous. Certainly Zinfandels from Sonoma's Dry Creek Valley have distinctive raspberry flavors that you don't find in Zins from Howell Mountain. Russian River Pinot Noirs exhibit a recognizable cola flavor that's hard to find in Carneros Pinots.

Wineries up and down the state of California are trying various vineyard techniques to enhance terroir. One method that's being tried more frequently is organic grape farming and biodynamic techniques. The natural soil improvement that's at the heart of organic grape growing helps vines to express themselves and be all that they can be, so to speak. Biodynamics takes that idea a step further. It includes in its method the influences of the cosmos as it interacts with the earth. If that sounds New Age, it long predates the cosmic thinking that arrived with the advent of psychedelia in the 1960s. Biodynamics is a method of farming first proposed by Rudolph Steiner in the 1920s and has anthroposophy at its philosophical core. One of its tenets is that the health and character of a piece of land, such as a vineyard, can be strengthened and intensified by recycling all materials on that property within its boundaries. Mike Benziger of Benziger Family Winery in Glen Ellen, California, explained to me that by composting spent grape pressings,

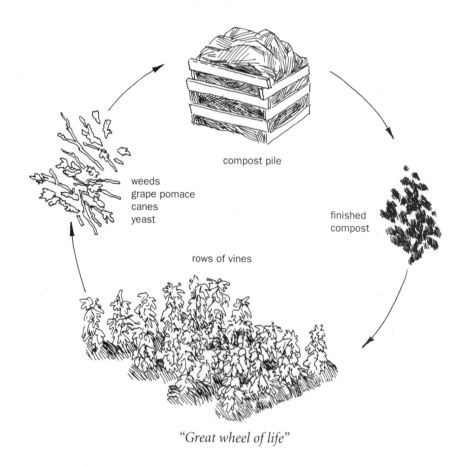

compost pile

weeds
grape pomace
canes
yeast

finished
compost

rows of vines

"Great wheel of life"

weeds, vineyard cuttings, and all other organic matter from a vineyard, the organic matter and the natural mix of microorganisms in that vineyard are recycled, and that enhances and strengthens the terroir of the wines grown there as time goes by. The yeasts that colonized the grapes return to the vines multifold. The soil bacteria around the vine roots are given renewed health by the compost that has formed on the property by the organic matter taken from that property. It all becomes a giant wheel of life, cycling and recycling in the vineyard, driven by the natural engines of sun, moon, stars, rain, wind, and weather — and by the natural web of life on that spot.

That's the idea, anyway. Sounds right to me somehow. Some of the finest vineyards in France are handled biodynamically and many, many more are organic. Do such techniques improve the flavor of a wine? Do they really help the wine to express the place where it is grown? Winemakers I talk to tell me that they do. "Organics isn't about ideology," John Williams said. "It's about making the best wine I can make."

So when a wine exhibits terroir, frequently one of its components is that minerality that started this discussion. I've seen various wine writers describe this quality as "washed stone," "liquid minerals," and "slate." I'm never quite exactly sure what they mean by these terms, but I understand minerality as a general concept and as a distinct component of a wine's flavor. It's most often found in white wines, especially a crisp Chablis, a sharp and refreshing Greco di Tufo, or even a Seyval Blanc from a vineyard like Franklin Hill in Bangor, Pennsylvania, where chunks of crystalline quartz the size of your fist protrude from the clay soil. Minerality is not fruit — it's pure earth.

Speaking of Bangor, Pennsylvania, the area around Bangor, Pen Argyl, Roseto, Wind Gap, Slatedale, and Slatington just south of Blue Mountain (with the Pocono Mountains to the north of Blue Mountain and the Lehigh Valley to the south) is an interesting area for wine production that I don't think has received enough attention. Like the steep slopes of the slate-littered hills along the Rhine River that's called the Rheingau in Germany, these slate soils have a decided south-facing aspect. This is the famous slate belt of eastern Pennsylvania. Just to its south are the cement-producing areas of Cementon, Northampton, and other towns to the west of the Delaware River.

Both concrete and slate are limestone sedimentary rocks (the former used for making cement and the latter used for making the finest roofing materials). Chardonnay is already grown successfully in Nazareth, one of the cement-producing towns. Why wouldn't Riesling, the vine that does so well in the slate slopes of the Rheingau, do well in the spoil banks and slate soils from Bangor west to Slatington? It grows well far to the north in the Finger Lakes region of upstate New York. I'd try it if I still lived back in Bangor.

The reason I bring up the example of the obscure viticultural potential of Bangor, Pennsylvania, is that the United States is full of undiscovered sites that someday will be counted among the sources of the finest wines of the world. It's obvious that Sonoma and Napa Counties in California are great regions for great wines, but many more sites that will be famous remain to be discovered, even there; and among those sites that are deemed worthy today, many will leap ahead in fame only after the vines that are now planted on them are pulled out. Then someone will figure out that a certain variety should go there, and when the site is replanted to that variety, the full potential of the vineyard will be realized and immense success will ensue. In Europe, thousands of years of viticultural trial and error have resulted in sublime pairings of vines to sites, with equally sublime results. The renowned wines of Domaine de la Romanée-Conti, Corton-Charlemagne, Chambertin, Château d'Yquem, Château Mouton, and so on are proof of the value of the process.

One of the links in the chain of processes and events that go into identifying the emergence of the great wines is the wine cellar of the knowledgeable wine lover. In these cellars, the mettle of the wines will be tried and true quality will emerge. The great wines will show well not only when young but also throughout a long life. It's the wine aficionado who will discover that certain unheralded wines have become exquisite, and who will begin to spread the word.

Though it seems that fine wines in the United States have long been with us, that really isn't the case. The years of Prohibition destroyed a vibrant wine industry in the United States, and only a handful of producers making "sacramental" wine kept going. Many other vineyard owners made and sold grapes for home consumption, much of which managed to be fermented, but few of those homemade wines could qualify as good artisanal wines, and there was no industry. American wine continued to languish from the end of Prohibition in 1933 until the mid- to late 1960s, when the industry began to reconstitute itself and reinvent itself in the French image. Vineyards were planted up through the 1970s and 1980s, and many mistakes were made in terms of which varieties went where. Besides the problems with Cabernet Sauvignon in Monterey County, for decades vineyardists in every California wine region have been diligently budding-over lackluster plantings to new scionwood (the top of the graft that produces the fruit), looking for the perfect match of vine to vineyard. The process continues, studded with great successes.

The scourge of the phylloxera root louse came back in the late 1980s and 1990s, and many of the vineyards in the Wine Country had to be ripped out and replanted on phylloxera-resistant rootstocks. This gave vineyard managers a chance to make better spacings, rethink trellising systems, make a better fit between clones of the various types of grapes and the vineyard soils and sites, and in general improve the vineyards and become less French and more Californian in approach. Now these new and improved vineyards are maturing and the decades of the early twenty-first century hold great promise. The proof of that promise will be realized in our wine cellars.

Bibliography

Adams, Leon D. *The Commonsense Book of Wine*. New York: McGraw-Hill Book Company, 1986.

Amerine, M. A., and M. A. Joslyn. *Table Wines*. Berkeley: University of California Press, 1970.

Amerine, Maynard A., and Edward B. Roessler. *Wines — Their Sensory Evaluation*. San Francisco: W. H. Freeman and Company, 1976.

Cox, Jeff. *From Vines to Wines*. North Adams, Mass.: Storey Publishing, 1999.

Gold, Richard M. *How and Why to Build a Wine Cellar*. North Amherst, Mass.: Sandhill Publishing, 1996.

Halliday, James. *Collecting Wine*. Sydney, Australia: HarperCollins, 1998.

Johnson, Hugh. *Hugh Johnson's Modern Encyclopedia of Wine*. New York: Simon & Schuster, 1983.

Kolpan, Steven, et al. *Exploring Wine*. New York: John Wiley & Sons, Inc., 2002.

Parker, Robert Jr. *Burgundy*. New York: Simon & Schuster, 1990.

Robinson, Jancis. *Vines, Grapes & Wines*. London: Mitchell Beazley, 1999.

———. *Vintage Timecharts*. New York: Weidenfeld & Nicholson, 1989.

———, ed. *The Oxford Companion to Wine*. New York: Oxford University Press, 1994.

Winkler, A. J., et al. *General Viticulture*. Berkeley: University of California Press, 1974.

Appendixes

WINE AROMA WHEEL*

The benefits of describing wines in specific terms, such as those on the Wine Aroma Wheel, are your greater enjoyment and appreciation of the wonderful world of wines, plus an enhanced ability to discriminate and remember wine flavors. Describing wine aromas is very simple with the help of this lexicon. Words are arranged in three tiers, from the most general in the center to the most specific in the outer ring. Terms for similar aromas are located adjacent to each other wherever possible. The distinctive aromas of varietal wines can often be recognized by the specific aroma notes listed below.

Much of the aroma in wine comes from the skins of grapes and contributes to their distinctive, varietal flavors. Winemaking operations modify these aromas in characteristic ways. Malolactic fermentation produces a buttery aroma, for example, while aging in oak cooperage contributes vanilla and clove notes to Chardonnays and most red wines. In contrast, Sauvignon Blanc, which may be oak-aged and may undergo malolactic fermentation, is recognizable by the presence of herbaceous (bell pepper or asparagus) notes that arise from the grapes.

Characteristic Varietal Wine Aromas

Cabernet Sauvignon, Merlot, Malbec, Cabernet Franc, (and red Bordeaux wines): Berry, vegetative or herbaceous (bell pepper, asparagus, olives), mint, black pepper, butter, vanilla, soy (in older wines).

Pinot Noir (and red Burgundies): Berry, berry jam (strawberry), vanilla, buttery, spicy.

Zinfandel: Berry, black pepper, raisin, soy, butter, vanilla.

Chardonnay (and white Burgundies): Fruity (apple, peach, citrus, pineapple), spicy (cloves), vanilla, butter.

Sauvignon Blanc: Floral, fruity (citrus, peach, apricot), vegetative or herbaceous (bell pepper, asparagus), vanilla, butter, spicy (cloves).

White Riesling (and white German wines): Floral, fruity (citrus, peach, apricot, pineapple), honey.

Gewürztraminer: Floral, fruity (citrus, grapefruit, peach), honey, spice.

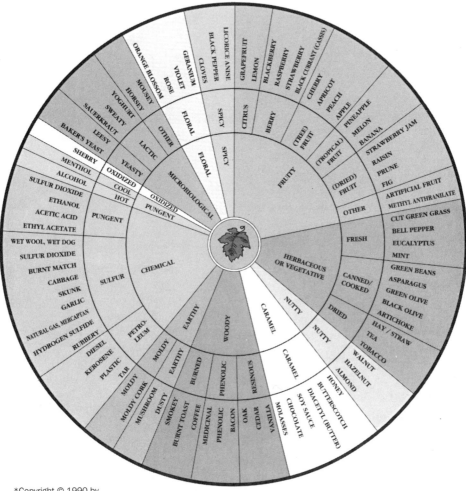

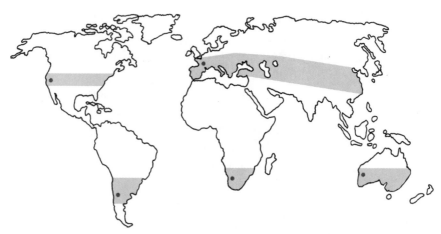

Most fine wine–growing regions are in bands of temperate climates north and south of the equator.

ITALY

SWITZERLAND
AUSTRIA
Veneto
SLOVENIA
Piedmont
CROATIA
Tuscany
CORSICA
Campania
SARDINIA
SICILY

Wine is made throughout Italy.

FRANCE

Fine wine areas are scattered around France.

SPAIN

Portugal and Spain, like Italy, have wine-growing regions throughout.

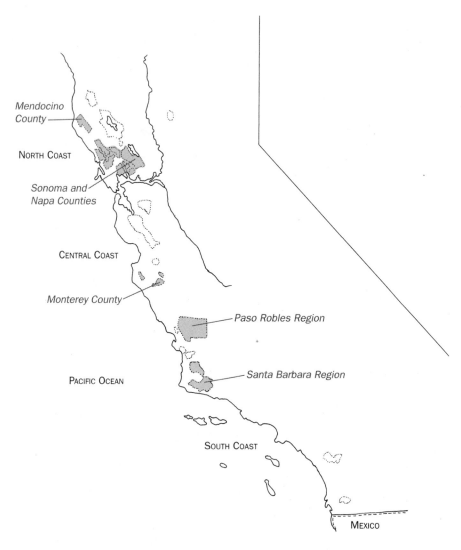

Mendocino
County

NORTH COAST

Sonoma and
Napa Counties

CENTRAL COAST

Monterey County

Paso Robles Region

PACIFIC OCEAN

Santa Barbara Region

SOUTH COAST

MEXICO

Wine-growing regions of California tend to hug the coast.

Resources

WINE EVENTS

The American Center for Wine, Food & the Arts
500 First Street
Napa, CA 94559
(888) 51-COPIA
(707) 259-1600
www.copia.org
A wonderful organization that connects love of wine to food and the arts.

Napa Valley Vintners Association
889 Adams Street, Suite H
St. Helena, CA 94574
(707) 963-3388
www.napavintners.com
The organization of Napa Valley's wine-makers; issues press releases and puts on wine events.

Sonoma County Wineries Association
5000 Roberts Lake Road
Rohnert Park, CA 94928
(707) 586-3795
www.sonomawine.com
The organization of Sonoma County's winemakers, issues press releases and puts on wine events.

MAIL-ORDER CATALOGS

International Wine Accessories
10246 Miller Road
Dallas, TX 75238-1206
(800) 527-4072
www.iwawine.com
Cabinets, corkscrews, coolers, and everything else you can think of in wine accessories.

Wine & All That Jazz
220 Tompkins Avenue
Pleasantville, NY 10570-3146
(800) 610-7731
www.winejazz.com
Cooling systems, racking systems, custom cellars, wine accessories, and more.

The Chicago Wine Company
5663 West Howard Street
Niles, IL 60714
(847) 647-8789
www.tcwc.com
Carries wines that are already well aged and new, hard-to-get wines.

Prime Wine
P.O. Box 373
LaGrange, IL 60525
(888) 867-9463
www.primewines.com
You can search their inventory online and place an order.

WineBid.com
P.O. Box 2550
Napa, CA 94558
(707) 226-5893
www.winebid.com
Auctions of wines.

Wine.com
(877) 289-6886
www.wine.com
Carries more than 5,000 imported and domestic premium wines. The site offers several very worthwhile features, including information on whether they'll ship wine to your state, online wine education, promotions and loyalty programs, sweepstakes events, and wine clubs and bulletin boards, as well as wine merchandise and accessories.

Wine House
2311 Cotner Avenue
Los Angeles, CA 90064-1877
www.winehouse.com
This Los Angeles–based store has an online presence. The site has a searchable catalog, message boards, tasting groups, and reviews of many wines.

The Wine Messenger
371 North Avenue
New Rochelle, NY 10801
(800) 760-3960
www.winemessenger.com
Specializes in wines from small producers around the world.

American Wine Essentials, Inc.
1472 N. Milpitas Boulevard
Milpitas, CA 95035
(877) 719-8486
www.winecabinets.com
Wine cabinets and walk-in cellars, storage racks, residential or commercial.

Napa Valley Wine Hardware
659 Main Street
St. Helena, CA 94574
(866) 611-9463
A full line of wine cellar accessories and equipment.

Sonoma Wine Hardware
536 Broadway
Sonoma, CA 95476
(866) 231-9463
A full line of wine cellar accessories and equipment.

Wine Cellar Solutions
P.O. Box 38373
Germantown, TN 38183-0373
(888) 649-9463
www.winehome.com
Custom wine cellars, wine storage systems, wine cooling units, wine cabinets, racks, stemware, accessories, and more.

Vintage Charts
www.vintage-charts.com
Burgundy, Bordeaux, Champagne, and port charts, plus links to online wine buying sites.

The Wine Institute
425 Market Street, Suite 1000
San Francisco, CA 94105
(415) 502-0151
www.wineinstitute.org
The trade and information organization for American wine.

**Robert Parker's Wine Advisor
and Cellar Manager**
www.winetech.com/html/rparker.html
*A powerful database of many thousands
of wines built from issues of* The Wine
Advocate, *with ratings, comments,
prices, and more, along with a pictorial
view of your own wine cellar in a
searchable database.*

The Uncorked Cellar
Uncork Pty Ltd
P.O. Box 1391
Narre Warren MDC
Victoria 3805
Australia
www.uncork.com.au/
*Australian software that gives ratings,
value guides, cellaring guides, winery
details, and winemakers' notes on more
than 27,000 individual vintages of
American, Australian, New Zealand,
and Canadian wines. Manages the
contents of your cellar.*

WineBase
www.winebase.com.au/
An Australian software database.

WineBook
www.winebook.de/wine/wine.html
*Wine cellar management and tasting
notes software made by a German firm.
Available in English, German, French,
and Italian versions.*

Wine Cellar Book
www.primasoft.com/wb.htm
*For Microsoft Windows only. Provides
fields for wine name, producer, style,
variety, tasting notes, rating, cost,
descriptions, etc. Automatically sorts
entries. A more powerful version is
called Wine Organizer Deluxe.*

Wineformation
http://wineformation.com/
*Wine cellar and information manage-
ment software for the accumulation,
analysis, and dissemination of wine-
related information.*

WineScore
www.winescore.com
*Ratings for 6,500 California and 3,000
French wines in software database for
handheld computing devices, such as
the Palm Pilot.*

Magorian Mine Services

P.O. Box 624
Foresthill, CA 95631
(530) 367-3636
Underground mining and tunneling.

Nordby Wine Caves

1550 Airport Boulevard, Suite 201
Santa Rosa, CA 95403
(707) 526-4500
Nordby digs underground wine caves throughout Northern California and is a good source of information on the process.

CUSTOM WINE CELLARS

American Wine Essentials, Inc.

1472 N. Milpitas Boulevard
Milpitas, CA 95035
(877) 719-8486
www.winecabinets.com
One-stop shopping for custom cellars, cooling units, wine cabinets and walk-in cellars, storage racks, residential or commercial.

Apex Saunas & Wine Co.

13221 Northup Way
Bellevue, WA 98005
(800) 462-2714
www.apex-sauna-wine.com/
Custom wine cellars and racking systems with nationwide service.

Paul Wyatt Designs

1097 Howard St., No. 104
San Francisco, CA 94103
(415) 626-9463
www.paulwyatt.com
Renowned for his beautiful and functional designs, Paul Wyatt is among the best designers of custom wine cellars.

Rosehill Wine Cellar and Renovation Group, Inc.

32 Howden Road, Unit 3
Toronto, ONT M87 2Z6
Canada
(888) 253-6807
www.rosehillwinecellars.com
A company that specializes in building wine cellars to your specifications.

Wine Cellar Innovations

4575 Eastern Avenue
Cincinnati, OH 45226
(800) 229-9813
www.winecellarinnovations.com
High-end custom wine cellars, kits, and racking systems. Computer-aided design includes three-dimensional virtual reality models of potential cellars. Sales reps in CT, FL, IL, IN, KY, MA, ME, MI, NH, OH, RI, VT, and WI.

Wine Cellars and Storage of Colorado

(303) 841-8989
www.wine-cellars.org
Manufacturer, distributor, designer, and contractor for wine cellar design services, wine cabinets, refrigeration, racking systems.

International Wine Accessories
10246 Miller Road
Dallas, TX 75238-1206
(800) 527-4072
www.iwawine.com
Cabinets, corkscrews, coolers, and everything else you can think of in wine accessories.

Silent Cellar
www.electrolux.com.
Electrolux makes this unit in three sizes. The medium size unit holds 150 bottles. Operates without motor or compressor.

Westside WineCellars
P.O. Box 5187
Beverly Hills, CA 90209
(888) 694-9463
www.westside-group.com
A fine selection of many dozens of different wine cabinets and their accessories.

Wine Cellars Unlimited
7262 Roos St.
Houston, TX 77074
(866) 856-4749
http://winecellarsunlimited.com/
Manufacturer and distributor of a wide variety of temperature- and humidity-controlled wine cellars, coolers, and storage equipment. Also manufacturers of custom wine cabinets and cellars.

WineCellarPro
28 Woodland Avenue
San Rafael, CA 94901
(800) 660-5758
www.winecellarpro.com
Bay Area provider of cellar doors, racking systems, cooling systems, and storage cabinets.

RFC Wire Forms, Inc.
525 W. Brooks Street
Ontario, CA 91762
(800) 334-0937
www.rfcwireforms.com
Cost-effective wire wine racks.

WineRacks.com
P.O. Box 67
High Falls, NY 12440
(888) 687-2517
www.wineracks.com
A nice line of wine racks and accessories. Located in the Hudson Valley.

WINE STORAGE FACILITIES

CAwinewarehouse
625 DuBois Street, Suite A
San Rafael, CA 94901
(415) 259-2860
www.cawinewarehouse.com
Twelve- to 300-case storage in redwood lockers for collectors. Maintained at a continuous 55°F.

The Strongbox Wine Cellar
1650 W. Irving Park
Chicago, IL 60613
www.winestorage.com
Chicago-based storage lockers kept at 55°F year-round. Open seven days a week.

The Wine-Storage Cave
77 McEntee Street
Kingston, NY 12401
(914) 340-9466
www.wine-storage.com
A large facility serving the Hudson Valley.

Glossary

aging on the yeast. Also known as *sur lies,* this is the time a bottle of sparkling wine spends in storage before the spent yeast of the in-bottle fermentation is disgorged.

ah-so. A type of cork puller that has two blades that slip into the neck of the bottle and grasp the cork, which can then be removed with a pulling-twisting motion. Its advantage is that corks can be reinserted in the bottles by reversing the motion.

anthocyanins. Phenolic compounds in a wine that are precursors to its final color, flavor, and aroma.

assemblage. French for the art of assembling the final mixture of still wines to be refermented in the bottle to make sparkling wine.

Auslesen. German for "selected." It means that certain very ripe bunches of grapes have been selected for separate vinification, leading to wines with some residual sugar.

balance. A trait of all great wines. Balance occurs when all the factors of the wine — acid, alcohol, pH, structure, flavor concentration, color depth, and so forth — are in harmonious proportions.

Beerenauslesen. German for "berry selected." It means that certain very ripe berries have been selected from within bunches of grapes for separate vinification, leading to concentrated, sweet wines.

botrytized. A wine is *botrytized* when the grape berries have been infected with the noble rot *Botrytis cinerea.* It can, with certain grape varieties, especially Sauvignon Blanc, Semillon, Riesling, and Gewürztraminer, result in dessert wines of intense flavor concentration, elevated sugars, and sublime quality.

bottle age. Time a wine spends in the bottle. With enough bottle age, the wine can be brought to its potential best, including the development of *bouquet,* the ineffable scent of well-aged wine.

bouquet. The characteristic, ineffable scent of well-aged wine.

Bretty. Winemakers' slang for a wine that has been infected with *Brettanomyces* yeast, giving it an off-flavor commonly referred to as "mousy."

bulked out. Term used by vineyardists and winemakers for rejected lots of grapes that are sold off to other wineries.

California cult wine. Wines made in small amounts from well-respected vineyards that attract a following of wealthy patrons who drive the price per bottle to absurd heights.

cap. Grape skins and other bits and particles of the fruit that float to the top during extended maceration.

captain's decanter. A glass decanter with a very wide bottom that allows it to stay on the table without tipping in a pitching, rolling ship.

cépage. French for "vine variety." Thus Chateau St. Jean's famous 'Cinq Cépage' Meritage is a blend of five varieties.

chai. French for an outbuilding used for barrel storage. A wine shed.

complex anthocyanins. Anthocyanins that have linked with tannins to form long-chain polymers that give wine much of its color, flavor, and aroma.

concentration. The intensity of flavor and color in a wine.

corked. A corked wine has the unmistakable stench of musty, wet cardboard that results from infection by organisms, supposedly residing in the cork, that produce trichloranisole.

crust. Port sediment. *See also* "throws a crust."

cultivar. A viticulturist's term of art meaning "a variety." It's a contraction of "cultivated variety."

decanting. Pouring clear wine off the deposits and sludgy material that form over time in bottles of unfiltered and unfined red wine.

disgorged. After sparkling wine has *aged on the yeast,* it is *riddled.* The neck is then frozen, the crown cap is pulled off, the ice plug and yeast pop out due to the pressure in the bottle, and the bottle is topped up with clean wine and given a "dosage" of sugar water with perhaps a drop or so of brandy, then corked and the wire hood fastened. The act of freezing and blowing out the ice plug is called *disgorgement,* and once the ice plug is out, the wine is said to be *disgorged.*

drying out. When, after extended aging, the color of the wine fades, the flavor thins out and becomes tea-like, and the aroma fades.

double magnum. See *jeroboam.*

ducted system. Also called *split air handler system.* A cooling system that operates like the split system, but cooling and moisture drainage in an evaporator, as well as the condenser operation, occur outside the wine cellar.

estate wines. Wines from a single vineyard.

extended maceration. Allowing the new wine to stay on the crushed skins and seeds and spent yeast for a period of time after fermentation stops. It can vary from a few days to many weeks and allows the wine to extract more flavor from the skins and for harsh tannins to smooth out.

fermentation. The action of wine yeast on sugary grape juice, turning the sugar into alcohol and the juice into wine.

field blend. A mixture of several types of grapes in a single vineyard. The vineyard is picked and the grapes are crushed together, creating a *field blend.*

fighting varietals. California wines in the $8–$12 range labeled by the grape variety from which they're made; "fighting" because of the stiff competition at that price range.

fining. The use of egg whites, isinglass, clay, or other agents to strip a wine of hazy particles and render it perfectly clear. Unless it's necessary to clear an obstinately hazy wine, it should be avoided, as it will remove some quality along with the cloudiness.

foxy. A descriptor of wine made from *Vitis labrusca,* the native American grape, or varieties derived from these wild grapes. Think Welch's grape juice.

futures. Paying now for wine that may still be hanging on the vine, usually at a worthwhile discount compared to the price at release.

garage wine. The French equivalent of California cult wine; so called because it is made in such small amounts that it could have been made in someone's garage.

grassy. An herbaceous or vegetative flavor found in Sauvignon Blanc.

hang time. The amount of time grapes hang on the vine from fruit set to harvest. Generally, the longer the hang time, the slower and gentler the ripening of the grapes has been and the greater chance that they'll reach maturity.

hot. A term for a wine with a strongly sharp and biting alcohol level.

imbottigliato. Italian for "bottled."

jeroboam. A three-liter bottle of wine, also called a *double magnum.*

Kabinett. The German equivalent of an American Reserve wine. See also *Reserve wines.*

lees. Spent yeast and other gunk that settles out as wine ferments. See also *aging on the lees.*

malolactic fermentation. A bacterial, not yeast, fermentation that occurs in wine — often with the assistance of the winemaker who adds the bacteria — that changes harshly acidic malic acid into softer-tasting lactic acid, thus smoothing an overly acidic wine.

maturity. In grapes, when the berries reach their flavor maximum and the tannins that coat the seeds turn brownish.

Meritage. A word devised in California in 1989 to denote a blended wine of Bordeaux varieties: Cabernet Sauvignon, Merlot, Cabernet Franc, Malbec, and Petit Verdot. Pronounced like *heritage.*

minerality. Wines exhibit this trait when they include flavors that give the impression of the minerals in the soils from which they sprang. Great wines often have both good fruit flavors and minerality.

must. Crushed grapes and juice either just before fermentation or during fermentation. Once fermentation stops, the must becomes wine.

native yeasts. Yeasts that are naturally present.

négociant-éleveur. A French wine merchant who buys grapes and vinifies them.

organoleptic. An adjective referring to the sensory impressions made on the taste buds and olfactory nerve by any food or beverage, including wine.

over-oaked. Wines kept in wooden barrels, especially new ones, too long can acquire too much oak flavor and are described thus.

plonk. Poor quality wine.

pumping over. The practice of periodically wetting the floating cap of skins during fermentation to prevent the growth of mold or any other unwanted organisms, especially by pumping wine from within the fermentation tank onto the cap. It's a rather harsh treatment that's being replaced in many wineries by gentler methods of wetting the cap, especially by "punching down" or submerging the cap in the must either by hand or machine.

punt. The indentation on the bottom of a glass wine bottle.

Qualitätswein. German for "quality wine," and given to almost everything German winemakers produce, so it doesn't really mean much at all.

Reserve wines. Supposedly the best wines of a vintage bottled separately from the main bottling, but sometimes this designation is just a sales gimmick.

riddle. To turn a bottle upside down so the spent yeast settles in the neck.

rim. By tilting a glass of wine above a white surface, the color of the wine becomes thinned out and more discernible at the rim, or the "edge" of the wine.

ripeness. In grapes, when sugar levels reach their optimum for wine quality, generally around 23.5 percent sugar (brix).

sherrification. A form of oxidation of wine that produces a sherry-like flavor and brownish color.

split system. Cooling system in which the condenser is located outside the wine cellar. Refrigerant is pumped from the condenser into an evaporator, air is drawn into the evaporator, where it is cooled by a coil, then blown back out into the wine cellar.

Supertuscan. A blend of Sangiovese, the traditional grape variety of Tuscany in Italy, with Cabernet Sauvignon or another of the five Bordeaux varieties that are now being grown in Tuscany.

sur lies. See *aging on the yeast.*

terroir. A French term meaning the unique taste of the place where the wines were grown. It's what may allow a connoisseur to taste a wine and name the vineyard where it grew. It includes all the factors of the site: climate, soil, grape variety, trellis system, nearby vegetation, native flora and fauna, types of microorganisms — everything that might bear on the development of the unique taste of a wine.

"throws a crust." When a port wine develops crusty deposits inside its bottle over time, it is said to do this.

tight. When a wine is *tight,* its tannins are gritty, and the fruit taste is hard and closed. Usually said of young wines.

titratable acidity. A measure of the total acid in a wine, expressed as grams per liter.

Trockenbeerenauslesen. German for "dried berry selected." It means that grapes that have been dried almost to raisins are hand picked from the ripest bunches and vinified separately, leading to wines of extraordinary lushness and honeyed quality.

ullage. The air space between the bottom of the cork and the top of the wine in an unopened bottle of wine.

umami. The fifth taste, after sweet, sour, salty, and bitter. It was discovered by a Japanese food scientist in the early twentieth century and is found in soy, roasted or fried potatoes, and most savory dishes. Also called the "yummy" taste. Monosodium glutamate enhances umami in food, which is why MSG is used in cooking.

valance system. A cooling system in which a water chiller is located outside the wine cellar, cold water is piped through an insulated hose to a valance unit at the top of a wall, and cold water is circulated through tubes with fins and returned for more chilling. Warm air rises, comes into contact with the cold water tubes and fins, and is cooled.

veraison. The time when young, green grape clusters start to show color.

vineyard-designated wine. A wine with the name of the vineyard where it was grown on the label; e.g., Heitz 'Martha's Vineyard' Cabernet Sauvignon.

vinification. The process of turning grapes and their juice into wine.

vin ordinaire. French for "ordinary wine." Wine of modest quality.

vinous. Meaning "of the vine," this term is used to describe the flavor of a wine that tastes like nondescript grapes, rather than blackberries, black cherries, and so on.

waiter's corkscrew. An excellent cork-removing device that includes a small blade to cut open the foil capsule that covers the cork, a wire helix that grasps the cork firmly, and a flange that fits over the lip of the bottle and allows the body of the corkscrew to act as a lever to pull the cork out.

waterfall refrigeration system. An in-room humidifier that maintains proper humidity, while an air handler cooling unit keeps the temperature in the wine cellar at a steady 55°F. A water chiller located outside the wine cellar delivers cold water to a cabinet topped with decorative granite or marble through which cold water is emitted, runs down to a collection basin, and then returns to the chiller.

Index

Numbers in *italics* indicate illustrations.

Other Storey Titles You Might Enjoy

Cordials from Your Kitchen by Pattie Vargas and Rich Gulling. Create delicious, elegant liqueurs for entertaining or gift giving. Includes more than 100 easy cordial recipes to suit every occasion. 176 pages. Paperback. ISBN 0-88266-986-9.

From Vines to Wines by Jeff Cox. With thorough, illustrated instructions for every step of the process, Jeff Cox offers a complete home winemaking education in one book — from planting vines to pulling a cork. Home winemakers, gardeners, and anyone with an appreciation for wine will find much to appreciate in this book. 256 pages. Paperback. ISBN 1-58017-105-2.

The Home Winemaker's Companion by Gene Spaziani and Ed Halloran. Here are 155 delectable wine recipes that guide you through everything from making your first batch of kit wine to mastering advanced techniques for making wine from fresh grapes. 272 pages. Paperback. ISBN 1-58017-209-1.

Making Wild Wines & Meads by Pattie Vargas and Rich Gulling. There's no end to the great-tasting wines you can make using ingredients (but not grapes!) from the local farmer's market, supermarket, or even your own backyard. 176 pages. Paperback. ISBN 1-58017-182-6.

These and other Storey books are available wherever books are sold
and directly from Storey Publishing, 210 MASS MoCA Way, North Adams,
MA, 01247, or by calling 1-800-441-5700.
Or visit our Web site at www.storey.com.